PLEASURE AND THE GOOD LIFE

PHILOSOPHIA ANTIQUA

A SERIES OF STUDIES
ON ANCIENT PHILOSOPHY

FOUNDED BY J. H. WASZINK† AND W. J. VERDENIUS†

EDITED BY

J. MANSFELD, D.T. RUNIA
J.C.M. VAN WINDEN

VOLUME LXXXV

GERD VAN RIEL

PLEASURE AND THE GOOD LIFE

PLEASURE
AND
THE GOOD LIFE

PLATO, ARISTOTLE, AND THE NEOPLATONISTS

BY

GERD VAN RIEL

BRILL
LEIDEN · BOSTON · KÖLN
2000

This book is printed on acid-free paper.

Library of Congress Cataloging-in-Publication Data

Riel, Gerd Van.
  Pleasure and the good life : Plato, Aristotle and the Neoplatonists / by
Gerd Van Riel.
     p   cm.—(Philosophia antiqua, ISSN 0079-1687; v. 85)
  Includes bibliographical references and indexes.
  ISBN 9004117970 (cloth : alk. paper)
  1. Pleasure. 2. Philosophy, Ancient. I. Title. II. Series.
B187.P57 R54   2000
171'.4'0938—dc21   00–029771
                                                                        CIP

Die Deutsche Bibliothek – CIP-Einheitsaufnahme

Riel, Gerd Van :
Pleasure and the good life : Plato, Aristotle and the neoplatonists
/ by Gerd Van Riel. – Leiden ; Boston ; Köln : Brill, 2000
   (Philosophia antiqua ; Vol. 85)
   ISBN 90–04–11797–0

ISSN   0079-1687
ISBN   90 04 11797 0

PRINTED IN THE NETHERLANDS

CONTENTS

Indices

PREFACE

This book grew out of a Ph.D. dissertation presented in 1997 at the Institute of Philosophy (Hoger Instituut voor Wijsbegeerte) of the University of Leuven (Belgium). Its most obvious difference from its ancestor is that of language, the dissertation being written in Dutch. More importantly, however, the "linguistic turn" from Dutch to English provided an occasion to modify the scope. The subject matter of the dissertation (parts of which have been published elsewhere) was Plato's *Philebus* and its influence in antiquity. The first part investigated the 'ethical' interpretation of the dialogue (i.e., the doctrine of pleasure), the second part examined the 'metaphysical' interpretation (i.e., the doctrine of the four 'causes', *Phil.* 23c-30d). In this respect, the scope of the present volume is narrower than that of the dissertation. Yet in another respect it is wider: for its investigation of the theory of pleasure is not confined to Plato's *Philebus* and its influence, but covers the general theories of pleasure of Plato and his successors. Thus, this book treats the problem of pleasure in the good life from a different perspective. Here the *Philebus* is but one of the relevant texts in a broader thematical study.

The research for this book was made possible by fellowships granted by the Fund for Scientific Research – Flanders (Belgium). I am very grateful to this Institution for its financial support. The present work benefited from the intellectual climate at the Institute of Philosophy, and in particular at its centre for the study of ancient and medieval philosophy (De Wulf-Mansioncentrum). This centre has built a solid reputation in the field of the study of the influence of ancient thought on medieval philosophy, in which Neoplatonism and Aristotelianism play a major role.

I owe my profound gratitude to Prof. Carlos Steel, whose enthusiasm, competence, and support were essential to the genesis of this work. I am also indebted to those who were kind enough to comment on and criticise draft versions of (parts of) the book: Prof. Richard Sorabji, Prof. Fernand Bossier, Dr. Jan Opsomer, Guy Guldentops, and Prof. Dominic O'Meara. I thank John Steffen, as well as Aaron Schuster, for correcting the English version. Finally, I am very honoured to have this work published in Brill's distinguished series

Philosophia Antiqua, and to have received a Humanities award of the Royal Belgian Academy (Koninklijke Vlaamse Academie voor Wetenschappen en Kunsten van België).

I dedicate this book to my wife Ann and to the memory of my parents.

Leuven, October 1999

INTRODUCTION

Very often in the historiography of philosophy a rigid opposition is drawn between hedonists and anti-hedonists: the former argue that pleasure is the ultimate good, whereas the latter adduce reasons to deny this claim. But, in fact, this characterization of the opposition between the two parties is too simple as it stands. On the one hand, if hedonists wish to participate in a philosophical discussion, then they have to accept that some rules governing the discussion — at least those concerning the reasonability and truthfulness of the discourse — are intrinsically valuable. If they think these rules are not valuable, then they will not be able to defend their hedonism as a philosophical position. On the other hand, non- or anti-hedonists have to accept some hedonistic arguments: to demonstrate that their own life choice is a better one, they have to argue that such a life is the most desirable one and thus that it promises, in one way or another, to yield pleasure. Of course, this does not mean that anti-hedonists in fact are (hidden) hedonists; there remain important differences concerning the role that is to be attributed to pleasure in this most desirable life. But, after all, when anti-hedonists want to present their own alternative, it is unavoidable that they use a hedonistic argument at a crucial moment in the discussion.

The present study will concentrate on this 'crucial moment', the point at which the philosophical analysis of the good life opens the door for pleasure, at which the life of the philosopher is argued to be the most desirable, and thus truly pleasurable, life.

We want to investigate more precisely how the Athenian Neoplatonists (i.e., the followers of Plotinus who worked in the Academy of Athens) faced this issue. The analysis of the authors belonging to this tradition can be seen as exemplary for the point we want to discuss. In fact, the Neoplatonists not only radically dissent from hedonism, they also — at first sight, at least — pay relatively little attention to the notion of pleasure, as it is situated at a very 'low' level of reality and thus falls outside of the real scope of their central ideas. This fact has two important consequences. First, it limits the relevant sources to only a few authors, viz. Plotinus, Proclus, and Damascius, in whose works a

consistent theory of pleasure can be found. In the works of other
Neoplatonic authors (at least in their extant works) the theme of
pleasure is devoid of all importance[1]. Second, due to the 'low profile' of
the theory of pleasure, the secondary literature has likewise paid but
scant attention to this feature. As we have indicated already, however,
the Neoplatonists have to argue for the occurrence of *true* pleasure in
what they consider to be the good life. In this sense, the theory of
pleasure becomes an important feature in their philosophy after all.

The first item to be discussed is the way in which the various authors
determine the nature of pleasure. Ancient philosophers in general established two specific models of pleasure. In the oldest model pleasure is
considered to be the replenishment of a lack, the fulfilment of a desire,
or the relief from distress. The central point in this model, defended by
Plato, to mention only the most important adherent, is that pleasure is
a movement that consists in the restoration of an original harmony: the
'natural condition'. Over against this view, Aristotle defends the theory
that pleasure is an additional element that occurs when an activity is
performed perfectly, i.e., without any impediment. In this case, pleasure no longer is a movement, but a certain 'additional element' that
flourishes once the natural condition is attained. We will closely
consider and evaluate both of these claims in the first chapter.

All ancient theorists of pleasure relied either on one of these two
paradigms or on a combination of the two. There was no third way of
explaining the nature of pleasure, and even in later philosophy there
does not seem to have existed a third alternative. It is important, then,
to get a clear view of both schemes, as this will enable us to understand
all later theories. Although the equation of pleasure with a replenishment certainly predates Plato[2], he gave the best and most elaborate
account of this model. The theory that pleasure follows upon unimpeded activity, on the other hand, was invented by Aristotle. With this
in mind, we will present in the first chapter a juxtaposition of the
theories of pleasure of the two major Greek philosophers, whose ideas
reappeared (in combination or in isolation) in the later tradition.

We will add some critical remarks regarding the claims of Plato and
Aristotle. In our opinion, they both accept a *necessary* link between

---

[1]   The case is different, of course, with the Commentators on Aristotle. They
essentially take over the Aristotelian theory of pleasure, constituting a different
tradition.
[2]   It is advanced already by Empedocles (Aëtius 4.9.15; cf. Dodds 1959, 304).

pleasure and either the replenishment of a lack or the perfect performance of an activity: that is, both philosophers hold that pleasure is guaranteed once the conditions outlined in the definition are fulfilled. But, as we will argue, this misrepresents the nature of pleasure: for it can always fail to occur, even if the situation perfectly coincides with the terms of the definition. Thus, for instance, the repetition of a pleasurable activity (or the recurrent replenishment of a lack) will become extremely boring, even if the activity itself remains unaltered (*casu quo* if the lack is not replenished). Against Plato one can adduce both that not every perceived replenishment of a lack is pleasurable and that pleasure might occur without any previous lack; against Aristotle one can state not only that pleasure is not guaranteed by a perfect activity, but also that it might just as well occur when an activity is not perfectly performed.

The juxtaposition of Plato and Aristotle also serves another aim: it will allow us to indicate the dependence of the Neoplatonists on both of them. Plato pays much attention to the role of pleasure within the good life. Indeed it is the central theme of one of his dialogues: the *Philebus*. This work also has the advantage of being the culminating point of the evolution of Plato's theory of pleasure; moreover, it is the most important work on which the Neoplatonists rely when treating the subject. Hence we will pay particular attention to this dialogue, without, however, leaving aside the discussions of pleasure found in the preceding dialogues (*Protagoras, Gorgias, Phaedo*, and the *Republic*).

Plato's discussion of pleasure, however, raises many problems. The most important one is that he pays more attention to the rejection of what he terms 'lower' pleasure than to the elaboration of his own alternative view of 'higher' pleasure. Exactly this problem challenges the hermeneutical skills of the Neoplatonists. The key that they use to disclose Plato's view of 'higher' pleasure is that offered by Aristotle. Although the latter dissents from Plato on almost every point of the theory of pleasure, the Neoplatonists use his ideas in order to clarify what they conceive to be the Platonic doctrine. Thus, it is important to have a clear view of Aristotle's theory in order to understand the Neoplatonic viewpoint.

After an excursus on the Stoics and Epicurus, the second chapter will highlight the standard Neoplatonic doctrine, as it can be retraced in the works of Plotinus (± 204/5 – 270) and Proclus (± 410 – 485). In essence they take over the Platonic definition of pleasure, but clearly confine it to corporeal pleasure. In their determination of higher pleasure, then, they make use of Aristotelian and (to a lesser extent) Stoic elements, stating that the activity of contemplation that constitutes the good life yields a very specific supervenient element: a 'well-being' (εὐπάθεια or εὐφροσύνη). When Plato labels this a pleasure (in his statement that the good life is the combination of pleasure and intellect), this can only have a metaphorical meaning. For it cannot be reconciled with the general definition of pleasure as the replenishment of a lack or the movement towards the natural condition, and thus it cannot be a genuine pleasure. This Neoplatonic analysis combines the opinions of Plato and Aristotle, leading to a very strange conclusion: the 'pleasure' that occurs in the highest activity is not a genuine pleasure.

Damascius (± 462 – 538 ?), on the other hand, whose opinion is discussed in the third chapter, is able to avoid this conclusion. His theory of pleasure is to be found in *In Philebum*, the only ancient commentary on the *Philebus* that is preserved. Damascius defends an essentially Aristotelian position, without, however, giving up the terminology of the Platonic tradition. This particularity causes trouble for the reader of the commentary, who at first sight is confronted with many contradictions due to the opposition between the language of tradition (and the omnipresent view of Proclus, Damascius' immediate predecessor) and his own innovative interpretation, without any clear indication of the differences between the two perspectives.

Damascius accepts that true pleasure (yielded by a state of intellectual rest) is genuine pleasure, since there does exist an activity (and, thus, pleasure) at rest. So he takes over the general idea of the Aristotelian theory, i.e., that the highest activity yields the highest (genuine) pleasure. Nevertheless he tries to safeguard the Platonic position by stating that this pleasure at rest actually is a replenishment. It is not, to be sure, the replenishment of a lack (as there is no lack in this state), but rather the gracious gift of something that was not previously missed. This interpretation is metaphysical, in that it emphasises the gift of the One Good to the intellect, but it can also be seen as a careful analysis of the nature of pleasure. Although Damascius refers only to *true* pleasure when making this statement, we should like to extend the idea to all kinds of pleasure: indeed pleasure often occurs as an unexpected visitor, as something that fulfils us without our directly aiming to achieve it. Conversely, however, the occurrence of pleasure can never be predicted. After all, no theory of pleasure can avoid the fact that in concrete circumstances pleasure can never be forced to occur.

CHAPTER ONE

TWO PARADIGMS: PLATO AND ARISTOTLE

I. Plato: The 'Replenishment Theory'

Plato never presented one consistent survey of his overall views on pleasure. As is the case with many other topics, his doctrines on pleasure are scattered throughout the dialogues, from the earliest to the latest. There is, however, one general element that makes it possible to bring at least some consistency in Plato's theory of pleasure. We will take it as the starting point of our present investigation: although Plato's theory of pleasure clearly evolved over time, his over-all understanding of pleasure as replenishment remained unchanged. Furthermore, the views presented in the early and middle period culminate in one dialogue in which pleasure figures as a central issue: the *Philebus*. This dialogue contains the most elaborate and balanced theory of pleasure Plato ever presented to his readers.

These two claims may seem a bit sketchy as they stand. We will try to elaborate on them in the present section. However, a preliminary remark should be made immediately: given the peculiar way in which Plato presents his ideas, the question of the extent to which his theories can be said to have evolved is difficult to settle. The particular contexts of the dialogues in which Plato discusses pleasure determine, in large part, the manner in which he treats the subject. He may have ignored aspects of the theory that are less relevant in the given context, although he did hold a certain view on these side issues when writing this particular dialogue.

Keeping this restriction in mind, we may take up our starting point: Plato always defines pleasure as the replenishment of a lack, and the manner in which this definition is elaborated evolves, culminating in the *Philebus*. Whereas in such earlier dialogues as the *Protagoras* and the *Gorgias*[1] this 'replenishment of a lack' is not qualified, such middle

---

[1] We adopt the 'standard chronology' of the Platonic works (as expounded, e.g., in Vlastos 1991, 46-47), since there is no reason to reject it from our point of view. On the contrary, the study of the various accounts on pleasure can only confirm the generally accepted chronological order.

dialogues as the *Phaedo*, and, in particular, the *Republic* show an interest in using this definition to draw a qualitative distinction between the different kinds of pleasure. A major puzzle, however, is not solved: the replenishment of a lack is always identified with 'relief from distress'. Apparently, then, one must admit that pleasure always coexists with pain, which makes it very difficult to explain 'pure pleasures' (i.e., pleasures that are not linked to a previous distress), the existence of which is affirmed in the *Republic*. The difficulty is solved, to a certain degree, in the *Philebus*, where Plato establishes a difference between, on the one hand, the scheme of lack and replenishment, and, on the other, pleasure and distress. By introducing this distinction between the occurrence of pleasure and pain, and the underlying physiological scheme, Plato renders it possible to qualify different states according to whether or not the lack and/or replenishment is perceived. 'Mixed pleasures' are states in which the lack, as well as the replenishment, is intense enough to be perceived, whereas in 'pure pleasures' only the replenishment is felt. Apart from these two states, there is a 'neutral state' in which neither the lack nor the replenishment is perceptible.

In this section, we will first trace this evolution in its broad outline through the *Protagoras*, *Gorgias*, *Phaedo*, and *Republic*, before offering a close reading of the *Philebus*. Finally, we will add some critical remarks on the physiological presuppositions of Plato's theory, and more precisely on the immediate link that he sees between pleasure and the (perceived) replenishment of a lack.

1. *From the* Protagoras *to the* Republic

Almost all passages on pleasure in Plato involve a discussion with the hedonists. The overall picture being that Plato rejects the thesis that pleasure is to be identified with the good (with nuances for each dialogue), the very first discussion of pleasure in the Platonic corpus (i.e., in the *Protagoras*) immediately presents a serious problem.

The position of hedonism in the *Protagoras* (352 a – 357 e) is much debated. Socrates seems to defend hedonism, accepting the thesis of his interlocutor that pleasure is the highest good, while at the same time urging him to admit that this thesis must be qualified. When it is made explicit, unconditional hedonism (ascribed to 'the many') necessarily is seen to be self-contradictory: for instance, in certain cases one will have to reject pleasure — and possibly even endure pain — e.g., if pleasure threatens to harm our health, which would eventually entail greater pain. It becomes very difficult, then, to maintain that pleasure is good unconditionally. The solution offered by Socrates is that the good life is guaranteed by an 'art of measuring' (μετρητικὴ τέχνη), which consists in weighing and comparing the quantity of present and anticipated pleasures and pains. Those who are 'overcome with pleasure' act as they do out of *ignorance*. They fail to reach the good life since they do not have any knowledge of excess and lack:

> Well then, gentlemen; since we have seen that the preservation of our life depends on a correct choice of pleasure and pain, be it more or less, larger or smaller or further or nearer, doesn't it seem that the thing that saves our lives is some technique of measurement, to determine which are more, or less, or equal to one another? — Yes, certainly. (357 a-b, trans. C.C.W. Taylor)

It is not at all perspicuous whether Socrates adopts hedonism here and, if he adopts it, why he does so, given his fierce reaction against hedonism in the treatment of pleasure that is to follow in the *Gorgias*, and given the recantation of the measuring technique in the *Phaedo*. Although the question remains unsettled, we would adhere to the view that Socrates does not himself accept hedonism here[2]. He appropriates the opinion of the many, he shows the difficulties and contradictions involved in it, and he presents a solution by which the contradictions can be avoided. This procedure does not entail that Socrates himself must be a hedonist. As is the case elsewhere in the *Protagoras*, Socrates and Protagoras act as the examiners of uncritical, popular conduct and beliefs.

Despite this problem, however, which makes it very difficult to determine the exact meaning of this passage, we can draw some conclusions from the way in which pleasure is discussed here. In the first place, although there is no real determination of the nature of pleasure, it is clear that Socrates makes no distinction between different kinds of pleasure. Pleasure is treated as a whole, and the only difference that is taken into account in the 'measuring technique' is a quantitative one (cf. 356 e; 357 a). Apart from this typically hedonistic idea, which is revoked in later dialogues, the passage also contains the foreshadowing of ideas that play an important role in later works. Thus, the *Protagoras* warns against a danger inherent in the measuring technique, namely, that a pleasure may be wrongly estimated when it

---

[2] Cf. Bidgood 1982, 46-124; A.E. Taylor 1926, 260ff.

is absent (e.g., pleasure in anticipation or in memory). This statement is taken up in the *Philebus*, where the wrong estimation of absent pleasures constitutes one of the kinds of false pleasures. Moreover, a typical argument in the later dialogues is foreshadowed here: the measuring technique implies that knowledge is needed to judge pleasure (357 b-e). It is not explained what kind of knowledge this could be, but, as Socrates himself says, for the argument it suffices to indicate that it is knowledge (357 b). In the *Protagoras* this enables him to state that nobody willingly errs: if one chooses the wrong pleasure, it is out of ignorance or, in this case, out of a wrong estimation of the pleasures and pains that are compared. In the general rejection of hedonism that follows in the later dialogues, this very idea is put forward to explain that the choice for pleasure is always subordinate to knowledge, which immediately dethrones the hedonists' highest principle.

The account in the *Gorgias* (492 e – 500 e) is much more straightforward. Here, Plato forthrightly refutes the hedonists' view. Moreover, we find here for the first time a clear conception of pleasure as the fulfilment of a desire, or the replenishment (πλήρωσις) of a lack. Socrates' interlocutor, Callicles, has just argued that the intemperate man (ἀκόλαστος) is the happiest of all, since he is able to fulfil all his desires. Socrates counters that the good life consists in the escape from the tyranny of desires, and he opens the discussion with a reference to two comparisons that he has once heard. According to the first one, the uninitiated (ἀμύητοι, which stands for the ἀνόητοι, the foolish) in Hades will try to fill a leaky jar (representing the appetites of their soul) with a sieve, whereas the jar of the temperate is adequately filled. The second comparison goes in the same direction: the temperate man has sound jars, full of many things, whereas the intemperate, having leaky vessels, is compelled to fill them endlessly or else to suffer the most extreme distress. The first one will be content and at peace, while the latter cannot but remedy his deficiencies. This, Socrates adds, should convince Callicles that the life of the temperate is much better than that of the intemperate. But Callicles does not agree. The life of the temperate man is not happy at all, since:

> ...that one who has filled up has no pleasure at all any more. It is (...) living like a stone once he has filled up, with no more enjoyment or distress. No; living pleasantly is in this — in having as much as possible flowing in. (494 a-b, trans. Irwin)

Pleasure, then, is the central theme of the discussion. The paradigms of pleasure are drinking when thirsty, eating when hungry, and scratching when itchy. Only physical pleasures are discussed here, but the scheme may be applied to pleasures of the soul as well (cf. 496 e 7-8: εἴτε ψυχῆς εἴτε σώματος, οὐδὲν γὰρ οἶμαι διαφέρει). According to Callicles, constant replenishment gives rise to pleasure, which in turn guarantees the goodness of this kind of life. This hedonistic position makes no distinction between different kinds of pleasure. Socrates, however, urges him to accept two claims. (1) If pleasure and pain occur together (which they do — though not at the same time and in the same respect — since pleasure is the replenishment of a painful lack; 496 e), then pleasure cannot be identical with well being (τὸ εὖ πράττειν), as the latter cannot coincide with its opposite, κακῶς πράττειν. (2) If a brave and wise man is a good man (which Callicles accepts), and if, on the contrary, the coward or foolish man is bad, then pleasure cannot be the criterion for being good, since the coward or foolish man experiences at least as much pleasure as does the brave one. Strangely enough, then, Callicles, who has been reluctant to continue the discussion, suddenly changes his opinion by stating that his view has always been that some pleasures are better than others. This inconsistency is rebuked by Socrates, who shows that it renders untenable Callicles' hedonism: if one pleasure is preferred to another, it is implied that this preference is guided by a criterion external to pleasure: it is the aim that is served by the choice for one specific pleasure rather than another. And since this criterion or aim is the good, pleasure can no longer be said to be identical with the good. Finally, the distinction between goodness and badness is said to be the work of specialists. The life of the 'hunters for pleasure', on the contrary, is fully empirical, without *knowledge* of what is better or worse.

The main points to be extracted from this passage are that a definition of pleasure is established, identifying pleasure with a replenishment (πλήρωσις); although this definition primarily concerns physical pleasure, it can be extended to include pleasure of the soul (see 496 e 7-8). Besides, we find here for the first time a clear assessment of the necessity of introducing a qualitative difference between pleasures. Socrates forces his hedonistic opponent to admit that pleasure is not identical *qua* pleasure, which in the end means that the choice between pleasures is made on the basis of a criterion external to pleasure. If one reads the entire *Gorgias* as a debate on the question 'How should we organise our lives? πῶς βιωτέον;' (Is it better to commit injustice than to undergo it, and who is the happier man, the tyrant versed in rhetoric or the philosopher?), we here find the partial answer that pleasure cannot guarantee the goodness of the good life. The life of those who only strive for pleasure is marred by two fatal errors: in the first place, such a life is like a leaky jar, which never attains complete repletion. In other words, it will never be satisfied, as it lacks measure. Moreover, it is only based on experience, and does not contain knowledge. It is, then, a life of ἄγνοια, and will never know how to distinguish good and evil. These two central claims are at the core of Plato's reaction against hedonism, and they contain a suggestion of the alternative that he has in mind: in order to be an acceptable part of the good life, pleasure has to be *measured*; the unlimited pleasure at which the hedonists aim never leads to satisfaction. Furthermore, pleasure has to be governed by *knowledge* of good and evil; those who prefer a life with only pleasure are never able to make this distinction. These two criteria can be found already in the *Protagoras*, albeit in a less elaborate form: the measuring technique implies that the choice for pleasures (which are measured, at least regarding their quantity) must be governed by knowledge. In later dialogues, these ideas get their full elaboration.

The *Phaedo* is as rigid as is the *Gorgias* in its opposition to those who strive for physical pleasure, but nevertheless it contains some hints of a more positive evaluation of higher pleasure. In the opening scene, Phaedo remarks that 'it's always the greatest of pleasures for me to recall Socrates' (58 d, trans. Gallop), and that the visit to Socrates caused him a strange mixture of distress and pleasure: the painful awareness that this would be Socrates' last day was combined with the pleasure of knowing that Socrates would be a happy man in Hades. However, the pleasure he used to feel while having a philosophical discussion was absent under these circumstances (58 d – 59 a). This leaves no doubt as to the real existence of higher pleasures. The problem with the *Phaedo*, however, is that Plato nowhere explains how this higher pleasure is to be understood.

At 60 b-c, Socrates, who has just been released, wonders about the correlation between pleasure and pain: although they do not want to be present at the same time, they are so strictly linked that the person who wishes to have one of them will have to endure the other as well. This seems to be the assessment of a central point in the discussion of pleasure that follows: pleasure is always linked to distress. Although they do not coincide, the presence of one entails the presence of the other.

In the main discussion on pleasure (64 c – 69 e) it is argued that the body is a hindrance to the aspirations of philosophers. What philosophers aim at is real knowledge, without bodily perception; the different affections of the body (including pleasure) prevent, rather than stimulate, the attainment of this higher goal. In addition to this claim, Plato establishes a comparison between the virtues of philosophers and the virtues of the general public. The paradoxical conclusion is that the virtues of non-philosophers appear to be self-contradictory. Thus, for instance, courage is generally said to be the overcoming of the fear of death. Now, since the fear of death is the consequence of an attachment to the body, the philosopher, who feels no sorrow for the body, is courageous to the highest degree. Similarly, temperance is generally defined as 'not being excited over one's desires, but being scornful of them and well-ordered' (68 c, trans. Gallop). If this is true, Plato suggests, then philosophers will certainly be temperate, as they are highly indifferent to bodily desires. When tested, the so-called courage and temperance of non-philosophers is self-defeating. For non-philosophers are courageous when they want to avoid things that are worse than the present dreadful situation. But then they are courageous because they fear the worse. That is to say, their courage is caused by fear. And those who are temperate abstain from certain pleasures because they desire other ones, of which they fear to be bereft. Their abstinence with regard to one pleasure, then, is caused by their not being able to refrain from another pleasure. Or, in other words, their temperance with respect to the given pleasure is due to an intemperance with respect to a pleasure that they do not want to miss.

The conclusion is that the exchange of pleasures and/or pains cannot be the right path to virtue. The only valuable currency (νόμισμα) is understanding (φρόνησις), which leads to true virtue, whether pleasure is added to it or taken away from it. This leads to a clear revocation of the 'measuring technique' as it was presented in the *Protagoras*. Although there, too, Plato makes it clear that knowledge is needed in order to make the right choice between pleasures, in the *Phaedo* he indicates that this measuring technique does not lead to the good (or virtuous) life. Measuring, weighing, and comparing pleasures and pains does not result in happiness. It is understanding, and understanding alone, that renders our lives good. Apparently this implies that pleasure is not needed in the good life, notwithstanding the omnipresent (but implicit) acceptance of the existence of higher pleasures. The point seems to be that the philosophical life might yield pleasure, but that this is not an essential requirement for qualifying this life as the good life. After all, pleasure is not a preoccupation of the philosopher.

This harsh claim is softened in the subsequent treatments of pleasure. The *Republic* and *Philebus* reveal an increasing awareness of the need to regard pleasure, or at least certain pleasures, as an essential component of the good life. In the *Republic*, the discussion of pleasure (IX, 580 d – 588 a) is intended to support the claim that the life of the philosopher is the happiest life of all. Plato here starts from the tripartition of the soul, as established in the fourth book. Each of the three parts has its typical pleasure, desire, and governing principle. For the part governed by the faculty of learning (ᾧ μανθάνομεν), the desire and pleasure is philosophical; the second part, led by passionate spirit, has its desire and pleasure in power, success and honour; the third part, the appetitive, has its desire and pleasure in money and gain. On the basis of this tripartition, mankind can be classified into three categories, according to the predominance of one of the three parts in each individual. Every person, then, prefers the pleasure of his or her own category, while despising the other pleasures. A true judgment about pleasure, however, can only be made on the basis of experience, understanding, and reasoning (582 a: ἐμπειρίᾳ τε καὶ φρονήσει καὶ λόγῳ). Since these are the privileges of philosophers, the latter will be the best judges: not only are they governed by understanding, they also have experienced the two other kinds of pleasure from childhood; and although they consider many of these pleasures to be necessary, they despise most of them. The other two, on the contrary, might know each other's pleasures, but they never attain the 'delight that the contemplation of reality brings' (582 c).

As an additional proof of the philosopher's happiness, Plato argues that only the wise man's pleasure is true and pure, while that of the others is illusory. To support this claim, he first shows that there is an intermediate state between pleasure and pain, in which the soul experiences neither of them. It is a state of rest (ἡσυχία), whereas both pleasure and pain consist in movement (κίνησις — 583 e). This state, then, cannot be a pleasure or a pain, but it is mistakenly regarded as a pleasure by those who are in pain, and vice versa. In these cases, pleasure and pain are merely appearances, without any reality.

Socrates points out that, in contradistinction to these illusions, there are real pleasures and pains, which do not consist in the cessation of their counterpart. The typical example is the pleasure produced by smells, and there are plenty of other cases too. Pleasures of this kind are true pleasures:

> without any preceding pain there do suddenly arise incredibly intense pleasures, which leave no distress behind when they are over. — That is true, he said. — So we must not believe that pure pleasure is escape from pain, and pure pain is escape from pleasure. (584 b 6 – c 2, trans. Waterfield)

This notion of pure pleasure is immediately contrasted with the 'so-called pleasures', which involve an escape from pain, and which are now said to be caused by the body. The satisfaction of bodily desires, however, is unreal, since the objects of these desires do not have a steady subsistence. This is to say, there is never a complete satisfaction of these desires. On the other hand, the emptiness (κενότης) of the soul (like absence of knowledge, ἄγνοια, or of understanding, ἀφροσύνη) can be truly satisfied, since its objects neither alter nor perish, and are never deceptive.

This analysis is put at the service of a distinction between three states, the lowest of which receives particular attention: in this state people are captivated by the quest for immediate satisfaction of their bodily desires. They are compared to cattle, 'spending their lives grazing, with their eyes turned down and heads bowed towards the ground and their tables' (586 a 7-8). Their pleasures are 'combinations of pleasure and pain, mere effigies of true pleasure' (586 b 7-8, trans. Waterfield). The highest point they ever reach is the 'intermediate state', the state of rest when a desire is satisfied for a moment, which in their eyes constitutes the highest pleasure. But they always fall back, as their unreal desires are never fully satisfied. The third and highest stage is not explicitly described, but it clearly concerns true pleasure in its physical occurrences (as in the example of smell) as well as in the form of satisfactions of the desires of the soul.

This stage, then, is claimed to be the specific domain of the philosopher, the only person to be led by wisdom and truth. It is the result of a harmony in the soul, when its three parts fulfil their proper function under the leadership of the intelligent part. If this harmony is disturbed, the dominating part will lead the entire soul to unsuitable, false pleasures. The passage closes with a witty calculation of the difference between the happiness of the dictator (who is even 'beyond the spurious pleasures') and the king (or the philosopher), whose life is '729 times more pleasant than a dictator's'.

This discussion offers a further elaboration of the ideas presented in the *Phaedo*: the assessment that the three parts of the soul have their own pleasures and desires — with the clear superiority of the intellectual part — parallels the thesis that the philosopher is able to take distance from the desires that originate in the body. It is not clear whether Plato wants us to think that pleasure is a necessary ingredient in the good life of philosophers, or rather that, as suggested in the *Phaedo*, although the pleasure of the philosophers is the highest one, they could be happy without pleasure. This question will be asked and answered in the *Philebus*.

Indeed, in many respects the theory found in this passage is the immediate predecessor to the elaborate theory of pleasure in the *Philebus*. We find here in the *Republic* the three main elements (mixed pleasure, the neutral, intermediate state, and true pleasure) on which the doctrine of the *Philebus* will be based. But the ideas are not completely developed in the *Republic*[3]. In the first place, one feels that Plato is very keen to describe the lowest stage, whereas he explains the middle by contrast with the lowest, and he only mentions the highest. This again reveals the general tendency to suggest the desirability of a higher pleasure through the negative description of the lower. As we have said already, it is obvious that the highest stage, which is the life of the philosopher (devoted to knowledge and understanding), involves true pleasures. But, then again, this causes a problem. Pure pleasures are introduced as pleasures that are not the relief of a preceding distress, so, at first sight, they are not the satisfaction of a desire. But in the description of the life of the philosopher, the definition of pleasure as a πλήρωσις is extended to the level of the soul, explicitly combining it with the notion of true pleasure (585 a 8 – b 11)[4]. Thus, it is stated that true pleasure consists in a satisfaction of the 'emptiness' of the soul by means of objects that are not perishable and not deceptive. In this sense, then, true pleasure would be the fulfilment of a desire after all (its truth being due to the truth of its objects), and we are left with a

---

[3] Cf. Annas 1981, 306-314.

[4] Cf. Gosling-Taylor 1982, 105 (discussing the *Republic*): 'Plato is trying to extend the physiologically inspired replenishment model of pleasure beyond the physiological sphere ... This gives him a general theory of pleasure'.

contradiction. Moreover, the problem is made worse by the juxta-position of the statement that true pleasure is the pleasure of the soul (complemented with the assessment that mixed pleasures originate in the body) and the statement that the pleasure procured by smells is the paradigm of true pleasure. So the class of true pleasures is not confined to pleasures of the soul. But, conversely, it does not seem to be the case that all pleasures of the soul are true pleasures. Many of them (if not the majority) are mixed, preceded by a distress. There is, then, a conflict between the classification of pleasures under the headings 'physical' and 'belonging to the soul', on the one hand, and the organization of pleasures into 'true' and 'mixed' ones, on the other hand. These two classifications are certainly not coextensive, although at first sight Plato seems to suggest that they are.

In our opinion, at the time of writing *Republic* IX, Plato did not have an answer to these problems (provided that he was even aware of them). As has been said earlier, in the *Philebus* he will offer a solution by introducing a difference between the escape from pain and the replenishment of a lack, although this does not mean that every problem will be solved in the *Philebus*.

2. *The* Philebus

The *Philebus* presents many difficulties. One of the major problems, which is not often treated in the secondary literature, resides in the very title of the dialogue. Strangely enough, the title character refuses from the outset to partake in the discussions. His follower Protarchus has to take his place. The quite exceptional interventions of Philebus are questions for clarification or morose remarks against Socrates; they seem to be meant in the first place to remind us that Philebus is still there. Why does he remain silent? Or rather, if his role is to remain silent, how are we to explain the title of the *Philebus*? The less obvious a title, the greater its importance for the interpretation of the work.

Therefore, it is important to examine the extent to which we are informed about Philebus. He is clearly characterised as a hedonist. Maybe he is not a teacher, but at least he is presented as an authority concerning pleasure: the anti-hedonists are called 'Philebus' enemies' (44 b 6)[5]. He adores pleasure as 'his' goddess (12 b). Before the actual

---

[5] A.E. Taylor 1956, 11-12 opposes this view by stating that Philebus must have

beginning of the dialogue he had stated in a discussion with Socrates that pleasure is the good[6]. Thus, paradoxically enough, Socrates' interlocutor is a hedonist who remains silent. The fact that Philebus' name is given to the dialogue indicates that Plato wants to question hedonism as such.

As we have seen, this is not Plato's first reaction against hedonism. The discussion with the partisans of pleasure runs throughout the entire earlier work of Plato, but a real solution is never given there. The discussion always ends as a kind of trench warfare in which each party stubbornly defends its conviction[7].

In the *Philebus* Plato makes the question about the relation between pleasure and intellect in the good life the central theme of the dialogue. The status quo of the previous dialogues is the starting point of the *Philebus*[8]. This is confirmed by the formal structure of the work. The dialogue starts *in medias res*, at a point where the discussion between Socrates and Philebus has already come to an end. According to several references made in the dialogue, the discussion reached a deadlock in a stubborn confrontation between Philebus' hedonism and Socrates' intellectualism. This reflects the situation of the earlier dialogues, but it is only the beginning of the dialogue: Protarchus will take over the position of his master. This indicates that Plato wants to get further than the initial status quo. What he wants to do here is to criticise hedonism from within, starting from the premises that the hedonists themselves accept, and without a priori denying the importance of pleasure in the good life. At a certain point, Socrates will suddenly break through the sterile opposition sketched at the beginning. He remembers that the good life does not consist in pure pleasure or pure intellect. Rather it is a mixture of both, or at least of certain kinds of pleasure and intellectual activity (20 b – 23 b). Plato thus displays a certain favorableness towards pleasure, and changes the

---

been a young fellow. The question is not very important, but one should nevertheless view Philebus as a serious man who is able to account for his opinions. If not, a refutation of his hedonism would not make much sense. As Diès (1941, LIV) remarks, hedonism is not the privilege of Philebus, 'ἀλλὰ καὶ ἄλλων πολλάκις μυρίων' (66 e 3). So Plato reacts against a widespread uncritical hedonism.

[6]   This previous discussion is referred to several times in the dialogue: 11 a – 12 b; 18 d – 19 e; 59 d – 61 c.

[7]   Frede 1993, LXIX; 1992, 433-437; Gosling-Taylor 1982, 45-128; Diès 1941, XXXV-XL.

[8]   Cf. Guthrie 1978, 202.

tone of the discussion. The central question, 'Is the good life a life entirely devoted to pleasure or to intellect?' is now turned into the problem of which component of the mixed life is more responsible for this life's being good. Plato's answer consists in a mild intellectualism, together with the acknowledgment of the importance of pleasure. In the meantime, however, the initial consensus with the hedonists serves as a basis on which to criticise their claims. This presupposes that Socrates' analysis of pleasure is accepted by the hedonists themselves. Therefore it is essential that Socrates' interlocutor is (at least at the outset) a convinced hedonist, and that he feels the authoritative presence of his master Philebus. On one single occasion the latter himself expresses his agreement with Socrates: he approves of the view that pleasure is unlimited (27 e 5-9). The hedonist's agreement is crucial here, since the unlimitedness of pleasure is later made an important criterion by which to assign to pleasure a lower position in the good life. Thus what might at first sight look like a minor detail is in fact of major importance in Plato's strategy.

Plato's critique not only is a direct attack of the content of the hedonistic position. It can also be deduced from stylistic elements of the dialogue, and in the first place from the problem concerning the title. At the outset, Philebus definitively entrenches himself in his position: 'My view is, and always will be, that pleasure is the un-doubted winner' (12 a 8-9, trans. Gosling). Young Protarchus takes over as Socrates' interlocutor, and initially defends the views of Philebus. But he gradually comes to understand Socrates' arguments; eventually he leaves his trenches and goes over to the enemy. Plato very skillfully depicts this evolution. To the question of whether there is any need for intellect and the like in the good life, Protarchus initially answers without restraint: 'Why? I should have everything if I had pleasure!' (21 b 2-3). At a later stage, however, he does not venture to contradict Socrates: 'Socrates is right, Philebus, we must do as he asks' — to which Philebus sneers: 'Well, haven't you undertaken to answer for me?' — 'I have indeed,' poor Protarchus answers, 'but I am in something of a quandary' (28 b 4-7). Finally, he surrenders: 'So far as I can see, Socrates, anyone who proposes pleasure as our good is involved in considerable absurdity' (55 a 9-11).

In the dramatic setting, the reader is the witness of an intrigue, a triangular relationship in which Socrates eventually courts the favour of Philebus' pupil. It is amazing that Philebus allows this to happen, since the signs are clear enough. Why does Philebus not intervene when he sees that Protarchus is leaving him? Thus, the problem of his abstention is reinforced: it brings him into an isolated position, and undermines his authority.

We would like to argue here that the silence of Philebus is functional within Plato's refutation of hedonism. Philebus remains the main character, the model hedonist. In a radical and uncritical way he continues on his way from one pleasure to another, wandering about in the pursuit of an indeterminate desire. This is a weak position, as it condemns him to a solipsistic pleasure: only what he finds enjoyable is worthwhile, and he cannot explain his pleasure to others. But his weakness is his strength. He can never be obliged to question his life choice, if he refrains from all criticism.

Protarchus, on the other hand, is willing to discuss, and wants to found his hedonism on sound arguments. Such 'philosophical' hedonists are in a stronger position, as they present themselves as interlocutors in the philosophical discussion. But their strength is their weakness: they are prepared to accept criticism, and to account for their convictions, which means that they might — and will — eventually be defeated.

2.1. *The Definition of Pleasure*

In the *Philebus*, the analysis of pleasure (31 b – 55 c) starts from a definition of the term under discussion. Socrates takes a pragmatic starting point: we should concentrate on the clearest forms of pleasure, i.e., those that are generally regarded as genuine pleasures. This certainly is the case, Socrates suggests, with the pleasures associated with eating and drinking, so long as one is not yet satiated. So, if we can infer anything about pleasure from these instances, it should be that pleasure is the replenishment of a lack. Eating or drinking is pleasurable only insofar as we are first hungry or thirsty. Once we are satisfied, our pleasure comes to an end. Pleasure, then, is coextensive with the restoration of a state of satisfaction, which Plato calls the 'natural condition' (κατὰ φύσιν). But the satisfaction is never definitively attained: the process of the replenishment of a lack is always thwarted by a new lack, and so on. Our life is a permanent flux between a 'preternatural' and a 'natural' condition, and pleasure and distress are to be situated within this flux. Socrates recapitulates his definition in the following way:

To sum up, don't you think it's a fair argument that as regards the form of things whose natural combination of indeterminate and determinant makes them alive my point holds, that when this form is disrupted, the disruption is distress, but the move to their own proper way of being, this return, is always by contrast a pleasure?[9]

We find here a clear statement of the definition of pleasure that was present (implicitly or explicitly) in previous dialogues. For a correct understanding of this definition in the *Philebus*, however, one should also take into account the physiology upon which it is based, and which is presented in the immediate context (*Phil.* 32 c – 36 c). Socrates here makes a clear distinction between pleasure (or distress) and lack (or replenishment). One should acknowledge, he points out, that the flux of lack and replenishment is inevitable and continuous, whereas (obviously) we do not feel pleasure and distress all the time. Not all bodily affections (παθήματα) penetrate the soul. When a stimulus vanishes before reaching the soul, it is not perceived. Thus, a lack that is too small to be perceived will not cause distress, and neither will a replenishment that is too small to be perceived give rise to pleasure.

Although this physiological analysis is presented in the context of a 'different kind' of pleasure, i.e., the pleasure in memory or anticipation of a replenishment, it does not imply a new definition. For the specific pleasure in memory or anticipation always presupposes a previous genuine replenishment. This, by the way, is the argument used to distinguish between memory and recollection (ἀνάμνησις): for the latter no sense perception is needed, whereas the former presupposes perception as a *conditio sine qua non* (34 a 10 – c 3). Elsewhere, too, Plato emphasises the link between memory and sense perception: our memory might be mistaken, since, being like a painter (39 b), it may draw a situation that never existed nor ever will exist. If we enjoy this fictitious memory or anticipation, our pleasure is false (36 c – 41 a). Pleasure in anticipation, then, always presupposes the general defini-tion of pleasure as being the replenishment of a lack. It can only be termed pleasure if it refers to a genuine replenishment. There is, then, no new definition involved. Only the terms, and the physiological

---

9   32 a 8 – b 4: καὶ ἑνὶ λόγῳ σκόπει εἴ σοι μέτριος ὁ λόγος ὃς ἂν φῇ τὸ ἔκ τε [Ast: τῆς mss. + Stobaeus] ἀπείρου καὶ πέρατος κατὰ φύσιν ἔμψυχον γεγονὸς εἶδος, ὅπερ ἔλεγον ἐν τῷ πρόσθεν, ὅταν μὲν τοῦτο φθείρηται, τὴν μὲν φθορὰν λύπην εἶναι, τὴν δ'εἰς τὴν αὐτῶν οὐσίαν ὁδόν, ταύτην δὲ αὖ πάλιν τὴν ἀναχώρησιν πάντων ἡδονήν (trans. Gosling). The same definition is to be found at *Timaeus* 64 a – 65 b. Cf. infra, p.27.

basis, of the definition are adapted here to a pleasure other than one
that is strictly corporeal, and within this enlargement Socrates adds a
point that is essential for the entire theory.

Contrary to what most commentators hold, this definition in the
Philebus is not confined to bodily pleasure alone. Although bodily
replenishment is its basis and starting point, Plato does extend the
definition to all kinds of pleasure. The pleasure that the body takes in
eating and drinking has been chosen as the starting point exactly
because everyone agrees that this involves genuine pleasure (31 e 2-3).
The analysis would have been less perspicuous if another example
were chosen as the starting point. But this does not mean that the
definition must be restricted to bodily pleasure alone. One can inspect
a whole series of examples in the *Philebus* that make it clear that the
definition is never recanted.

   After the presentation of the definition, Plato discusses examples of
mixed pleasures (46 c – 50 e), i.e., pleasures that are always inter-
mingled with distress. This presupposes the definition of pleasure as a
(perceived) restoration of a (perceived) lack. The first group of examples (46 c – 47 b) concerns pleasure of the body as such, without
any intervention of the soul (like scratching as a relief of itching, or like
being warmed when one is cold). We have both contrasting perceptions[10] (hot and cold, itching and scratching) at the same time,
sometimes both being equally balanced, sometimes one of them being
preponderant. The second group (47 c – d) presents the mixed pleasure of the combination of body and soul. According to Socrates, these
examples have been treated before. They must be, then, the pleasures
of memory and anticipation, presupposing a genuine bodily replenishment (cf. 35 e 9 – 36 c 1). The third group (47 d – 50 e) exemplifies the
pleasures of the soul alone, without the intervention of the body. This
group is discussed extensively, but in an incredibly superficial manner.
Apparently, Plato wants to prove that emotions and passions (anger,
fear, love, etc.; see 47 e 1-2) are a mixture of pleasure and distress.
One example is chosen as being the most difficult one, and thus
serving as the touchstone, a clear understanding of which will enable

---

   [10]   This 'perception' of course implies the functioning of the soul. Plato cannot
mean that 'pleasure of the body without intervention of the soul' is fully detached
from the psychic functions. He rather wants to indicate the 'place' where this affection initially occurs: in the body, in the soul, or in the combination of both.

us to extrapolate the typical elements of all other kinds of emotions (48 b 4-6). This example is the emotion of the spectators of plays, and more precisely of comedy. Plato indicates that the pleasure we take in a comedy, on seeing the misfortune of our neighbours, is caused by a lack in our soul: jealousy (φθόνος, 48 b 8 – c 1). Here, again, laughing (pleasure) is seen as the replenishment of a lack (revealed in jealousy). The analysis, though, is fairly unsatisfactory: Plato nowhere explains how laughing stems from jealousy, whether jealousy is the only impulse that makes us laugh at a comedy, and whether this really is a replenishment: does our jealousy come to an end (i.e., is it replenished) when one laughs at the misfortune of one's neighbours? Furthermore, what would be the ethical value of such a position? Contrasted with, e.g., Aristotle's analysis in the *Poetics* of the effect of tragedy (and this may doubtlessly be inferred also for his analysis of comedy), this passage is extremely shallow. One can only notice, together with Dorothea Frede, that Plato indicates that the allegedly innocent pleasure in a comedy actually reveals a moral shortcoming, and that 'Plato may intend to show there are no innocent emotions'[11]. But even if one takes this for granted, the thesis is put forward in a rather elusive way.

But nevertheless, we can deduce from this passage — and this is of main interest here — that the general definition of pleasure remains unchanged, even at the level of the affects of our soul. In all cases (Plato cites only a few examples, but indicates that the analysis holds for all emotions), pleasure coincides with the replenishment of a lack.

Further on in the dialogue, in the discussion of true pleasure (50 e – 53 c), the definition is restated. In addition to the mixed pleasure discussed until now, there is, Socrates says, a kind of pleasure that is completely devoid of distress. This pure, or unmixed, pleasure is true pleasure. After an enumeration of pleasures falling within this class (pleasure caused by beautiful colours, forms, smells and sounds[12]), Plato generalises the issue:

> and generally [true pleasure consists in] any [state] where the deprivation is imperceptible and which supply perceptible replenishments which are both without pain and pleasant. (51 b 5-7)

---

[11]   Frede 1992, 451.

[12]   51 b 3-5 (further elaborated at 51 c 1 – e 5). Later on, 'pleasure at studying' (ἐν τοῖς μαθήμασιν) is added to the list (51 e 7 – 52 b 9).

The essential feature here, which constitutes a major improvement compared to the parallel account in the *Republic*, is the reference made to the condition of perceptibility of a lack or replenishment that lay at the basis of the definition: not all affections penetrate the soul. If they languish before reaching our perception, they will not cause distress. This, of course, does not mean that man is able to escape from the flux of lack and replenishment after all. It only reveals the possibility of lack and replenishment being present without causing pleasure or distress, viz. when they are too minor to be perceived.

In the case of true pleasure, the lack is not felt, whereas its replenishment is. Hence it is possible to feel a pleasure without any previous distress. The clearest example is the replenishment of forgetfulness (51 e 7 – 52 b 9). By its very nature, the process of forgetting is not perceived: if one were aware of it, there would be no forgetfulness. If, then, one enjoys remembering, one feels true pleasure — with one important restriction: the memory should be sudden and unexpected; if one had to make an effort in order to remember, then the sensation of a lack (and hence distress) was involved, which would prevent the pleasure from being true.

Another consequence of the scheme that lies at the basis of the definition is that true pleasure, by its very nature, never can be violent. Violent pleasure, Plato intimates, completely belongs to the class of the unlimited, the 'more and less', whereas true pleasure is essentially 'moderate' (ἔμμετρα, 52 c 1 – d 2). Perhaps Plato was thinking that, if true pleasure consists in the replenishment of a lack that was too small to be perceived, then the replenishment itself will not be violent either. Apparently, a slight difference between the perceptibility of lack and the perceptibility of replenishment is possible, since in the case of true pleasure the lack is not felt, whereas the replenishment is; but the discrepancy cannot be such that the lack is not felt, whereas the replenishment is violent. True pleasure, then, will by definition be a non-violent pleasure. This qualifies the earlier claim that pure pleasure is 'incredibly intense' (ἀμήχανοι τὸ μέγεθος, *Rep.* 584 b 7). In the new scheme presented in the *Philebus*, true pleasure cannot be intense, although one can still say that it remains the greatest possible replenishment of the least possible lack.

On our view, however, this thesis, which is the immediate consequence of the definition, is erroneous. Nothing prevents a true pleasure (a pleasure without distress) from being violent. It is very well possible that one is truly exalted by a pleasure that is not preceded by distress. As we will explain in detail later on, this misconception is due to the acceptance of an automatic link (or even an identity) between replenishment and pleasure as postulated in the definition.

The same line of argument recurs at 42 c – 44 a, where Socrates and Protarchus discuss the neutral state, the misconception of which is one of the forms of false pleasures. The passage starts with an explicit reference to the definition of pleasure:

> We have often said that when a thing's constitution is being disrupted by compression or dissolution of elements, or by satiety or deprivation, or by excessive growth or wasting, then distress, pain, suffering, every-thing of that sort, follow these in their train. — Yes, that's familiar doctrine. — But when a thing's proper constitution is being restored we agreed among ourselves that this restoration was pleasure? — We did. (42 c 9 – d 9, trans. Gosling)

Here, the definition is used as an argument for the possibility of a state in which neither the lack nor the replenishment is felt. This application is immediately met by the objection that a state without lack or replenishment is impossible, since, 'as the experts say, everything is in a constant flux and reflux' (43 a 1-3). So the flux of lack and replenishment is inevitable, and the very idea of a neutral state seems to be erroneous. But Socrates says that this ought not to be a fatal objection, and he makes his point by referring to the underlying physiological scheme. If one admits that the flux of lack and replenish-ment is inevitable, one can still defend the view that sometimes neither of them is perceived. For, Socrates adds, we have seen that affections must be intense enough to be perceptible (43 a 10 – c 7). If they are not, we will feel neither pleasure nor distress. The neutrality of this state indicates that we attain here an interruption of the whirl of pleasure and distress, but not, of course, of lack and replenishment.

Could one say, then, the interlocutors wonder, that such a life without distress is the most pleasurable? In that case, pleasure would be nothing other than freedom from distress. This opinion has always been strongly refuted by Plato. As we have seen, in the *Republic* he indicated that this intermediate state, between pure pleasure and pleasure that is always mixed with pain, cannot itself be pleasure. It can only mistakenly be seen as pleasure when compared with the lower pleasures, by those who, immersed in mixed pleasures, believe that the removal of all pains will constitute the highest pleasure. In the *Philebus*, the situation is clearer still, precisely because Plato adds the new element of physiology, which enables him to explain the continuity of the three stages elaborated in the *Republic*. For on the basis of the physiological scheme the highest pleasure can be qualified as pure pleasure since in this case the lack is not felt, whereas there is pleasure in the perceived replenishment of the lack. At the lowest level, both lack and replenishment are perceived, which means that we feel pleasure as well as pain. The intermediate level is a disposition in which neither lack nor replenishment are perceived, although both are present. One must, then, draw a clear distinction between this neutral or intermediate state and the highest pleasure.

The opinion defended here is later rejected by Epicurus, who refuses to accept a neutral state between pleasure and distress. In its stead, he distinguishes between two kinds of pleasure: the 'kinetic' and the 'katastematic'. Kinetic pleasure (pleasure in movement) consists in the escape from pain. But the highest pleasure, the katastematic, is a condition (κατάστημα) of balance that occurs when all pain has been removed. According to Epicurus, then, the absence of pain itself is a pleasure, and even the most desirable kind of pleasure[13].

On Plato's view, this is an untenable position. By definition, this neutral state is neither pleasure nor distress. How, then, could one maintain the idea that it constitutes pleasure — let alone the highest pleasure! The absence of distress is not necessarily pleasurable. Those who think they feel pleasure, when they are only free of pain, err: their pleasure is false (43 d 4 – 44 a 11).

This statement can be seen as a corollary of Plato's definition of pleasure. If indeed pleasure is entirely linked to the movement towards the natural condition, and thus to the replenishment of a lack, then it is impossible to situate pleasure in a condition beyond all lack. But, on the other hand, the natural condition *in se* is inaccessible: our life is always in movement (i.e., the aforementioned flux), and we will never attain a state in which all lack will be resolved. One must, then, in considering Plato's view — and this has not been sufficiently acknowledged by most commentators[14] — make a clear distinction between the neutral state and the natural condition. The absence of pleasure

---

[13]   For a discussion of Epicurus' theory of pleasure: cf. infra, p.79-87.

[14]   The identification of the neutral state with the natural condition is made by ancient as well as contemporary commentators, e.g., for the contemporaries: Frede 1992, 440 and 448, and Dillon 1996, 106; for the ancients: Speusippus (fr. 77 and 84 Tarán; cf. Dillon 1996, 100 and 105-106; Tarán 1981, 437), Alcinous (*Didasc.* 185.24-187.7), and also Damascius, as we will see later on.

and pain is fundamentally different from the absence of lack and replenishment. The latter state is strictly impossible, whereas the former is attained intermittently.

Thus, the natural condition being inaccessible, the neutral state is nothing but a kind of contentment, and not at all a pleasure. To the contrary: as pleasure is absent here, this state cannot be a modality of the good life, which should always be a combination of pleasure and intellect. On Plato's view, the highest pleasure is true or pure pleasure, which in its turn is to be distinguished from the natural condition as well as from the neutral state[15].

From this survey we may conclude that the definition of pleasure remains unchanged throughout the *Philebus*: as in the former dialogues, pleasure always is the replenishment of a lack, with the additional qualification that the replenishment should be perceived in order to yield pleasure. Against this conclusion one might object that Plato here does not present his own ideas: given the context of the *Philebus*, which largely consists in the conversion of a hedonist, one might argue that, for polemical reasons, Plato presents a definition he himself does not agree with. The definition would then only serve as an argument *ad hominem* against the hedonist. This is the view defended by W.K.C. Guthrie[16]. However, that this is definitely not the case is made clear by the earlier dialogues, which also contain just one definition of pleasure. Moreover the *Timaeus*, which is almost contemporary with the *Philebus*, presents the same definition, without any reference to an anti-hedonist polemic:

> The nature of pleasure and pain, then, must be conceived as follows. An affection which violently disturbs the normal state, if it happens all of a sudden, is painful, while the sudden restoration of the normal state is pleasant; and an affection which is mild and gradual is impercep-tible, while the converse is of a contrary character.[17]

---

[15] This point is confirmed in the *Republic* (where the neutral state is intermediate between lower, or mixed, and pure pleasure, cf. supra), and in the *Laws*, where Plato affirms that 'we desire that pleasure should be ours, but pain we neither choose nor desire; and the neutral state we do not desire in place of pleasure, but we do desire it in exchange for pain' (V, 733 b, trans. Bury).

[16] Guthrie 1978, 199.

[17] *Tim.* 64 c 7 – d 3: τὸ δὴ τῆς ἡδονῆς καὶ λύπης ὧδε δεῖ διανοεῖσθαι· τὸ μὲν παρὰ φύσιν καὶ βίαιον γιγνόμενον ἀθρόον παρ' ἡμῖν πάθος ἀλγεινόν, τὸ δ' εἰς φύσιν ἀπιὸν πάλιν ἀθρόον ἡδύ, τὸ δὲ ἠρέμα καὶ κατὰ σμικρὸν ἀναίσθητον, τὸ δ' ἐναντίον τούτοις

The emphasis on the sudden character of pleasure and pain, which is likewise present in the *Republic* (584 b 6-7; cf. supra), is to be contrasted with the immediately following assessment that gradual affections are imperceptible. Thus, if an affection were not sudden, it would not cause pleasure or pain. There is, then, no difference at all between this definition and the one presented in the *Philebus*; and this even holds for the physiological basis upon which the definition is built. Plato thus makes it very clear that he does accept it unconditionally.

At first sight, one might be tempted to conclude that here Plato has found the magic potion that makes pleasure manageable: if pleasure occurs in the movement towards the natural condition, it may suffice to know the way to the natural condition, in order to provoke our pleasure; nothing seems to prevent us, then, from attaining the perfect pleasure.

But Plato is not so optimistic. He never defines the natural condition. What, in any case, could be the full repletion or the ultimate abolition of all lack? And how would we experience that? If pleasure occurs in the restoration of the natural condition, then the natural condition itself is devoid of all pleasure. Apart from the fact that a life without pleasure is rejected throughout the *Philebus* (since it is not desirable for human beings), the natural condition must logically be an unattainable state, as it is the absence not only of pleasure and distress, but even of the underlying lack and replenishment. It was clearly stated that in our concrete life this total escape from the flux of lack and replenishment is impossible. The natural condition is a limit, a horizon that we will never attain in its pure form[18]. We are bound to a

---

ἐναντίως (trans. Cornford, modified).

[18] Perhaps 'purity' is the most problematised term in the *Philebus*. Everywhere in the dialogue, the notion of the 'mixed' occupies the central position in the argument: the mixture of limit and limitlessness, of pleasure and intellect, of body and soul, of lack and replenishment, of being and becoming. Thus, the *Philebus* counters other dialogues, e.g. the *Phaedo*, where the possibility of the purification (κάθαρσις) of the soul is evidenced. However, Dorothea Frede 1993, LXIX indicates that this does not mean that the *Philebus* would constitute an "exception": the same attitude towards purity is found in the *Symposium*. Thus, according to Frede, Plato shows "that humans are forever in-between creatures, between the mortal and immortal, the finite and infinite, the good and bad". This remark is made also by H.-G. Gadamer 1931, 176: "Die ganze Fragestellung des *Philebos* beruht auf der Voraussetzung, daß wir nicht göttliche Wesen, sondern Menschen sind". See also Guthrie 1978, 201.

mixed, concrete (in the etymological meaning of the term) life, in which the replenishment of a lack is always thwarted by a new lack. We are imprisoned in our condition of lack and replenishment. But this does not mean that our life would be a vale of tears: it is owing to this very fact that we are able to feel pleasure.

2.2. *Plato's Critique of Hedonism*

In the *Philebus*, the definition of pleasure, which is the starting point of the examination of pleasure, constitutes a point on which both Socrates and Protarchus agree. The discussion, then, starts from a consensus between the hedonist and his opponent. In the meantime, however, the claims of radical hedonism and radical intellectualism are disproved by the acceptance of the mixedness of the good life. Those who recognise only one of the components (whether it be pleasure or intellect) deny our concrete human situation. This central idea forces the interlocutors to reconsider their claims and restate the problem. The ante no longer is the first prize, but rather the second: which of the two is more responsible for the goodness of the good life?

But, after all, the hedonist seems to defend a lost cause. One finds, in the initial consensus, all of the elements that will eventually force him to forsake his thesis. This conclusion is not achieved by positing a rigorous intellectualism against the hedonists. It follows rather from a stringent analysis of the implications of the definition of pleasure.

In the first place, Plato's intellectualism is very modest in this dialogue. The choice for intellect is made only through the denial of the claims of pleasure, rather than by elaborating a positive counterpart. In this sense, the witticism of Protarchus, 'It shows good sense that intellect didn't claim first prize' (23 a 1-2), can be seen as a declaration of the platform.

As in the earlier dialogues, Plato here advances the idea that the intellect is required both to moderate pleasure and to make a right choice between different pleasures. In this dialogue (*Phil.* 23 c – 30 e), he expresses this idea by regarding intellect as belonging to the class of the cause, which brings together limit (measure) and the unlimited (pleasure). But, so it seems, Plato wants to confine the analysis of intellect to this point. If intellect can be shown to be that which imposes limits on pleasure, its superiority to pleasure is demonstrated, and no further examination of intellect is needed for the present purpose.

This is confirmed elsewhere in the dialogue. Plato's examination of the different kinds of intellectual activity (55 c – 59 d) is fairly super ficial. Apparently, the passage is only meant to balance the analysis of pleasure. Intellect is reduced to 'the different sciences', culminating in Dialectics as the highest and purest of all (57 e 6 – 59 c 6). Plato nowhere specifies how these sciences relate to 'intellect'. Besides, it is remarkable that he does not use one unequivocal term to indicate what, thus far, we have called 'intellect'. He variously calls it 'understanding' (φρόνησις or τὸ φρονεῖν), science (ἐπιστήμη), memory (μνήμη and τὸ μεμνῆσθαι), and intellect (νοῦς)[19], without clarifying the difference between these terms. In the final classification, however, there seems to be an important difference between intellect (νοῦς) and understanding (φρόνησις) on the one hand, which obtain the third prize, and the sciences (ἐπιστῆμαι), on the other hand, which, together with the skills (τέχναι) and right opinions (δόξαι ὀρθαί), are put at the fourth level (66 b 5 – c 2). This difference is not explained. The contrast with the rigorous severity towards pleasure is obvious. Clearly, it is not intellect that is at stake in the *Philebus*.

If Plato had defended an extreme intellectualism against the hedonists' claim, then he himself would have committed the error that he charges them with committing. His most important reproach — against both extremes — seems to be, not that they offer this or that description of the good, but that they present any unequivocal determination of it at all. The good, he says, cannot be determined by one single term. Our 'way leading to the good' (61 a 7) does not bring us beyond the 'threshold of the good' (64 c 1). Apparently, its dwelling place is too remote to be accessible to us[20]. Of course, one can affirm, as Plato does at the outset of the dialogue (20 c – 23 a), that the good must be sufficient (ἱκανόν), desirable (ἐφετόν), and perfect (τέλειον). But these are only formal criteria, which do not determine the essence of the good. On the other hand, we do have some adequate criteria by which to judge whether a mixture is good:

> If we cannot use just one category to catch the good, let us take this
> trio, beauty, proportion, truth, and treating them as a single unit say

---

[19] Apart from these, he also uses σύνεσις, τὸ νοεῖν, and τὸ λογίζεσθαι, and often resumes them using the formula 'καὶ πάντα τὰ τούτων συγγενῆ' (thus, e.g., 11 b 7; 13 e 4; 19 d 5 ; 21 a 14).

[20] Cf. Bidgood 1982, 189-190.

that this is the element in the mixture that we should most correctly hold responsible, that it is because of this as being good that such a mixture becomes good (65 a 1-5).

Thus, a mixture is as it ought to be, if it is well proportionate, beautiful and true. If one of these elements is lacking, the mixture cannot be sufficient, desirable or perfect.

Once agreement has been reached on this point, the solution to the initial problem lies near at hand. The goodness of the good life is due to that component of the mixture which is most akin to the three characteristics of the good. If, then, we judge pleasure by this standard, its inferiority is obvious. Being unlimited and indeterminate in itself, it is totally devoid of truth and proportion. And beauty is denied of it in the following way:

> ... we even experience shame ourselves [i.e., when noticing someone indulging in the most intense pleasures]. Indeed, so far as possible, we try to keep them out of sight, confining all that sort of thing to the hours of darkness on the ground that it is not proper for the light of day to see them. (66 a 1-4, trans. Gosling)

In the attribution of the three characteristics to intellect, Plato's account is much less precise. Only the link between truth and intellect is well-founded: intellect is always led by truth; it is the privileged place in which to find truth. Beauty and proportion of intellect, however, are merely claimed, but not argued for. Again we must notice that the analyses plead against pleasure rather than in favour of intellect.

Does this account suffice to convince the hedonist? Protarchus at least is converted. But is he the representative of hedonism here? We might consider him to be too compliant, which would considerably weaken Plato's critique: it would then prove to be strong enough to unsettle *some* hedonists, without however refuting hedonism as such. Indeed, hedonists could maintain that the alleged priority of the intellect only indicates that the intellect is an instrument by which to reach the ultimate good, which after all is pleasure. But, in fact, Plato's critique is much more thoroughgoing. His analyses allow us to infer that no hedonist accepts that the criteria used to pursue certain pleasures lie within pleasure itself. Hedonists, too, will implicitly subordinate their pleasure to external factors.

This point can be clarified by a thorough consideration of the opposition between the purity and intensity of pleasure that is a direct consequence of the definition of pleasure. Hedonists will point out that the only criterion by which to make a choice between different pleasures is quantity or intensity. For, qualitatively they are all identical; there is no difference between pleasures *qua* pleasure. According to the definition, however, the choice for the most intense pleasure entails an acceptance of the most intense distress, since the intensity of pleasure is proportional to the magnitude of the lack that is being replenished. The more pleasure that hedonists want, the more they will have to endure distress. At first sight, this is an acceptable consequence: if an intense distress eventually leads to more pleasure, then this distress is instrumentally good, and hedonists may choose it because of its pleasurable effects. But the *Philebus* intimates that this leads to an internal contradiction within hedonism. If hedonists pursue pure or true pleasure, unmixed with distress, then they should acknowledge that pure pleasure is always measured or moderate (cf. supra), and thus cannot be the most intense pleasure — although intensity is claimed to be the only criterion by which to judge pleasure. Hedonists, then, will have to admit that their choice for a pure pleasure is dependent on other criteria than the quantitative calculus. Even more so: the choice for pure pleasure is by definition opposed to the choice for the most intense pleasure.

This problem lies behind the discussion at the beginning of the dialogue, concerning whether all pleasure is identical qua pleasure. Against this starting point of the hedonist, Socrates points out that pleasure is a genus containing different species that can contradict each other (12 c – 13 e). Protarchus is not immediately convinced, and Socrates finds himself obliged to introduce another point. According to hedonists, all pleasure is good. But must they not concede that there are differences in goodness between different kinds of pleasure? Protarchus restates the thesis that there is no difference between kinds of pleasure in as far as they are pleasures. This is followed by a sophistical argument of Socrates: if one maintains this thesis, one could as well say that 'the different is most identical to the different'. For if A differs from B, and B differs from A, then both share a common element: they are different. 'Qua different', then, A and B will be identical ... 'and then, our discussion will get hissed off the stage' (13 d 6). Eventually, Protarchus surrenders on the ground of an entirely external argument, namely, Socrates' concession that intellect is not an undifferentiated whole either (13 e 9 – 14 a 9).

It has often been emphasised that Protarchus is extremely compliant here[21]. Without Socrates adducing any valid argument, Protarchus concedes that pleasure is not identical qua pleasure. He could have maintained his initial position, since no argument has revealed that the difference between pleasures is due to pleasure itself, rather than to the pleasurable object. But, in fact, the situation is much more intricate than it appears at first sight. The discussion here announces an issue that will be put forward (implicitly) in the course of the examination of pleasure: one cannot but accept that there are differences within the genus of pleasure, whether these differences concern the intensity or purity of the pleasure, or the difference of pleasurable objects. Protarchus is willing to admit this, but he does not immediately foresee the consequences of this concession. If there is a difference, one should look for the criteria that explain this difference. If, then, hedonists stick to the view that the difference is external to pleasure, they actually recognise that the criterion used to choose one pleasure rather than another is not inherent in pleasure. Their choice is guided by factors that are not reducible to pleasure itself. In other words, the hedonists' pursuit of pleasure is subordinate to criteria different from pleasure itself, which in fact renders their hedonism self-defeating.

At this early stage in the dialogue there is no question of Protarchus betraying one of the fundamental claims of hedonism. It is only demonstrated that hedonists, notwithstanding their thesis that pleasure is identical qua pleasure, will have to make a well-founded choice for one pleasure and against another in concrete situations. Protarchus agrees on this point, but is not aware of the consequences of this concession (see 13 a 6: ἴσως, ἀλλὰ τί τουθ᾽ ἡμῶν βλάψει τὸν λόγον;).

One should not, however, give Plato credit too soon. Apparently, he holds the view that pleasure occurs automatically with the replenishment of a lack. But this is too optimistic. The replenishment of a lack does not immediately lead to pleasure. Our eating or drinking — and, by extension, every replenishment of a lack — is not pleasurable per se. Pleasure might occur, but it might as well fail to appear. We will elaborate this critique in due course; for the moment, suffice it to say that Plato's identification of pleasure with the replenishment of a lack causes problems: the link between them is not guaranteed. This entails

---

[21]   Hackforth 1945, 14-15 and 16 n.1; Guthrie 1978, 206-207; Frede 1993, XIX.

that true pleasure does not necessarily have to be linked with the
replenishment of merely a small lack. Plato suggests that this link is
exclusive: true pleasure cannot be intense, since the preceding lack was
too slight to be felt. However, if one no longer automatically links
pleasure with the replenishment of a lack, then it appears well possible
that we do not at all feel pleasure with the replenishment of an intense
lack; on the other hand, we do feel an intense pleasure without there
having preceded an intense lack to our pleasure. True pleasure, then,
can no doubt be an intense pleasure.

However, Plato's critique of hedonism is not weakened by this
objection; on the contrary, it is made stronger. The thesis (against
Plato) that true, or pure, pleasure does not have to be a slight pleasure
entails the affirmation (against hedonism) that pure pleasure does not
have to be intense. There is no automatic link between truth (or purity)
and intensity of pleasure. Purity, in either case, is a criterion that
cannot be derived from the intensity of pleasure.

Thus, Plato confronts hedonists with a dilemma: by which criterion
will they decide when they are obliged to make a choice between a
pure, but slight, pleasure and an impure, but intense, one?

Hedonists might opt for the pure pleasure, regardless of its intensity,
thereby restating their position as a 'qualitative hedonism', as J.S. Mill
will have it. This thesis implies that pleasure is ranked not only
according to its quantity, but also according to the qualitative
differences between the different kinds of pleasure[22]. Following the line
of Plato's argument, however, this is an untenable position. For what
would guide our preference for pure pleasure? If we agree that
pleasure as such only differs according to its intensity, then how can
the quality of pleasure ever lie within pleasure itself? Qualitative
hedonism de facto bases its choice for pleasure on external criteria,
which, accordingly (at least in the Platonic conception) are to be
ranked higher than pleasure itself.

The hedonists might also unconditionally opt for intensity as a
criterion. They might hold that speaking about the truth of a pleasure
is absurd: all pleasure is equally true. Pleasure might be contaminated
by distress, but this contamination does not affect pleasure itself.
Distress is a disturbing element added to pleasure from the outside.
Taking pleasure in itself, one should abstract from the distress and

---

[22] J.S. Mill, *Utilitarianism*, ch. 2. Cf. A.E. Taylor 1956, 55-56; Edwards 1979, 112.

recognise that pleasure *qua* pleasure always is pure or true[23]. The hedonistic calculus, then, comes down to calculating the particles of pleasure and of distress mixed in one experience. In other words: we always prefer a maximum of pleasure, without taking into account its admixture with distress, but of course it is better that an experience contains as little distress as possible.

Plato's arguments, however, lead us to conclude that this statement, too, is based on an incomplete analysis. Why is a pleasure that is less contaminated with distress preferable? The choice cannot be based on intensity: it is not necessarily so that pleasure is more intense just because there is less distress involved. Intensity alone does not render a pleasure good.

Moreover, our experiencing pleasure implies that we know that we are enjoying the pleasure: a certain degree of consciousness, i.e., a function of intellect, is needed to recognise pleasure as pleasure[24]. Although Plato's description of truth and of the role of intellect is too cognitivistic, he does make a correct analysis in intimating that our spontaneous choice for (or against) a certain kind of pleasure is what we would call a 'propositional attitude'[25]: our behaviour implies a judgment and classification of pleasure based on the criterion of truth and, along with this, of the good[26]. It does not work, then, to qualify this judging ability as 'instrumentally good', taking pleasure as the ultimate end. Against the claim of hedonists, practical norms do not have pleasure as their starting point. On the contrary, any pleasurable experience presupposes the existence of practical norms by which the choice for this particular pleasure is made. Intellect (in the Platonic terminology) is, then, intrinsically superior to pleasure, just as truth is intrinsically superior to intellect.

Thus, on both horns of the dilemma, the unlimited pleasure at which hedonists aim appears to be an illusion. Our choice for a certain

---

[23] Cf. J. Bentham, *An Introduction to the Principles of Morals and Legislation*, 30.

[24] A hedonist will have no problems to agree with this. As a defender of hedonism would have it: 'The pleasure and pain in which the hedonist is interested are inner qualities of feeling, and some small introspective ability is required in order to focus attention upon pleasures and pains in the relevant sense. If introspective psychology is thrown out completely, then hedonism in its classical sense is thrown out with it' (Edwards 1979, 27).

[25] Cf. Frede 1992, 442-448.

[26] The same analysis will be made by Plotinus. Cf. infra.

pleasure is always regulated by an external measure and is never evaluated solely on the basis of its intensity. So not every pleasure is equally true or pure; nor is every pleasure equally good.

On the basis of these analyses, Plato, when making a final ranking of the ingredients of the good life, attributes the first prize (i.e., within the mixed life) to 'measure, everything that is moderate and appropriate (καίριον)' (66 a 6-8). It is surpassed only by the absolute good, of which we have reached the threshold. Thus, Plato indicates that the norm, or measure, involved in the mixed life is the most important criterion for goodness. For intellect and pleasure are discussed only at a lower stage: intellect at the third and fourth rank (respectively as 'intellect and understanding', and 'sciences, skill and right opinion of the soul'), and pleasure (at least, true pleasure) at the fifth and last rank (66 b-c). The second rank is taken by 'the proportionate, the beautiful, the perfect and sufficient and everything which pertains to this class' (66 b 1-4). The list seems to be cumulative: the lower rank is admitted on the ground that it contains within itself the characteristics of the higher.

At the end of the dialogue Protarchus is convinced: 'We are now all agreed, Socrates, on the truth of your position' (67 b 8-9). He must confess that his hedonism was based on incoherences and incomplete arguments. Once confronted with the consequences of his thesis, he cannot but conclude that he too did in fact subordinate pleasure to criteria irreducible to unlimited pleasure itself.

This conversion is not exclusively the result of arguments concerning the content of his position. One might say that even to participate in the discussion presupposes a conversion. When are hedonists prepared to discuss? The answer is well known: they might wish to argue or to convince insofar as it is instrumentally good, leading to a maximisation of pleasure. But is this the case in the given circumstances? Engaging in a debate is not without obligations. Participating in a discussion supposes that one gives a justification of one's views; in a debate there are laws that are more important than the proper views of the interlocutors, even if the result would be that the proper view appears to be untenable. Hedonists might consider this to be instrumentally good, except, or so it seems, in one case: in a discussion about pleasure itself. If they are prepared to discuss their central thesis, they must take their beloved goddess off her pedestal and make her obey the laws of the debate, even before one single word has been said. But she will not have the last word either: the conclusion, whatever it may be, will have to give account to the truth and reasonability of a discourse.

Essentially, then, the participation in a discussion about pleasure presupposes that one has already abandoned radical hedonism, in this sense, that one considers as intrinsically good not only pleasure, but at least also the reasonability of a discourse — if one takes the debate seriously, of course. Perhaps, in this sense, no 'philosophic' hedonist is a (radical) hedonist. Hence the inevitability of Protarchus' conversion: in his very willingness to participate in the debate, he renounces Philebus and his goddess, and accepts the importance of truth. Philebus refuses to do this: for a radical hedonist, a serious discussion about pleasure is *taboo*. The problem is not that he might be refuted; it is much more fundamental: he would a priori have surrendered, by his very participation in the discussion. Thus, Philebus cannot discuss pleasure. He must perforce remain silent.

But why would he want to discuss? Philebus is the uncritical hedonist who withdraws from any debate about his life choice[27]. He personifies the difficulty of arguing against hedonism, and confronts the philosopher with his own limits. For philosophers can only *hope* that their interlocutors are willing to engage in a discussion. But what if their interlocutors are not so willing, when they detect that this does not fit their radical hedonism? Will they not prefer pleasure and avoid philosophy, criticism, debate? They might perhaps read the *Philebus*. But if this does not secure them pleasure, they will not venture to do so. Their silence is their strength.

Can one really say, then, that Protarchus is converted? Insofar as he is willing to discuss, he by that very willingness renounces radical hedonism. Radical hedonists cannot be converted. Before giving one single argument in a discussion, they no longer are radical hedonists. What they can do to safeguard their hedonism, is to remain silent, as Philebus does, and (hopefully) to enjoy.

3. *An Evaluation of Plato's Theory*

3.1. *A Positive Doctrine?*

As we have seen above, Plato gradually develops the idea that a qualitative distinction between pleasures is necessary to assess the role

---

[27] He is like the 'amoralist' depicted by Bernard Williams 1972, 17-27.

of pleasure in the good life. This eventually brings him, in the *Republic* and *Philebus*, to reconsider the claims of hedonism, and to acknowledge that the very plea for the desirability of the philosophic life entails the admission of a certain kind of pleasure that renders this life choiceworthy. All the same, it remains very difficult to abstract a positive doctrine from the various discussions of pleasure in Plato's dialogues. His position, rather, is implicit and subordinate to his criticism of hedonism. It has been remarked more than once that (especially in the earlier dialogues) the rejection of the opponents' views is not counterbalanced by a clear alternative[28].

In the *Philebus*, Plato's central claim is clear enough: the good life is a mixture of pleasure and intellect; both terms are analysed separately, as is the mixture itself. At the end of the dialogue, Plato examines both the degree to which and the criteria on the basis of which a mixture can be qualified as good. However, if one examines more deeply which kinds of pleasure are combined with which kinds of intellectual activity, Plato's answer is much less perspicuous. All kinds of intellectual activity are admitted into the good life, from the 'intellect' (νοῦς) to the 'correct opinions'. Thus, any so-called 'intellectual activity' is good. Pleasure, on the other hand, is much less favoured. Only true and pure pleasure (and pleasure in virtue, health, and temperance[29]) is admitted, along with those 'necessary pleasures' that are not really good[30] but that cannot be avoided (61 b – 64 a). All other kinds are rejected.

What, then, is the relation between intellectual activity and pleasure? To put it concretely: the good life is a life containing all intellectual activities, combined with pleasure in virtue, health and temperance, pleasure in pure odours, colours, sounds and forms, and pleasure in studying, at least if such pleasure does not proceed from a previous distress, plus the (necessary) pleasures of eating, drinking, and sex. Apparently, Plato has in mind a purely external combination of the entire class of intellectual activities with only a part of the class of pleasures. An immediate relation between certain members of the two

---

[28] Thus, e.g., with the rejection of physical pleasures in the *Phaedo*. Although one feels Plato intimates a positive evaluation of 'higher', psychic pleasures, he does not really pay attention to them; cf. Bostock 1986, 32-35.

[29] It is not clear whether these pleasures should be considered as kinds of true pleasure.

[30] Hence, the necessary pleasures do not figure in the final hierarchy of good ingredients of the good life, whereas they were admitted in the good life.

classes does not seem to exist, although Plato does use the terms 'οἰκεῖαι ἡδοναί' (51 d 1) and 'σύμφυτοι ἡδοναί' (51 d 8)[31]. But since it is not clear whether the pleasure in pure forms, odours, etc. necessarily is true pleasure — it being very well possible that in some, if not in most, cases these pleasures remedy a previous distress, which prevents them from being true — one cannot infer that pure odours, etc. have true pleasure as their *natural* companion.

The same goes for pleasure in studying: it is true pleasure only if there was no previous distress, or 'longing for knowledge'. This is an important restriction that prevents us from considering all intellectual pleasure as true and even threatens to exclude the majority of intellectual pleasures from the good life: although some intellectual pleasures are pure, or true, this is not a distinctive feature of all intellectual pleasures. Many, if not most, of the intellectual pleasures are impure. So, although some true pleasures may be intellectual pleasures, not all intellectual pleasures are true pleasures. The categories are not coextensive, and we are not allowed to infer that true pleasure is the pleasure 'proper (οἰκεῖον) to' intellectual activity.

This shortcoming in the analysis, to which Aristotle will present a valuable alternative, renders it very difficult to extract a positive doctrine from the *Philebus*, and from Plato's treatment of pleasure in general. Does Plato intend to show that life devoted to intellect furnishes the highest (i.e., true) pleasure? This appears to be the aim, taking into account the continuous repetition that the intellect occupies a higher place than pleasure. But if the scope of the *Philebus* is a plea for the desirability of an intellectual life, one must realise that a life exclusively devoted to the intellect is repeatedly rejected as undesirable (and hence not good). The very logic of the *Philebus*, then, would require the complementary claim that the intellectual life procures a typical pleasure, which is not equalled by any other activity. Although there are some hints of this doctrine in the *Philebus*, as well as in the *Republic*, Plato did not develop these ideas.

Exactly this shortcoming in Plato's evaluation of pleasure forces later Platonists, who have read Aristotle's alternative, to give an account of Plato's view of higher or intellectual pleasure. The absence of a clear account in Plato himself leads to different solutions in the Platonic tradition.

---

[31] Also at *Rep.* 586 d-e.

3.2. *The Physiological Presuppositions of the Definition*

The major impediment to establishing an unconditional link between true pleasure and the intellect is the physiological scheme that underlies the definition of pleasure. Indeed, the scheme of lack and replenishment hinders a positive evaluation of pleasure — including true pleasure. For, starting from this basis, pleasure is always a 'process of becoming' that tends towards a being or essence situated elsewhere. Pleasure being only the replenishment of a lack, it vanishes once the lack is replenished. Pleasure, then, tends towards its own destruction, since it is directed to a condition beyond all lack (and thus beyond all replenishment). This renders it impossible to consider pleasure as an end in itself, that is, as a good. Plato explicitly makes this inference at *Phil.* 53 c – 55 c. True, he mentions only mixed pleasures here, and his argument concerns only this kind of pleasure[32], but insofar as true pleasure is also the replenishment of a lack — albeit a nonperceptible lack — it cannot escape from this general depreciation of pleasure.

Thus, Plato does not succeed in his attempt to designate pleasure (even true pleasure) beyond all doubt as a good ingredient of the good life, precisely because his presuppositions prevent him from drawing this conclusion. There seems to be no room for any pleasure 'at rest', i.e., any kind of pleasure that is not preceded by a lack — the paradigm of which would be intellectual pleasure.

3.3. *The Identity of Pleasure and Replenishment*

One of the strengths of the *Philebus*, which renders the doctrine much more sophisticated than as found in the previous works, is the distinction Plato here draws between the physiological scheme of lack and replenishment, on the one hand, and the definition of pleasure and distress, on the other. This enables him to explain the difference between pure pleasure, mixed pleasure, and the neutral condition.

However, this distinction, the essential implication of which is that pleasure can never be reduced to a strictly empirical level, is not completely worked out in Plato's analysis. Despite drawing the conceptual distinction, Plato does not seem to accept a real distinction between the two. Following his line of argument, once a replenishment is experienced, it is certain that we will feel pleasure. There is, then, a

---

[32]   Gosling 1975, 221; Guthrie 1978, 229.

necessary link (or even an identity) between an experienced replenishment and pleasure. This would imply that pleasure can be manipulated, that we know what to do in order to obtain pleasure.

But exactly here lies the central problem. We can never be certain that the replenishment of a lack will yield pleasure. It seems to be the case, rather, that pleasure cannot be attained except indirectly: it is only by aiming at something other than pleasure that we will reach pleasure itself.

As J. Elster has pointed out, many states in our human life are 'essentially by-products'[33]: of their essence, they can be reached only indirectly. The more we try to bring them about through a direct intention, the less we will actually attain them. Elster's paradigm is 'happiness': we cannot reach this end except through the performance of other activities. Sleep, too, is of this kind: we can fall asleep only when we forget our sleeplessness, and any attempt to sleep will rather have the opposite effect[34].

As we remarked, the same is true of pleasure. We never know exactly what we must do in order to reach pleasure; its occurrence depends on other activities, and a painstaking attempt to attain pleasure seems to prevent, rather than to stimulate, its occurrence. Eating and drinking — to confine ourselves to the typical examples chosen by Plato himself — do not *per se* give rise to pleasure. Pleasure does not consist in the movement itself; instead, it is — possibly — added to the movement. So it is not merely an empirical datum and cannot be identical with a physiological process. Pleasure seems to accompany the replenishment of a lack only if we are not obsessed by the lack, if, so to speak, the lack escapes from our attention. Of course we can manipulate the situation up to a certain degree, arranging things so that the occurrence of pleasure becomes more likely. But we can never be sure. Pleasure can occur, but it can as well stay away; its occurrence is never guaranteed. One should conclude, then, *contra* Plato, that it is impossible to identify pleasure with the experienced replenishment of a lack. It remains possible that we experience a replenishment without any pleasure. If this were not so, then one should accept, for instance, that a hungry homeless person would feel *pleasure* when eating his first bowl of soup after a long time without food — which would be a cynical misrepresentation of the man's

---

[33] Elster 1983, 43-108.
[34] Cf. Elster 1983, 45-46.

suffering. Feeling pleasure, then, seems to be a supplementary quality of some replenishments, but not of all. Moreover, pleasure is not always the same in identical circumstances; on the contrary, the permanent repetition of the same (initially pleasurable) effect will eventually be extremely boring. So even if we were to finally find a secure way to attain pleasure, the stability of its occurrence would not be guaranteed. It seems to be the case that pleasure only occurs *despite ourselves*, at that moment during which we do not aim at it. So there is no necessary link between replenishment and pleasure, and, in this respect, the Platonic position is highly questionable.

3.4. *Plato's Merits*

The most important merit of Plato's analysis of pleasure is the upgrading of pleasure that, despite all the difficulties, is implied in the notion of the mixed life.

But apart from this, there is another aspect of his theory that constitutes a remarkable contribution to the examination of pleasure, namely, the idea that the intellect must impose a certain measure on pleasure. The idea of μετριότης was already present in the philosophies of Plato's predecessors. Theognis, Democritus, and Aristippus[35] had pointed out that pleasure should be pursued in moderation (μετριότης). Plato takes over this central idea and further elaborates it. He points out that measure cannot follow from the definition of pleasure itself. The replenishment of a lack in itself does not involve moderation. On the contrary: according to the definition, pleasure should be as intense as possible. The qualitative difference between pleasures, however, on the basis of which their ethical value can be determined, is due to the imposition of a limit by the intellect (if not consciously, then at least in the introspection that is always required to feel pleasure).

There is, then, a tension between pleasure as such (which is unlimited) and the measure imposed by the intellect: pleasure always tends towards excess, escaping from the control of our intellect. It cannot be subdued unless our soul is in harmony with itself, i.e., unless the intellectual part of the soul governs the whole (to use the language of the *Republic*). In the case of pleasure, this 'government' comes down to the moderation imposed on the never ceasing movement of lack

---

[35] Cf. Festugière 1936[a], 235-239; 251.

and replenishment upon which pleasure and distress attend. In the *Philebus* this idea is expressed by stating that the proper mixture of pleasure and moderation, determined by the intellect, is the right combination (ὀρθὴ κοινωνία, 25 e 7) that holds the middle ground between the more and the less. It is an equilibrium that does not allow of gradations, as opposed to that which does not possess measure in itself (like health — one is healthy or one is not, there are no gradations —, as opposed to sickness, which can have many gradations)[36]. Hence it is understandable that, in the final ranking, 'τὸ καίριον (that which comes at the right time on the right place), τὸ μέτριον and the like' (66 a) take pride of place in the good life. It is the equilibrium between excess and shortness that primordially renders our life good, and both intellectual activity and pleasure must bear in themselves this measure in order to be acceptable in the good life.

Of course, the risk of a failure can never be excluded, and it always remains possible that pleasure escapes from its boundaries. As the limit imposed is external to the true nature of pleasure, there always will be a danger of missing the right measure in our pleasure.

II. ARISTOTLE: THE 'THEORY OF THE PERFECT ACTIVITY'

1. *Aristotle's Rejection of the Platonic Definition*

1.1. *The 'Platonic' Definition of Pleasure*

Aristotle's discourse on pleasure, in both Book VII and X of his *Nicomachean Ethics*[37], starts from a *status quaestionis*: the author first

---

[36]   This explains why Plato at *Phil.* 25 e – 26 d provides only *positive* examples of the μεικτόν: the ἄπειρον cannot be the continuum on which measuring unities are imposed (as in the case of, e.g., temperature, which is often erroneously considered to be the typical example of the ἄπειρον). In that case, *everything* would be a 'mixture', and there would be no reason to cite only positive examples. Rather, the ἄπειρον signifies anything that allows of a difference of 'more and less' (like sickness, licentiousness, etc.), whereas the μεικτόν is the equilibrium reached by eliminating all excess; cf. Moravcsik 1992, 237-239 (also 1979, 96-97); Frede 1993, XXXVI-XXXVII.

[37]   We cannot discuss here the differences between the two accounts of pleasure found within the same work (in *NE* VII 11-14, and X 1-5). The question has been dealt with many times, and it seems to be clear that, although both accounts cannot belong to the same work (because of the absolute absence of cross-references, which would hardly be possible if the same subject were treated twice within one and the same work), there is no essential difference of opinion between them; see esp. Owen

investigates some opinions defended by earlier thinkers and then proceeds to assess their merits as a means of establishing his theory of pleasure. In a very peculiar way, this *status quaestionis* dominates the whole discussion. In the first place, it sets the terms of the debate: it is not an investigation into the diversity of previous views on pleasure as such, but concerns mainly the relation between pleasure and the good. Thus it is stated, from the very beginning of the discourse, that its scope is to be the issue of the role that should be attributed to pleasure within the good life[38]. Secondly, the *status quaestionis* is present throughout the discussion: Aristotle goes on to criticise the earlier views (VII, ch. 12-14; X, ch. 2-3), and his positive account (X, ch. 4-5; in book VII it is even absent in this form) is basically intended to contrast the opinions quoted.

All this may only serve to emphasise the polemical character of the Aristotelian discussion of pleasure, and, as a consequence, a close investigation of the positions that Aristotle rejects becomes very important. First, however, we need to notice that there is a slight difference in the presentation of the *status quaestionis* in the two passages. Book VII presents three different opinions:

1. pleasure cannot be good, under any circumstance, or in any form. This is the rigidly anti-hedonistic position, denying to pleasure any place in the good life. It is not necessarily the same, however, as saying that pleasure is evil[39].
2. some forms of pleasure are good, but most of them are to be rejected.
3. pleasure is not the highest good, but it may be good in itself.

Obviously, the fully hedonistic position is absent here, although the

---

1971-72, 135-152 [repr. 1977, 92-103].

[38] *NE* VII 11, 1152 b 4-24; X 1, 1172 a 25 – 3, 1174 a 11; this importance of the ethical evaluation of pleasure leads Ricken 1995, 208, to conclude that an examination of Aristotle's view should not be centered around the definition of pleasure, for '...die Frage nach dem Wesen der Lust ist vielmehr der nach ihrem Wert untergeordnet'. However, one should be aware of the fact that an investigation of the definition of pleasure, on which we will concentrate, immediately leads to the moral evaluation of pleasure. As we will try to show here, this is true especially when the Aristotelian definition is contrasted with the Platonic doctrine of pleasure.

[39] Thus, for instance, Speusippus (the anti-hedonist) will be said to have denied that pleasure is evil: *NE* VII 13, 1153 b 5-7. Rather it should be seen as opposed to the good as well as to pain (which is evil).

very terminology of the third alternative suggests it as a view that some might defend.

In Book X, on the other hand, the hedonistic position is one of the main issues. Aristotle here reduces the discussion to a straight opposition between two views: a rigid anti-hedonism and a strict hedonism, thus radicalizing, but at the same time simplifying, the main line of the discussion.

These doctrines have, with a great degree of probability, been identified, partly on the grounds of the scarce references given by Aristotle himself in his entire discussion of pleasure. Plato is named once[40], and so are Speusippus (VII 13, 1153 b 5) and Eudoxus (X 2, 1172 b 9). The views attributed to these three thinkers correspond perfectly with three of the opinions mentioned in both versions of the *status quaestionis*. Speusippus is presented as a rigid anti-hedonist[41], who holds that pleasure can in no way whatsoever be good; his thesis is mentioned as the first alternative in both passages. Eudoxus is a strict hedonist, and his name is explicitly attached to the second opinion mentioned in the tenth book, taking pleasure as the highest good. The first of the remaining opinions, the second opinion mentioned in Book VII, can be attributed to Plato ('some forms of pleasure are good, although most of them are to be rejected', which corresponds to the view Plato presents in the *Philebus*). One would expect the last of the quoted opinions (the third one listed in Book VII: pleasure may be good, though not the highest good) to be a reference to Aristotle's own view[42]. Indeed, in this form it does foreshadow the position that Aristotle will defend, but the identification is made difficult, if not impossible, by the argument quoted in support of this position: pleasure cannot be the highest good, because it is not an end, but rather a process of generation[43].

In any case, if we take the opposition in its most radical form, we must place Speusippus and Eudoxus at opposite extremes. Both Aristotle and Plato would occupy distinctive intermediary positions.

---

[40] *NE* X 2, 1172 b 29; Aristotle mentions Plato's predilection for the mixed life above pleasure, based on the argument that a combination of two good things is better than one single good; cf. *Philebus* 20 b – 23 b and 59 d – 61 a.

[41] For a careful evaluation of Speusippus' account on pleasure, see Dillon 1996.

[42] Thus, e.g., Festugière 1936[b], VIII; Joachim 1951, 235.

[43] VII 11, 1152 b 22. As we will see, this certainly is contrary to Aristotle's own view, and corresponds rather to the Platonic position; if this is so, however, it raises the problem that Plato is quoted twice in two different ways.

At the same time, Aristotle clearly sympathises with Eudoxus (although he does object to strict hedonism)[44], and shows no affinity whatsoever with the anti-hedonism of Speusippus. This is shown *inter alia* by the fact that Aristotle takes for granted the starting point of Eudoxus: all creatures naturally strive for pleasure[45]. Eventually, this will be the position he quotes, in a very typical procedure, as the 'ἔνδοξον' to which his own position has to accord, in order to 'save the phenomena'. Thus, he will justify the common belief that every living being strives for pleasure, by showing how this fits the general scheme of his own theory. Since, according to Aristotle, pleasure is the supervenient effect of an activity, one can explain that every living being seems to strive for pleasure, because they all want to perform the activity of living. Just as everyone enjoys to the highest degree the activity that is most proper to him (such as music for the musician, study for the studious), life, which is most proper to all living beings, will be pleasurable for each of them. So, Aristotle says, it is in accordance with sound reasoning (εὐλόγως) to state that everyone strives for pleasure, since it gives a supplementary value to our most proper activity, life[46].

This predilection for Eudoxus makes it very likely that it is Speusippus whose opinion is under attack here. And, indeed, Aristotle does react fiercely against an extreme anti-hedonism. This would give us a battlefield on which the (more or less extreme) 'partisans of pleasure' (i.e. Eudoxus and Aristotle) are fighting the (more or less extreme) anti-hedonists (i.e., Plato, and in particular Speusippus). The reaction against Plato, if indeed there is one in this scheme, would be merely incidental, that is, in the event that he holds a position similar to that of Speusippus.

There are, however, indications that the situation is more complex than the standard interpretation. Indeed, the reaction against anti-

---

[44]   Cf. Hardie 1968, 295; Merlan 1960, 31; Rorty 1974, 482.

[45]   Quoted in *NE* X 2, 1172 b 9-10. See also I 12, 1101 b 27-31.

[46]   X 4, 1175 a 10-21 (cf. II 3, 1104 b 34 – 1105 a 5). The question of which of the two (pleasure or life) is most 'desirable' is put aside here in a *praeteritio* (l.18-19). However, it is clear that life is the activity without which pleasure would not be possible; so life must be desirable, at least as a *conditio sine qua non* for pleasure. What Aristotle does not answer is the question of whether this would mean that our life is, after all, desirable merely as the instrumental precondition for pleasure — in which case, of course, hedonism would return.

hedonism is not quite at the heart of the argument. Much more so is the basic definition upon which this anti-hedonism is built. Thus, for instance, Aristotle refers to a distinction which was drawn within the context of the anti-hedonistic arguments between the 'process of generation' and the 'end'. He presents this distinction as the very first argument:

> The reasons given for the view that pleasure is not a good at all are that every pleasure is a perceptible process to a natural state, and that no process is of the same kind as its end, e.g. no process of building of the same kind as a house. (VII 11, 1152 b 12-14, trans. Ross)

Pleasure does not belong to the class of ends: it is only a process towards a certain end, exterior to pleasure itself. Since, then, an end is by definition something good, pleasure itself cannot be described as a good. This argument is present also in the *Philebus* (53 c 4 – 55 c 3), where Socrates refers to 'subtle thinkers' (κομψοί) whose position he adopts to show that pleasure cannot be good. This is generally regarded as a reference to Speusippus[47], but we are more inclined to accept Dorothea Frede's suggestion that it must be a reference to Plato himself[48]. Whoever is meant here, it is not the thesis of the subtle thinkers itself that is crucial, but rather the definition upon which it is built: one can accept that pleasure is not an end only if one agrees that it is defined as a kind of movement towards an end, viz. 'a perceptible process towards a natural state'. The same goes for the argument quoted by Aristotle: the process end distinction is given as an argument to support the anti-hedonistic thesis, but the central issue at stake here is the explicitly quoted definition, without which the argument would not hold water. It is this definition of pleasure as a 'perceptible process of generation' that lies at the heart of the problem: every criticism that Aristotle levels against his predecessors basically rests upon the refutation of the underlying definition of pleasure. All other arguments come down to this single criticism.

This point is of major interest within the context of Aristotle's discourse on pleasure: it proves that the position under attack is not Speusippus' radical anti-hedonism as such. Thus, Aristotle's polemical intentions, though apparently directed in the first place against

---

[47] Cf. A.E. Taylor 1956, 24-25; Gosling-Taylor 1982, 231-240.

[48] Frede 1993, 63 n.3: 'The addressee is no doubt Plato himself (...); the firm entrenchment of pleasure with generation is an innovation of the *Philebus*, and this is solemnly acknowledged here'.

Speusippus, have a much wider range, and concern also, if not mainly, the definition of pleasure advanced by Plato. We will refer, then, to the theory under attack as the 'Platonic' account, since Plato doubtlessly was the most authoritative (though not the only) defender of this thesis.

1.2. *Aristotle's Criticism*

The most important of Aristotle's criticisms, which dominates the entire discussion, is that the Platonic definition is based solely upon physiological processes in the body. On Aristotle's view, starting in this way from only one specific form of pleasure (the corporeal one) leads to an inadmissible generalization. Opposing this view, he argues that bodily pleasure must not be taken as the paradigm of pleasure, introducing his criticism in the following manner:

> They say, too, that pain is the lack of that which is according to nature, and pleasure is replenishment. But these experiences are bodily. If then pleasure is replenishment with that which is according to nature, that which feels pleasure will be that in which the replenishment takes place, i.e. the body. But that is not thought to be the case. (*NE* X 3, 1173 b 7-11, trans. Ross)

Here Aristotle objects, in the first place, to the purely physiological basis of the definition: pleasure and pain are considered to be merely bodily processes of lack and replenishment. This would imply that eventually the actual bearer of pleasure would be the body — a thesis that no one would accept. Indeed, Plato himself was convinced that it is the *soul* that feels pleasure: in his definition he explicitly mentions the 'ensouled species' (τὸ ἔμψυχον εἶδος, *Phil.* 32 b 1), and even purely corporeal pleasure, according to Plato, is not possible without a minimum of consciousness. So the conclusion Aristotle rightly draws from the premises of the Platonic definition is not acceptable to Plato himself. For the latter, too, pleasure and pain are expressions of consciousness and cannot be reduced to the purely corporeal.

However, once pleasure is situated somewhere other than in the body, the given definition no longer holds. Aristotle continues:

> Therefore pleasure is not a replenishment, though one would be pleased when replenishment was taking place, and when one cuts oneself one can feel pain.[49]

---

[49] *NE* X 3, 1173 b 11-13: οὐκ ἔστιν ἄρα ἀναπλήρωσις ἡ ἡδονή, ἀλλὰ γινομένης μὲν ἀναπληρώσεως ἥδοιτ᾽ ἄν τις, καὶ τεμνόμενος λυποῖτο (trans. Ross, modified). We agree

So, one must not identify deficiency and replenishment (purely corporeal processes) with pain and pleasure. There is a distinction between process and affect, between body and consciousness. Thus, the definition of pleasure based on physiology collapses: pleasure is not the replenishment itself, but an affect that is supervenient upon the replenishment[50]. Upon this very distinction Aristotle's own definition is based.

Before elaborating on his own alternative, however, Aristotle dwells on the causes of the misinterpretation of pleasure:

> This opinion seems to be based on the pains and pleasures connected with nutrition: on the fact that when people have been short of food and have felt pain beforehand they are pleased by the replenishment. But this does not happen with all pleasures; for the pleasures of learning and, among the sensuous pleasures, those of smell, and also many sounds and sights, and memories and hopes, do not presuppose pain. Of what will these be the coming into being ? There has not been lack of anything of which they could be the supplying anew. (X 3, 1173 b 13-20, trans. Ross)

The source of the misunderstanding is thus an exclusive focus on the pleasure associated with eating and drinking. This, indeed, was presented by Plato himself as the basis of his definition of pleasure: for he had Socrates remark that in the examination of pleasure one should take as one's starting point those situations in which the occurrence of pleasure is generally recognised — which indeed is the case with eating and drinking (*Phil.* 31 e 3 – 32 a 1).

As regards food and drink, Aristotle holds that the given structure is correct: a previous lack is replenished, and this process causes pleasure. But he immediately adds that this cannot be the paradigm for all pleasure. He cites cases of such strictly intellectual pleasure as those associated with studying, memories, and hopes. But many forms of pleasure in the realm of sense perception likewise do not fit the given definition. None of the cases mentioned can be considered to be the replenishment of a previous lack.

---

with Gauthier-Jolif 1959, II 829, that the term 'τεμνόμενος' does not necessarily indicate a surgical operation, as most commentators hold. It may simply mean 'cutting oneself' or 'being cut' as a model for bodily processes in which a deficiency of the natural state occurs. Aristotle points out that the 'cutting' itself is not pain, but that pain can (possibly) occur as the consequence of being cut. Likewise, pleasure is a possible accompaniment of a replenishment, and not the replenishment itself.

[50] Cf. Frede 1992, 453.

The forms of pleasure cited here as examples are strikingly close to the examples of true pleasure given by Plato in the *Philebus*[51]. Plato did realise that these should occupy a specific place: indeed they do not imply a previous pain. But still, as we have already discussed, he did include them in his theory. That there is no previous pain, he said, does not mean that there is no previous lack. Indeed there *is* a lack (this is inherent in our human nature: we never escape from the flux of lack and replenishment), but in this case it is not experienced because it is too weak. The pleasure that we do experience is, then, in any case the replenishment of a lack. It is typical for this kind of pleasure to experience the replenishment while the lack remains unnoticed (cf. supra, p.23-25).

Aristotle rejects this explanation. It is nothing more than an extrapolation from bodily pleasure; and, in order to safeguard his thesis, Plato had to prove that all kinds of pleasure remedy a previous lack. But, Aristotle claims, there are pleasures that exist *without any previous lack*. It is not that this lack is not experienced: it is simply absent. In other words, the Platonic definition disregards the true nature of many pleasures. It thus misses the very essence of pleasure by assuming a wrong starting point. The kind of bodily pleasure associated with eating and drinking is just one possible example of pleasure and must not be taken as its paradigm. Instead, the definition must be made much broader, based on the statement that pleasure is a perfection that supervenes on the perfect performance of an activity[52].

2. *A New Model*

2.1. *Aristotle's Definition of Pleasure*

In the context of his Book VII refutation of Speusippus' anti-hedonism, Aristotle points out that the distinction between process and end plays no role in the examination of pleasure. There is no need, he says,

---

[51] In the *Philebus*, the following examples of true pleasure are mentioned: pleasure in beautiful colours and (mathematically exact) forms, 'most of the pleasures of smell' and of (pure) sounds (*Phil.* 51 b 3-5; elaborated in 51 c 1 – e 5); later, pleasure in studying is added to the list (51 e 7 – 52 b 9).

[52] See the definition discussed below. We intend to show that in Book VII, where this definition is presented, Aristotle suggests a straightforward identification of pleasure with the perfect activity, whereas in Book X he clearly shows that they are not identical. The latter view is more consistent with the general outline of the theory; cf. Van Riel 1999[c].

to postulate something better than pleasure, as some do when they state that the end is better than the process:

> For pleasures are not really processes, nor are they all incidental to a process: they are activities, and therefore an end (VII 13, 1153 a 9-10).

With this remark, Aristotle gets to the heart of the matter. Pleasure, he maintains, does not occur in attaining or restoring the natural condition of our faculties, but rather in using these faculties[53]. As a consequence, pleasure is not directed towards an external end. This leads him to the elaboration of a new definition:

> διὸ καὶ οὐ καλῶς ἔχει τὸ αἰσθητὴν γένεσιν φάναι εἶναι τὴν ἡδονήν, ἀλλὰ μᾶλλον λεκτέον ἐνέργειαν τῆς κατὰ φύσιν ἕξεως, ἀντὶ δὲ τοῦ ʼαἰσθητὴνʼ ἀνεμπόδιστον.

> This is why it is not right to say that pleasure is perceptible process, but it should rather be called activity of the natural state, and instead of 'perceptible' 'unimpeded'. (VII 13, 1153 a 12-15, trans. Ross)

Aristotle clearly points out in what respect his formula differs from the one he rejects. Pleasure, so he claims, is the unimpeded activity of a disposition (ἕξις) in its natural state, i.e., a disposition that functions as it should. In other words: pleasure occurs when a faculty of a living organism can perform its activity without any obstruction. The possible obstructions are to be situated in the subject as well as in the object. When my ear, for example, hears beautiful sounds in a perfect way its activity of hearing yields a specific kind of pleasure (and the same goes for any other faculty). The perfect hearing of ugly sounds is not pleasurable, and neither is the imperfect hearing of beautiful sounds.

With this argument, Aristotle finally refutes the Platonic theory of pleasure. Pleasure is not the return to the natural condition; on the contrary, it is the perfect realization of the activity that is inherent in the natural condition itself.

The scheme of the repletion of a lack can be brought into harmony with this new model, but merely as one possible instance in which the definition can be adopted; and it is not even an important one, as we will see later on.

---

[53] VII 13, 1153 a 10-11. At *Rhet.* I 11, 1369 b 33-35, Aristotle seems to accept the Platonic account. This can be explained, however, as a reference to the 'scholastic' definition that circulated in the Academy. It does not entail that Aristotle agrees with it; cf. Gosling-Taylor 1982, 196-198.

2.2. *Pleasure as a 'Supervenient Element'*

Early in the Aristotelian tradition, the problem was raised of how the relation between a perfect activity and the pleasure it yields should be understood. Is pleasure identical with the unimpeded activity of a disposition in its natural state, or is it a complementary effect of the perfect performance of an activity (and if so, how is one to understand this 'supervenience')? Both positions have their authoritative defenders, and the debate between them has not yet come to an end[54].

At first sight, Aristotle seems to have entertained both options in describing the relation between pleasure and unimpeded activity, and the difference between these options marks the distinction between the two accounts of pleasure found in his *Nicomachean Ethics*. In his 1971-72 article 'Aristotelian Pleasures', G.E.L. Owen argued that the two discussions of pleasure, although they certainly cannot belong to the same work, do not present an essentially different view of pleasure. There is only a difference in perspective: whereas Book VII mainly investigates the nature of what is enjoyable, Book X focuses on the question of what the nature of enjoyment is.

Once this shift in perspective is acknowledged, it is understandable that Aristotle did not pay much attention to the relation between activity and pleasure in the seventh book: he identified them without much further ado. One should say, then, that he did not hold the view that perfect activity and pleasure are identical (as we put it); he simply did not raise the question. Indeed an explicit choice for this view would lead to a serious inconsistency, since a simple identity of pleasure with unimpeded activity would in the end mean that pleasure is to be identified with happiness: as the good for man is the highest actualization of his highest faculty, this would *ipso facto* be identical with the highest pleasure. The position of Aristotle would, then, despite his own objections to hedonism, turn out to be a form of hedonism: pleasure (at least one kind of pleasure) is the highest good.

In the tenth book, however, Aristotle seems to be much more sensitive to the problem, and he sees himself obliged to give a more nuanced explanation of the mutual role of activity and pleasure. In

---

[54] Gosling-Taylor 1982, 249-250 and 264 state that Aristotle's position comes down to a straightforward identification of pleasure with the perfect activity. Their opinion is criticised by Urmson 1984, 215-216, and intimated, but not defended by Broadie 1991, 336 and n.21. The question of the relation between pleasure and activity is also treated, though from a different point of view, by Bostock 1988 and by Gonzalez 1991.

doing so, he clearly rejects the view that pleasure and activity are identical[55]. Instead, as we will see, he argues for a very close, and even inseparable, connection between activity and pleasure, thereby avoiding a hedonistic position[56].

In Book X, after having criticised other philosophers' views on pleasure, Aristotle takes as the starting point of his positive account of pleasure an examination of the faculties of sense perception. The most perfect activity of these faculties of perception is attained when both the faculty and the perceived object are in an optimal state. This perfect activity is *per se* the most pleasurable. However, this scheme covers not only sense perception: all intellectual activities yield a specific pleasure when both the faculty and the object are perfect[57].

How, then, are pleasure and activity linked together ? Aristotle says:

τελειοῖ δὲ τὴν ἐνέργειαν ἡ ἡδονή. οὐ τὸν αὐτὸν δὲ τρόπον ἥ τε ἡδονὴ τελειοῖ καὶ τὸ αἰσθητόν τε καὶ ἡ αἴσθησις, σπουδαῖα ὄντα, ὥσπερ οὐδ᾽ ἡ ὑγίεια καὶ ὁ ἰατρὸς ὁμοίως αἴτιά ἐστι τοῦ ὑγιαίνειν.

Pleasure perfects the activity, not in the same way, however, as the object perceived and the faculty of perception, if optimal, perfect it; just as health and a doctor are not in the same way the cause of being healthy. (X 4, 1174 b 23-26, trans. Rackham, modified)

Most commentators interpret this passage in the following way: the doctor is the efficient cause, and, in a similar way, the perfect condition of faculty and object is the efficient cause that perfects the activity. 'Health' signifies the *formal* cause: it is the form of a healthy man insofar as he is healthy[58]. Festugière[59] takes over this position, but

---

[55] Cf. Owen 1971-72, 143-145.

[56] Gauthier-Jolif 1959, II 780-781 deny that this would solve the problem: according to them, hedonism is not avoided by 'loosening' the ties between pleasure and activity. On Aristotle's view of happiness, they claim, there is after all an unbreakable link between the two. It does not make any difference, then, whether one considers pleasure to be identical with activity or takes it as 'a necessary consequence' of it. This criticism, however, is unjust. Indeed, as we will see, pleasure does provide an activity with a supplementary perfection, and so happiness too will obtain a supplementary quality when pleasure is added to it. But pleasure is in no way the proper finality of happiness; *eudaemonia* remains the highest goal in itself and does not require pleasure to be attained.

[57] X 4, 1174 b 14-23.

[58] Michael of Ephesus (*In Eth. Nic.* X, CAG XX, 557.24-558.12), Thomas Aquinas (*In Eth. Nic.* X, lect. VI n.2027), Grant 1885, *ad loc.*; Tricot 1959, 495 n.1; Burnet 1900, 453; Irwin 1985, 376. The two last mentioned, however, do not take the analogy seriously, saying that though the doctor is the efficient, and health the formal, cause, both kinds of perfection of an activity are *final* causes (Irwin), or that

he also acknowledges that pleasure (analogous with health in the example) is explicitly called τέλος a bit further on[60], and thus is considered as a *final* cause. A healthy condition, as Festugière explains the passage, is brought about by two *efficient* causes: the doctor who intervenes and the subject that bears in itself the possibility of being healed. Health, then, perfects the healthy condition, as a *formal* and at the same time *final* cause. As a formal cause it determines the form of the perfectly healthy condition, and as a final cause it stands for the perfection to which every condition aspires. So end and actual condition coincide in this case. This is a perfection 'au sens propre': without this health, the concrete healthy condition would never be perfect. Pleasure, too, is of this kind: a final and formal cause by which an activity is perfected 'au sens propre'. Gauthier and Jolif [61] reject this explanation; and, in doing so, they belong to a long tradition of commentators whose explanation of the passage in question has hardly been less influential than the aforementioned[62]. According to them, the doctor indeed stands for the *efficient* cause, but health cannot be but the end to which we aspire, the *final* cause. They argue that, although Aristotle often uses health as an example of the formal cause, in most cases it serves as a model of final causality. Aristotle's reference to pleasure as a τέλος in the immediate context is for them the ultimate argument for identifying pleasure with the final cause. Gosling and Taylor[63], however, attack the cogency of these arguments: against the statement that health is the model of final causality, they raise the point that it remains possible after all to consider health as a formal cause: 'If we have two people, one of whom, *A*, is constipated, the other, *B*, is without digestive troubles, and ask 'Why is *A* having such

---

the analogy is with perception and the object perceived, not with pleasure (Burnet).

[59]   Festugière 1936[b], 44-46 n.37; in the second edition of Hardie 1968 [1980[2]], the author takes over the main lines of the thesis of Festugière (p.409-411), although in the first edition he had followed Hackforth in amending the text. He changed 'ὥσπερ οὐδ᾿' in 'οὐδ᾿ ὥσπερ', meaning 'nor as health and the doctor are causes...' instead of 'just as health and the doctor are not in the same way the cause...'. In this case, of course, there would be no problem at all with this passage.

[60]   In X 4, 1174 b 31-33, quoted below.

[61]   Gauthier-Jolif 1959, II 839-841.

[62]   Cf. Albertus Magnus, *Super Ethica*, lib. X lect. 7, 730-734 (ed. Colon.); Henricus Bate Mechliniensis, *Speculum divinorum et quorundam naturalium*, lib. XV, cap. 6 (ed. forthcoming in the series 'Ancient and Medieval Philosophy, De Wulf-Mansioncentre, ser. I'); Johannes Buridanus, *Super decem libros Ethicorum*, lib. VII quaest. 26 (ed. Paris. 1513).

[63]   Gosling-Taylor 1982, 244-247.

trouble while *B* has none ?' the answer may be not that *B* is being helped along by a mixture of medicaments, but that *B* is healthy. Here *B*'s health is the formal cause of his digestive peace'[64]. The other argument quoted is countered by Gosling and Taylor with the thesis that τέλος means 'perfection', and thus can signify final as well as formal causality: both an end that should be strived for and an actualised condition. Their conclusion is that pleasure can only be a formal cause: the perfect state of a disposition.

None of these explanations, however, is satisfying. To be more precise, two objections can be made. First, pleasure cannot straight-forwardly be considered as a *final* cause: it is not the end to which an activity aspires. Clearly, we do not always perform all our activities in order to obtain pleasure. It even seems to be the case that a straight-forward aspiration to achieve pleasure would in fact prevent us from obtaining any pleasure whatsoever. As we will see in a moment, Aristotle indeed makes this inference. So if the reference to pleasure as a τέλος implies final causality, this may not be taken in a strict sense. Second, pleasure can neither be taken as the *formal* cause of a perfectly performed activity. The form of this activity is not pleasure. If, for example, at a certain moment I enjoy a piece of music (i.e., if my activity of listening is performed optimally and directed towards an optimal object, taking into account my natural preferences and abilities), then the activity I perform is not in the first place *enjoying*, but rather *listening*. The form of my activity does not change when it is optimised; I do not pass from listening to enjoying. If this were the case, there would be a sudden and totally inexplicable shift within the performance of a certain activity. In fact, those who accept the option that pleasure is identical to the perfection of an unimpeded activity end up saying that the form of a perfect activity (i.e., enjoying) is different from the form of the activity before it reaches perfection (e.g., listening), which clearly is absurd. Besides, when I stop listening, the pleasure connected with listening also disappears. Of course, I can enjoy the pleasure of remembering, but the same scheme returns here: remembering is primordial; when it disappears, pleasure disappears along with it. So the activity that yields pleasure is substantial; its perfect actualization itself, and not pleasure, is the formal cause.

The analogy Aristotle presents here must not be over-interpreted. Pleasure is not a cause, since, as we will see in a moment, it is only a

---

[64] Gosling-Taylor 1982, 245.

supervenient element. J.M. Rist even calls pleasure 'parasitic'[65]
(although the negative connotations of this metaphor impair its suit-
ability). So from the very beginning, the comparison with the causal
role of health does not hold, and it is a wrong starting point to search
for an identification of pleasure with a certain type of causality. The
passage presents only a loose parallel that is to a certain extent
forced[66].

All the same, it is possible to get a bit further with the given
example. The goal to which doctors aspire clearly is the health of their
patients[67]. But they cannot attain this goal directly. All they can do is
create the conditions for health: they cannot create the healthy state
itself. Or, in Aristotelian terms, they cannot directly impart the form of
health to their patients. They can only attain this goal by fulfilling a
number of conditions for health. They perform activities that aspire to
this ultimate goal, but of which the intrinsic goal is not health itself.
Administering potions, medical interventions, and so on do not in
themselves have health as their goal; health is rather the goal to which
the combination of all these activities, or the adaptation of a certain
activity to a certain case, is directed. In other words: health is the
ultimate finality of activities performed by doctors, *in addition to* the
finality and form that the activities have in themselves.

In a similar way the analogy with pleasure can be understood:
pleasure yields a *supplementary* perfection, in addition to the perfection
that an activity always has in itself. The example, however, is neither
transparent nor completely apt, since health remains, after all, the
ultimate *goal* to which doctors aspire[68], whereas pleasure always
remains a supervenient effect, and not a goal. So the emphasis in this
interpretation should be on the additional character that pleasure and
health have in common. When the passage is explained in this way, its

---

[65]   Rist 1989, 109.

[66]   I owe this idea to a personal communication of J. Cleary. Cf. also Hardie
1968, 313: 'We should then have to explain the apparent contradiction [i.e. between
the acceptance that pleasure is a formal cause and the later statement that pleasure is
an epiphenomenon] by saying that the first passage does not give a final or strictly
accurate answer but is a dialectical move towards the strict answer'.

[67]   Cf. *NE* I 1, 1094 a 8: [τέλος] ἰατρικῆς ὑγίεια.

[68]   Thus, in the context of the given analogy, health serves as the *final* cause,
aimed at by the doctor; it remains possible, however, to hold the view that in *other*
contexts health is a formal cause, e.g., in the example given by Gosling and Taylor.
But neither of these modes of causality is exemplified in pleasure, so this cannot be
the scope of the analogy.

function in the context is at least made clearer. The summary with which Aristotle closes this passage indeed stresses the supervenience of pleasure upon an activity, which in itself has *a different* inherent perfection:

> τελειοῖ δὲ τὴν ἐνέργειαν ἡ ἡδονὴ οὐχ ὡς ἡ ἕξις ἐνυπάρχουσα, ἀλλ᾽ ὡς ἐπιγιγνόμενόν τι τέλος, οἷον τοῖς ἀκμαίοις ἡ ὥρα.

> The pleasure perfects the activity, not as the disposition does which is already present in the activity, but as a supervenient perfection, like the bloom in those who are vigorous. (X 4, 1174 b 31-33, trans. Rackham, modified)

This passage, too, has often been misunderstood, particularly concerning the meaning of 'ὥρα' and 'ἀκμαίοις'. There is no reference here to the beauty of youth, as the standard interpretation would have it[69]. ᾽Ακμή᾽ means rather the 'vigour' of life, i.e. between, say, the ages of forty and fifty, when human life reaches its pinnacle[70]. '῏Ωρα', then, although it *can* have the meaning of 'bloom of youth', should be understood in another way here. The central notion is 'ἀκμαίοις', and it is difficult to combine this with the 'bloom of youth'. '῏Ωρα' must have a more general meaning in this context: namely, a 'flourishing' that is not confined to youth. So its meaning is not beauty here, but rather the effects of the culminating point of life: success, strength, prestige, etc. This 'bloom' is not necessary for life, but, when it is present, it gives a supervenient quality to our life, a perfection that cannot be reached in any other way[71].

---

[69]   See, e.g., Owen 1971-72, 146, who translates ὥρα as 'beauty', and ἀκμαίοις as 'prime'. Irwin 1985, *ad loc.*, has 'bloom', resp. 'youths'. Most translators (Ross 1925; Tricot 1959; Ackrill 1973; Barnes 1984; Broadie 1991, 336) render ὥρα as 'bloom of youth', but translate ἀκμαίοις as 'those in the flower of their age'. This traditional view is also taken over by LSJ, who quote this passage as an example of ὥρα meaning *the bloom of youth*. There is, then, a shift in the argument, unless one takes it that 'the flower of the age' refers to youth (which would be erroneous). If, however, it refers to the vigorous age (as it does), the example implies two distinct ages (which, then, suggests an interpretation *à la* Gosling and Taylor, implying the succession of two chronologically distinct perfections; see below, n.71).

[70]   See *Rhet.* II 14, 1390 b 9-11: the body reaches its pinnacle (ἀκμάζει) between the ages of thirty and thirty-five, the soul about the age of forty-nine. Cf. Gauthier-Jolif 1959, II 842: 'l'*akmè* est la force de l'âge, non la jeunesse'.

[71]   We cannot agree with the interpretation of Gosling-Taylor 1982, 211-212 (cf. also 241-242), according to whom 'one perfection per actualization is enough', i.e., the perfection of the activity itself and the supplementary perfection of pleasure (if it is supplementary at all) must be chronologically distinct. The phrase 'οἷον τοῖς ἀκμαίοις κτλ.' should be understood thus: the 'spring of youth' perfects the 'prime of

Pleasure is of this kind: it is not the intrinsic perfection of an activity, but rather a surplus, a quality that supervenes on it. Aristotle thus clearly acknowledges that activity and pleasure are not identical. Pleasure may be an extremely desirable and gratifying surplus, which makes us perform an activity even more ardently[72], but the activity as such can be performed without pleasure[73].

2.3. *The 'Proper Pleasure'*

Notwithstanding the clear distinction he draws between pleasure and activity, Aristotle does accept an internal correlation between an activity and a certain pleasure: every activity has one single 'proper pleasure' (οἰκεία ἡδονή). Apart from the rejection of physiology as a basis of the theory of pleasure, this notion may be considered as the main advance made on Plato's theory of pleasure. Although the term itself, οἰκεία or σύμφυτος ἡδονή, figures in Plato (*Phil*. 51 d 1 and d 8, cf. supra, p.39), the latter did not elaborate on the notion. In the end, his view of the relation between pleasure and intellect remained unclear. Intellectual pleasure was not at all coextensive with true pleasure; there were many other types of pure pleasures, and moreover, many, if not most, intellectual pleasures were impure. After all, Plato's

---

youth', because a perfect bloom of youth implies that one has passed through the *previous stage*, the 'spring of youth'. Some people, so they say, pass from winter to autumn, which prevents them from 'perfecting' their life; 'to go through spring is to go through a season of perfection' (212). So, the first perfection is only an intermediary stage, needed to reach the later 'supervenient' perfection. This interpretation presents two problems. In the first place, Aristotle clearly does not imply a chronological sequence of perfections of an activity: pleasure is a supervenient perfection that goes together with the perfect performance of the activity proper. If this were not the case, Aristotle would be saying that pleasure is a state we reach after having performed an activity. We would, then, experience the pleasure of our eyes only *after* having seen a beautiful form. Such an explanation would attribute too counter-intuitive an argument to Aristotle. Moreover, ἀκμαίοις certainly does not mean 'the prime of youth', as Gosling and Taylor maintain.

   [72] Cf. X 5, 1175 a 31-36.

   [73] The inference of Gosling-Taylor 1982, 252, reverses this reasoning: 'Lack of impediment is required for perfect actualization which constitutes *eudaimonia* (...). But lack of impediments entails pleasure, and so pleasure is required for *eudaimonia*.' One must not, however, make this reversal. Lack of impediments is indeed a condition for happiness, but this does not mean that pleasure — which also occurs when all impediments are removed — would also be a condition for happiness. It is consequential to it (a supervenient perfection), and not conditional.

good life consisted in a loose combination of two vague components, 'pleasure' and 'intellect'.

Aristotle, by comparison, presents a much more refined account, based on the central claim that any activity can yield pleasure. For if pleasure perfects a certain activity, then this pleasure must of necessity be very peculiar for each type of activity (X 5, 1175 a 29 – b 1). Elsewhere, Aristotle remarks that no one can experience the pleasure of a musician or of a just man, unless one is a musician or a just man himself (X 3, 1173 b 28-31, also II 8, 1109 a 7-21). In other words, the link between an activity and the 'proper pleasure' is exclusive.

The nature of this proper pleasure, moreover, has repercussions for the performance of different activities. The specific pleasure of one activity impedes the performance of another. Thus, the effect of the proper pleasure of a different activity is the same as the effect of distress: it hinders the 'unimpeded performance of a certain activity'. For instance, when a lover of music, while studying, suddenly hears the music of a flute, he will be distracted from his work insofar as he is more fond of music than of studying: pleasures impair each other and the corresponding activities (X 5, 1175 b 1-27).

Of course, this entails that pleasure is also dependent on the natural disposition of the subject. The proper pleasure, Aristotle says, differs from species to species. Every living being has its own 'natural function' (ἔργον), and, along with this, its activities will differ from the activities performed by other beings[74]. Heraclitus knew already that an ass 'would prefer chaff to gold'; the proper pleasure of man is not the same as that of a horse or a dog (X 5, 1176 a 3-9). And even within the species there are differences: not everyone enjoys the same things, and sometimes what one person finds pleasurable may even disgust another person. What, then, is the norm? Which criterion allows us to decide whether something is a real pleasure?

> We hold that in all such cases the thing really is what it appears to be to the righteous man. (X 5, 1176 a 15-16)

The good person is the one whose natural disposition is well ordered: they know what is truly important, and they will be the norm by which to judge possible perversions.

One might question this starting point: is it not an illusion to think that this ideal will ever be attained by any individual? But perhaps this

---

[74] Cf. *NE* I 7, 1097 b 25 – 1098 a 20.

is not what Aristotle meant: his righteous person is 'the good man, *qua* good' (X 5, 1176 a 18: ἀγαθός, ᾗ τοιοῦτος). In other words, the norm need not be fully realised in order to be the norm. Perhaps the righteous person is never perfectly good; still, their judgment remains decisive. Their authority covers the areas in which they are truly righteous. Moreover, 'righteousness' should be understood primarily as a good disposition that may be adapted to all human faculties. It concerns, for instance, the correct disposition of the perceiving faculties, in which case the righteousness is easily recognised. When adapted to human conduct, the case is made more difficult: how is one to judge whether someone's deeds are as they ought to be? Isn't this judgment of righteousness always subject to another norm, which remains implicit in Aristotle's analysis? There is the risk that Aristotle's starting point is a *petitio principii*: the good person is the norm for judging morality, but, in the meantime, the good person is good because he is righteous. The morality that is judged is nothing else but the norm itself. Apparently, Aristotle was aware of this difficulty. He is rather pessimistic about the 'makability' of the good person: understanding and implementing a moral norm presupposes that one possesses moral excellence already[75].

In any case, on the basis of the theory of pleasure elaborated here, it is possible to establish a *moral* distinction between the different kinds of pleasure. The bottom line is fairly clear: pleasure that is detested by anyone is no pleasure, unless it is so for the depraved. Their enjoyment is due to a perversion of their nature — and many corruptions and illnesses threaten our human nature (X 5, 1176 a 20-24; cf. X 3, 1173 b 20-25). But what is the highest, typically human pleasure? The answer to this question parallels the ethical status of the activity by which the pleasure is yielded. As we saw, this can differ along with the disposition both of the subject (the degree of accuracy of perception etc., as well as the degree of development of the natural faculties) and of the object (an activity that has an inferior object is inferior itself). The highest activity, or eudaemonia, will be the one that perfectly satisfies these conditions (X 4, 1174 b 14-23). This highest human activity is the activity of contemplation: here the rational faculty, being the natural and proper end of man, reaches its highest performance. Due to the nature of pleasure, this highest activity will yield the highest pleasure, compared to which all other pleasures are inferior. But, as we

---

[75]   Cf. Sullivan 1977, 111-112.

saw, this condition cannot be reached by just anyone. Any one who is not aware of the moral norm will not attain the morally superior pleasure. On the other hand, morally inferior pleasure will be a hindrance to the attainment of moral excellence. Hence, the interference of moral quality and pleasure is decisive for the possibility of attaining eudaemonia.

Notwithstanding his pessimism concerning the attainability of morally superior pleasure, Aristotle did manage to positively evaluate pleasure — something Plato had failed to do — through the notion of proper pleasure. This pleasure does not impede the activity, not even the highest activity; on the contrary, it even stimulates our performance of the activity. Thus, the pleasure that accompanies a good activity will be good *in se*.

3. *Consequences of Aristotle's New Model*

Starting from his new definition of pleasure, Aristotle goes on to elaborate his criticism of the Platonic theory of pleasure. One can highlight three main consequences: (1) pleasure cannot be a movement; (2) nor can it be excessive per se; and (3) although the notion of pure pleasure can be employed, it must be reconsidered.

3.1. *Pleasure is not a Movement*

Aristotle rejects the opinion that pleasure is a process of becoming, holding instead that pleasure is always perfectly realised, just like the activity of seeing. Every concrete act of seeing is a perfect performance of the sensory faculty of the eyes. It is possible, of course, to see either many or only a few objects, or even to see well or to see badly. *Qua* seeing, however, every actualization of this faculty is perfect: there is nothing between seeing and not seeing. The same goes for pleasure: if it is present, it is perfectly realised. It can be more or less intense, and it can occur quickly or slowly[76], due to the activity by which it is yielded and to the dispositions of the subject: lovers of arts rather than of sports will have more intense pleasure and have it more quickly in arts than in sports. But within pleasure as such (whether it be in arts or in

---

[76] Cf. X 3, 1173 a 31 – b 4.

sports) there is no difference in speed or intensity; *qua* pleasure it is fully actualised in every moment of its existence. All this is contrasted with the activity of building, where a project is realised step by step and progressively. The project is not perfected until the last stone is laid, after the completion of all stages in the realization of the house. Every stage is a means to the attainment of the ultimate goal[77].

This comparison, however, is elusive. It cannot mean — although this would seem to be a necessary implication — that pleasure itself is an activity: it does not have an independent existence, and neither is it doing something[78]. Aristotle rather seems to mean that pleasure is 'something like' an activity, insofar as it is neither a means to the realization of an ultimate end nor a process of becoming. In this way, pleasure (something like an activity) occurs as a supervenient element in an activity. The question, then, becomes how it is possible that the activity and the pleasure — both of which are perfect and ends in themselves — are inseparably combined?

Clearly, pleasure is distinct from the perfect actualization of a certain activity. Aristotle points out that an activity and its proper pleasure (οἰκεία ἡδονή) are so closely linked together that one could be tempted to say that they are identical:

> Pleasure is closely linked to the activity, indeed so inseparable from it as to raise a doubt whether the activity is not the same as the pleasure.[79]

Aristotle himself, however, immediately rejects this option: it would be absurd, so he says, to regard pleasure itself as identical with a thought or perception. So there always remains an irreducible difference between an activity and its proper pleasure. Undoubtedly, the pleasure that is taken in a cognitive activity can itself be described as cognitive, but it is fundamentally different from the activity as such. Their alleged identity is due to a misunderstanding of their inseparability[80].

---

[77] X 4, 1174 a 14 – b 9.

[78] Cf. Sparshott 1994, 311-315.

[79] X 5, 1175 b 32-33: αἱ δὲ [as opposed to the more loose relation between desire and activity] σύνεγγυς ταῖς ἐνεργείαις, καὶ ἀδιόριστοι οὕτως ὥστ᾽ ἔχειν ἀμφισβήτησιν εἰ ταὐτόν ἐστιν ἡ ἐνέργεια τῇ ἡδονῇ (transl. Rackham). Cf. 1175 a 19-21: συνεζεῦχθαι μὲν γὰρ ταῦτα φαίνεται καὶ χωρισμὸν οὐ δέχεται· ἄνευ τε γὰρ ἐνεργείας οὐ γίνεται ἡδονή, πᾶσάν τε ἐνέργειαν τελειοῖ ἡ ἡδονή.

[80] X 5, 1175 b 34-36.

Of course, in arguing thus, Aristotle cannot avoid the problem that if indeed pleasure and activity are not identical, then what makes them inseparable? Moreover, the case is made even more difficult by Aristotle's assertion that pleasure, too, is a perfect activity. To this Aristotle, in fact, offers no clear answer, but one could explain his position (to a certain degree at least) from the general outline of his theory. The activity, which is the actualization of a natural disposition (ἕξις), is self-sufficient and bears its end in itself. The pleasure that accompanies this activity is likewise perfect and has its end in itself, but it is not self-sufficient; it completes the unimpeded activity and gives it a supplementary perfection, but its existence is fully dependent on the activity. From an analytical viewpoint one can separate them; but in fact the second (pleasure) is always inseparably linked to the first (the activity), and they both have their origin in the same natural disposition of the subject[81] (with the nuance, however, that for pleasure the disposition alone is not enough: an actual realization of the activity is also needed for pleasure to be possible). Thus, for Aristotle, pleasure as such is an empty notion; it can exist only in combination with a perfect activity, to which it is inseparably linked.

The consequences of Aristotle's rejection of pleasure as movement are very important. Confronting an additional argument of Speusippus, who apparently had held the view that pleasure could not be the good because it is not stable, Aristotle gives the following explanation. The lack of stability in pleasure is due to the fact that our nature is not simple, at least insofar as it is perishable. When the 'first part' (the soul, no doubt) is active, the activity of the 'other part' (presumably the body) is impeded, and vice versa. When both are in balance, there is neither pleasure nor distress. If our nature had been simple, one and the same activity would always and continuously yield pleasure (VII 14, 1154 b 20-25). A few lines further, our longing for a variation of pleasure is said to be the effect of a perversion of our nature (1154 b 28-31), by which Aristotle presumably means that the longing for variation is rooted in an excessive inclination to corporeal pleasure.

This is a puzzling argument. It implies that the boredom that occurs in the repetition of pleasurable activities is due to our composite nature, and more precisely to the material element in it[82]. If our nature

---

[81] Cf. Broadie 1991, 338.
[82] Cf. *Met.* XII 2, 1069 b 15-20; *Phys.* I 7, 190 b 10-11: variability always

were simple, we would not require any variation. This can only mean that intellectual pleasure as such is always stable. But, since we have bodily needs as well, we cannot but refrain from our intellectual activity every now and then to satisfy them. If so, then the variance of pleasure is inherent in our human nature. But, in that case, can it still be called a perversion? Aristotle here presents an unmistakable dualism that cannot be reconciled with the doctrine of man as a hylemorphic unity, which he defends in his mature works. Indeed, it is not at all clear how the activity (as well as the proper pleasure) of the body could be *by its nature* a hindrance to the soul, and vice versa. On the contrary, genuine pleasure, as defined by Aristotle, seems to be possible only if the body and soul are brought into harmony (whereas, in this passage, this condition is said to yield neither pleasure nor distress).

Aristotle's position can be defended by arguing that his theory of proper pleasure plays a role here: since corporeal and intellectual activities have their own specific pleasure, there might be an opposition and a mutual hindrance between them. But this ought not to be due to their very nature. It is very well possible that some pleasures can appear together without impeding each other, even when one is intellectual and the other corporeal. Someone who enjoys both smoking and studying may be capable of smoking and studying at the same time, and even of enjoying them both. Corporeal pleasure, then, does not per se impede intellectual pleasure, let alone intellectual activity.

This dualistic remark, however, is less important than a distinction that Aristotle draws, as it were, in the margin: the activity of the body is activity in movement, whereas intellectual activity is essentially stable (or at rest). Aristotle adds the following remark:

> Hence god enjoys a simple single pleasure perpetually. For there is not only an activity of motion, but also an activity of immobility, and pleasure exists rather in rest than in motion. (VII 14, 1154 b 26-28)

Aristotle here draws a distinction between two kinds of activity: activity at rest and activity in movement[83]. By definition, then, they both can

---

presupposes the potentiality of matter.

   [83] Cf. *Phys.* III 2, 201 b 31; *Met.* XI 9, 1066 a 20-21; *De an.* 431 a 6. This account is not fully coextensive with the distinction made at *Met.* IX 6, 1048 b 18-35; 8, 1050 a 23 – b 2; see Urmson 1988, 99-103; Ricken 1995, 214-216; Rist 1989, 108-111;

afford pleasure. Hence there is a distinction between pleasure in movement and pleasure at rest. This enables Aristotle to integrate Plato's model within his own: pleasure-in-movement, taken as a paradigm by Plato, can be regarded as a kind of pleasure, since movement, too, is a kind of activity — and an activity yields pleasure. But this pleasure in movement must not be taken as the paradigm of pleasure. As Aristotle indicates, pleasure exists in rest rather than in motion. For the movement, i.e., the restoration of a lack, is inferior to the attained natural condition itself. Moreover, according to Aristotle, this activity in movement is only pleasurable *per accidens*:

> The processes that restore us to our natural state are only incidentally pleasant; for that matter the activity at work in the appetites for them is the activity of so much of our state and nature as has remained unimpaired; for there are actually pleasures that involve *no* pain or appetite (e.g. those of contemplation), the nature in such a case not being defective at all.[84]

To support this view, Aristotle points out that we do not enjoy the same thing *during* and *after* the repletion. After the repletion, we take pleasure in that which is *absolutely* pleasurable. During the repletion, on the contrary, we can take pleasure in things that are not absolutely pleasurable: when we are ill we might swallow sour or bitter potions that in themselves are not pleasurable at all (VII 13, 1153 a 2-6).

The incidental character of pleasure in the repletion of a lack is indicated here in a very compact way, but the reasoning can be developed thus: we can feel pleasure only insofar as we are healthy; no deficiency of our natural state could ever be pleasurable. But how, then, is it possible that we do feel pleasure in the repletion of this deficiency? Apparently, for as long as the repletion is taking place, a certain lack remains, which makes it almost impossible to enjoy the repletion. Aristotle himself offers a solution: pleasure is possible in this situation because our constitution is not wholly deficient. A part has

---

Ross 1953, II 251; Bostock 1988, 251-272; Liske 1991; Polansky 1983.

[84] VII 12, 1152 b 34 – 1153 a 2: κατὰ συμβεβηκὸς αἱ καθιστᾶσαι [*sc.* ἡδοναὶ] εἰς τὴν φυσικὴν ἕξιν ἡδεῖαί εἰσιν (ἔστι δ᾽ἡ ἐνέργεια ἐν ταῖς ἐπιθυμίαις τῆς ὑπολοίπου ἕξεως καὶ φύσεως)· ἐπεὶ καὶ ἄνευ λύπης καὶ ἐπιθυμίας εἰσὶν ἡδοναί (οἷον αἱ τοῦ θεωρεῖν ἐνέργειαι), τῆς φύσεως οὐκ ἐνδεοῦς οὔσης. We interpret the text in the manner of Festugière 1936[b], 17-18 n.3: ἔστι δ᾽ἡ ἐνέργεια ... φύσεως is a parenthetical remark that explains the preceding phrase. The next sentence ἐπεὶ καὶ ... ἡδοναί stands in opposition to the previous one, and is also followed by an elucidation: τῆς φύσεως οὐκ ἐνδεοῦς οὔσης.

remained healthy, and it is under the instigation of this part that the replenishment takes place. The pleasure we seem to feel in the replenishment, then, is not to be situated in the replenishment as such, but rather in the activity of that part of us that has remained healthy. In this sense, a repletion is pleasurable only *per accidens*: the pleasure we feel is not caused by the part of our body in which the replenishment takes place. This means, in other words, that pleasure as such is *not* to be found in the repletion of a lack, but exclusively in the faculties or dispositions that function as they should. The activity of the latter, then, is pleasurable per se.

This *incidental* pleasure should not, however, be understood as if it concerned only the affect of the body, whereas the soul would have *absolute* pleasure in the same activity. An example might help clarify this. Our pleasure in eating does not come, as we saw, from that part of our body in which we feel the lack (hunger). In appeasing our hunger it is not our stomach, but rather our (vegetative) soul, that enjoys the activity of eating; the pleasure belongs to a part of our constitution that did not suffer from any deficiency. It would, then, be possible to say that our body's pleasure is only incidental, while the soul's activity is pleasurable *per se*. But one must acknowledge that the activity of our soul in which we took pleasure in this case is *essentially modified* by the lack we felt: the repletion can be pleasurable only because of, or thanks to, the previous lack. In brief, in the absence of hunger, eating is not pleasurable. So there are activities that we never enjoy *as such*, but the pleasure of which depends on circumstances external to the activity itself (as hunger is a necessary condition for enjoying the activity of eating). In this sense, pleasure in eating, and generally speaking every repletion of a corporeal lack, even though it belongs to an activity of the soul, is pleasurable only *per accidens*.

The distinction between the pleasurable per se (or at rest) and per accidens (or in movement) does not, however, involve two different definitions, nor even two distinct kinds of pleasure. The pleasure we take in the repletion of a lack is due to the perfect, natural condition of a different faculty. We do not enjoy the replenishment as such, but rather the actual functioning of the faculty that provides the replenishment. So, in the end, there is only one kind of pleasure, which is to be situated in the natural condition, i.e., a disposition that functions in a perfect way.

Thus, Plato's paradigm of pleasure is reduced to a mere side issue of the broader theory Aristotle presents. Plato ignored the fact that pleasure can never be situated in a disposition that is in any way deficient, and thus neither in the restoration process that this deficient disposition undergoes. If pleasure occurs in such a situation, it is due to the perfect activity of another disposition that does function as it should.

3.2. *Pleasure is not Excessive per se*

A second corollary of Aristotle's new definition consists in his rejection of the alleged excessive character of pleasure. Again, this criticism can be traced back to the rebuttal of the underlying definition, and can thus be seen as directed against Plato's *Philebus* rather than against Speusippus. Indeed, this was an important element in Plato's theory of pleasure in the *Philebus*. Pleasure, he said, cannot be investigated in a proper way except by examining its most intense forms. Socrates appropriates this starting point from the 'enemies of Philebus', who hold the view that pleasure does not exist at all, because it is only the escape from distress[85]. This thesis, Socrates adds, is too radical to be acceptable. All the same, its starting point is valuable, namely, that in order to get a correct view of pleasure one should investigate its most extreme forms, where the proper characteristics are most clearly present[86]. From this starting point, however, Plato arrives at his own drastic conclusion: all forms of pleasure share the characteristics of this real, excessive pleasure — albeit in a more moderate form. Even true pleasure, since it remains, after all, the repletion of a lack, is subject to the general thesis that pleasure *in se* is *unlimited*: it always admits of 'the more and the less' (*Phil.* 27 e 5 – 28 a 4). The risk of excess can never be excluded.

To this analysis Aristotle will object that the alleged excessive nature of pleasure is due again to the pivotal role attributed to bodily pleasure (VII 14-15, 1154 a 8 – b 31). His first argument is rather

---

[85] *Phil.* 44 b 6 – c 4. Most commentators identify these 'enemies of Philebus' as Speusippus *cum suis* (cf. Schofield 1971, 2-20 and 181; Dillon 1996, 104-114, who gives a survey of the relevant literature; see also the survey in Tarán 1981, 79 n.379, who agrees, however, with Diès (1941, LVII-LXII) in rejecting the standard interpretation and considering the 'enemies of Philebus' to be non-philosophers). However, although we see no reason to reject this identification, this does not mean that Aristotle is attacking only Speusippus. Essentially, his reaction is directed against the thesis that Plato himself takes over from the 'enemies of Philebus', namely, that the true nature of pleasure is to be found in its most intense forms.

[86] *Phil.* 44 a 12 – 45 e 8; in 45 e 9 – 50 e 4 Plato exemplifies this assumption.

superficial and serves as an *entrée en matière*: bodily pleasure should not be seen as something bad. No one would stay alive without replenishing his bodily needs; and how, indeed, could something that belongs of necessity to nature be bad? Moreover, if bodily pleasure is bad, then how can its opposite, pain, still be considered as something bad? Should not the opposite of something bad always be good ? (VII 14, 1154 a 10-11). Although one cannot deny that this argument is directed primarily against Speusippus' rejection of pleasure as such, a hint of this negative view of pleasure is present also in the *Philebus*. Plato did admit 'necessary' pleasure into the good life, not because it is good, but because it is inevitable (62 e). That it is not in Plato's eyes good can be inferred from the fact that necessary pleasure is absent from the 'final classification of all good ingredients of the good life' (66 a-c); on the side of pleasure, only the true and pure pleasure of the soul is mentioned. Thus, the negative evaluation of necessary pleasure is implied in the *Philebus*.

The reaction against Plato comes to the fore in Aristotle's second argument, directed against the thesis that pleasure would be excessive by its very nature. He points out that not all movements or activities that yield pleasure admit of excess[87]; so, too, neither is pleasure excessive in those cases. In some cases, excess is possible, but even regarding these Aristotle cannot agree with Plato. That the replenishment of corporeal needs admits of excess does not mean, he says, that corporeal pleasure itself is excessive. Excess is due not to the nature of pleasure, but to a perversion of our desire. So one must not regard all pleasure (under the paradigm of bodily pleasure) as something bad simply because it might be excessive. The case of distress, however, is different: one avoids not only excessive pain, but all pain as such. The opposite of excessive pleasure is not pain (except for those who strive for excessive pleasure only; see VII 14, 1154 a 20-21). Aristotle's point here is that the assertion of an opposition between excessive pleasure and pain is too simple: the absence of excessive pleasure is not at all the same as pain. Opposed to excessive pleasure is not pain, but rather *pleasure without excess*, and this pleasure cannot but be good.

---

[87] Aristotle does not give examples, but seems to have in mind the activities of 'seeing', 'hearing', and the like: activities that do not allow for degrees. One cannot see, hear, taste, etc. in an excessive way, even if, say, a curious person wants to see an excessive number of things: this does not imply that the act of seeing itself allows for excess.

This misunderstanding is due, Aristotle maintains, to the assumption that one normally strives for pleasure *in contrast*: the experience of excessive distress causes one to search for a remedy (ἰατρεία) by striving for pleasure in an excessive way. But one must not generalise this: it is only the case for some individuals in some situations. Moreover, an excess is only possible in one kind of pleasure, i.e., that which is preceded by a distress (and this, as we saw, is not even pleasure in the proper sense of the word):

> But the pleasures that do not involve pains do not admit of excess; and these are among the things pleasant by nature and not incidentally. By things pleasant incidentally I mean those that act as cures (for because as a result people are cured, through some action of the part that remains healthy, for this reason the process is thought pleasant); by things naturally pleasant I mean those that stimulate the action of the healthy nature. (VII 14, 1154 b 15-20, trans. Ross)

The distinction between things incidentally and naturally pleasant is here put to the service of the explanation of excessive pleasure. The latter is possible only, Aristotle says, in those things that are pleasurable *per accidens*: pleasure that occurs in the restoration of the natural state. Naturally pleasant, on the contrary, are those things that stimulate the activity of a given nature: it belongs to the natural state of a certain disposition. So, since the incidentally pleasant yields only a derived form of pleasure, one should conclude that excess does not belong to the nature of pleasure itself.

In Book X, Aristotle discusses a closely related topic: Plato's argument that because pleasure admits of 'the more and the less', it is unlimited. Aristotle can agree with this, but not without essentially modifying the theory: pleasure, so he says, does admit of more and less, if one considers the act of enjoying. But this would also go for virtue and the like: because one individual is better predisposed than another, the practice of justice, virtue in general, and so on, no less than pleasure, will admit of more or less. In other words: one person will by nature enjoy more, and enjoy sooner, than another, but this does not mean that the nature of pleasure itself is unlimited. Moreover, a fixed condition such as health also admits of more and less in this sense: not everyone is healthy in the same way, nor does health remain unchanged. When we become ill, we do not lose our health all at once: it changes, remains for a while, and then disappears in a certain respect. Likewise, one can say that pleasure admits of more or less if one takes into account the factor of time: at one moment we feel more pleasure than at another (X 3, 1173 a 15-28).

Aristotle here modifies Plato's analysis of the 'more and less' of pleasure by introducing a non-individual and diachronic viewpoint: one person enjoys more, another less, and at one moment pleasure is greater than at another. He does not accept, however, that there is a 'more and less' within pleasure itself. So, for Aristotle, pleasure is not excessive *in se*. Excess is possible only in the pleasure in movement; moreover, excess is not inherent in the nature of pleasure itself. It is due to a perversion of certain desires, brought about by external causes. Therefore, Aristotle concludes, Plato went wrong (with Speusippus following in his wake) in taking excessive pleasure as the paradigm under which to investigate the nature of pleasure.

One may question, however, the validity of this Aristotelian analysis: does the excess lie outside pleasure, as Aristotle maintains, or is there something within pleasure that always tends to excess? In our opinion, the Platonic account is the more correct one. Pleasure never remains constant; to maintain an equal degree of enjoyment (and to avoid the boredom which threatens all pleasure) the requirements are always increased. Pleasure itself seems to demand that the limits of enjoyment are always shifting.

3.3. *'Pure' Pleasure*

Finally, Aristotle modifies Plato's criterion of the *purity* of pleasure, in order to harmonise it with his own views. Plato considered a pleasure to be pure when it was totally devoid of its counterpart. This condition could, then, only be fulfilled in the case of true pleasure, because here the previous lack was too small to cause distress. Thus, in Plato, the criteria of the purity and of the truth of pleasure coincided.

Aristotle, on the contrary, who does not take over the definition of pleasure as the perceptible replenishment of a lack, implicitly assumes a hedonistic argument: if there is any pleasure present, it will always be pure. Even if it goes together with distress, the purity of pleasure in itself is not abolished. It would, then, be meaningless to use the criterion of purity in its Platonic form: in an Aristotelian context, every pleasure is pure in this sense.

Aristotle does, however, continue to use this criterion from a different perspective. According to him, there is a difference in purity between different activities, and thus also between the pleasures that accompany those activities. Seeing, he maintains, is purer than touching, and hearing and smelling are purer than tasting (X 5, 1175 b 36 – 1176 a 3). The norm for this distinction seems to be the degree to which an activity is able to grasp the *form* and to detach from matter. Pure pleasure is, then, the pleasure that is detached from material things. It reaches its highest realization in the pleasure of God, completely devoid of the instability of matter[88]. This also has consequences for man, who is the bearer of a divine element: man must strive to achieve immortality (at least as far as possible) by living in accordance with the highest part of himself. And this highest, divine element in man is intellect[89]. Because a life in accordance with the intellect is the realization of the highest human activity, it automatically yields the purest, most stable pleasure:

> At all events the pursuit of it [philosophic wisdom] is thought to offer pleasures marvellous for their purity and their enduringness. (X 7, 1177 a 25-27, trans. Ross)

This implies that, in the end, the criteria of the purity and the truth of pleasure converge in Aristotle, as they did in Plato, albeit in a totally different context.

4. *An Evaluation of the Aristotelian Account*

If one reads the Aristotelian account of pleasure from the perspective we have presented, it becomes clear that it is closely related to the Platonic viewpoint. Admittedly, there is no reason to deny that Aristotle's objections might just as well be directed against Speusippus' theory of pleasure. But eventually all his criticisms concern the definition of Plato. The latter serves as the negative background against which Aristotle wants to elaborate his views. The entire analysis, then, seems to serve two ends: first, to show the failure of Plato's definition; and, second, to provide an alternative that makes possible a better understanding of the true nature of pleasure. When he takes over

---

[88] Cf. VII 14, 1154 b 26-28; see also *Met.* XII 7, 1072 b 24-25.

[89] *NE* X 7, 1177 b 30-34: εἰ δὴ θεῖον ὁ νοῦς πρὸς τὸν ἄνθρωπον, καὶ ὁ κατὰ τοῦτον βίος θεῖος πρὸς τὸν ἀνθρώπινον βίον. οὐ χρὴ δὲ κατὰ τοὺς παραινοῦντας ἀνθρώπινα φρονεῖν ἄνθρωπον ὄντα οὐδὲ θνητὰ τὸν θνητόν, ἀλλ᾽ ἐφ᾽ ὅσον ἐνδέχεται ἀθανατίζειν καὶ πάντα ποιεῖν πρὸς τὸ ζῆν κατὰ τὸ κράτιστον τῶν ἐν αὑτῷ. Cf. *Met.* XII 7, 1072 b 22-24.

central notions from the Platonic account (such as pure pleasure), he does not do so without thoroughly modifying them.

One may say that Aristotle does succeed: his account is more consistent than that offered by Plato. By connecting pleasure to an activity instead of to the replenishment of a lack, Aristotle is able to provide a better understanding of the nature of the higher forms of pleasure. This enables him to give a positive account of those forms of pleasure (something very difficult indeed in Plato's theory, based as it is on physiology), without at the same time disconnecting them from lower pleasure. Particularly, the possibility of a pleasure at rest is a very important improvement on Plato's theory: true and pure pleasure is no longer the replenishment of a lack, but rather the highest performance of our highest activity, a state of rest that occurs when our faculties are perfectly functioning. This insight has had a decisive impact on the later tradition: all later theorists of pleasure, even those who call themselves 'Platonists', copy this Aristotelian canvas to establish a close relation between the absolute desirability of higher reality and an absolutely desirable form of pleasure.

The central point in Aristotle's divergence from Plato is the new conception of the natural condition, on which they both build their definition of pleasure. Plato describes this natural condition as an abstract ideal, a state devoid of lack and replenishment, which we will never attain in its purity. Pleasure is the movement towards this condition, which implies that an actual attainment of this condition (even if it were possible) would no longer yield any pleasure. As a consequence, a divine life, without lack and thus without repletion, is doomed to be a life without pleasure.

Aristotle, on the contrary, does not regard this natural condition as an abstract ideal, but rather as the perfect development of a natural faculty. R.J. Sullivan summarises this view in the following way: 'The nature of a thing is defined by its function, the function of a thing is its excellence'[90]. In other words, the natural condition is an attainable and utterly desirable state. It is the condition to which every faculty naturally tends. This automatically implies that we do feel pleasure when this state is attained, and that pleasure is no longer confined to the movement towards it. Even more so: pleasure in the natural condition is more genuine pleasure than is pleasure in the replenishment of a lack. Contra Plato, Aristotle holds that god does experience

---

[90]   Sullivan 1977, 95.

pleasure: god's is even the most stable pleasure, because his natural condition is always perfectly established. This divine pleasure is true and pure pleasure. Through intellect, man partakes in this divine gift, and his intrinsic finality is to fully develop this highest faculty as far as possible. He thus reaches true and pure pleasure in the life devoted to contemplation.

There are, however, weak points in Aristotle's account. Without attempting to be exhaustive, we would like to consider three imperfections.

1. It has already been pointed out by many commentators that Aristotle's attitude *vis-à-vis* pleasure in movement is too negative. This criticism is found in its clearest form in J.O. Urmson[91]. He argues that Aristotle's interpretation of the term 'process', or 'generation' (γένεσις), is too narrow. Aristotle sees it as the 'movement towards an external end', as a kind of activity that is not an end in itself, but only serves to achieve something else (as in the case of building a house). However, as Urmson makes clear, there are activities that are essentially a process but are performed for their own sake: 'It is not usually the case that people solve crossword puzzles solely for the pleasure of contemplating the finished product or for putting it to some use'[92]. So the pleasure taken in this kind of activity cannot only be situated in the final result, and neither can one say that it consists in the replenishment of a lack. Apparently, Aristotle does not take into account this kind of pleasure in movement, although he does give an example of it: the pleasure in listening to music. This is not the affect that remains when the process has come to an end, and neither is it the replenishment of a lack[93]. On the contrary: listening to music is a process performed for its own sake, and in which the activity itself is essentially (not incidentally) pleasurable. Even intellectual pleasure, highly esteemed by Aristotle, belongs in some cases to this class: for example, we do not take pleasure in the state attained by reading, but rather in the process, in the reading, itself.

---

[91] Urmson 1988, 101-103. This criticism was already formulated in Urmson 1967, 327-328.
[92] Urmson 1988, 102.
[93] Cf. Gosling-Taylor 1982, 314.

We do not wish to enter into the debate that has arisen since Urmson first published his criticism[94], nor can we dwell here on the relationship between *energeia* and *kinesis*[95], an issue that is essential to the discussion. We have only touched upon the criticism precisely because it shows how Aristotle's account of pleasure in movement is highly dependent on Plato's statement that this kind of pleasure is always the replenishment of a lack[96]. Aristotle's reaction against the generalization that Plato developed from this starting point blinded him to the possibility that there are other forms of process-like activities than those which Plato had in mind. After all, his reaction against Plato prevented him from considering the possibility of an alternative interpretation of the pleasures in movement. His aim was to show that the sort of pleasure in movement that Plato took as the paradigm did not cover all kinds of pleasure. In so doing, however, he did not question the validity of Plato's arguments in his own field: he simply took over the Platonic account of pleasure in movement, and rejected it as a whole in order to replace it by his own interpretation of the nature of pleasure.

2. The main problem we would like to address is a point that we raised already when discussing Plato's views. Just as Plato accepts a necessary link between the replenishment of a lack and pleasure, Aristotle seems to accept that there is a *direct* link between a perfect activity and the corresponding pleasure, which would imply that an unimpeded activity *necessarily* yields pleasure. But is that position tenable? An unimpeded functioning will surely stimulate the occurrence of pleasure, but this does not necessarily mean that we *will* enjoy any unimpeded activity. Suppose my favourite music is Beethoven's fourth Piano Concerto, and I have the occasion to listen to it performed by a great soloist. I listen carefully, and there is not the slightest impediment to my activity of listening. Does this guarantee my pleasure? All conditions seem to be fulfilled, and yet it remains possible that I will not

---

[94] See Sullivan 1977, 47 n.36 [p.58]; Gosling-Taylor 1982, 312-314; C.C.W. Taylor 1988; Gonzalez 1991, 147 n.11 (basing himself on Bostock 1988).

[95] For this issue, see the texts quoted above, n.83.

[96] Cf. Broadie 1991, 326: 'Aristotle rejects the assumption [viz. that the only pleasures are the gross and often violent physical ones], but he has something of the neutralists' [i.e. those who adopt the view that the highest human activity is neither pleasurable nor painful] negative attitude to those pleasures'.

enjoy the music at all. The question, then, is when and how pleasure comes in.

Unlike Plato, Aristotle seems to have been aware of the difficulty. The essential feature of Aristotle's account is that pleasure is an effect that is never attained except indirectly: the subject can reach pleasure only through the detour of a perfectly performed activity. Thus, the very notion of supervenience that is essential for Aristotle's doctrine shows that he would agree with the thesis with which we confronted Plato earlier on, that pleasure is 'essentially a by-product'. Since pleasure is a supervenient perfection of the performance of a certain activity, the only thing we have in hand is the performance of the activity itself, not the addition of pleasure to it. Moreover, in Aristotle's account, pleasure does not exist in isolation, i.e., without an activity upon which it is added as a supervenient perfection.

Despite this merit, however, one can criticise Aristotle for not having followed his analysis to its final consequences. For, although he makes a clear distinction between activity and pleasure, he nonetheless implies that the perfect performance of an activity *necessarily* yields pleasure. Even if we cannot directly aim at it, pleasure still occurs of necessity when we attain the perfect performance of the activity. So, although the direct access to pleasure is denied, its occurrence is guaranteed after all, through the detour of the perfect realization of an activity. This does not mean that we will perfectly realise every activity, but it does mean that we *will* have pleasure once the perfection of an activity is attained.

But, as we saw, this is an untenable position. There is no clearcut answer to the question of when and how we will attain pleasure. Like happiness, it is something we may hope to attain, without ever being sure how to behave in order to guarantee its attainment. Even if we know exactly what to do to perfect the performance of an activity, we cannot be sure that pleasure will be added to it. Moreover, the very fact that a perfectly realised activity will eventually cease to yield pleasure, when it is repeated too many times, proves that the perfection of an activity as such is not enough to explain the occurrence of pleasure[97].

---

[97] Aristotle's own answer to this central question (at least, central in our account) is fairly superficial and starts from a rather gratuitous dualistic perspective (cf. supra, p.63-64): our desire for variation in our pleasures is due to our composite nature: 'whenever one of the two elements is active, its activity runs counter to the other, while when the two are balanced, their action feels neither painful nor pleasant'. If

There is, then, no direct access to pleasure. Although Aristotle seems to be aware of this problem, it is not taken into account in his solution: as it stands, the theory suggests that an indirect aspiration to pleasure (through the detour of a perfectly performed activity) does guarantee my pleasure after all. But if this perfect activity necessarily yields pleasure, in what sense, then, would this differ from a direct access to pleasure?

As a matter of fact, we can never be sure what to do in order to attain pleasure: it is never guaranteed. As an additional element, pleasure might occur, but it might as well fail to appear. Let us return to Beethoven's fourth Piano Concerto. It is not certain that I will experience pleasure in attending a performance of this work. Even if all the circumstances are in an optimal state, I cannot be sure that I will enjoy the concert. Aristotle might object that the absence of pleasure would be due to the fact that not all of the conditions for a perfect performance of the activity are fulfilled. Perhaps the concert hall was too cold, which distracted my attention from the music. Or maybe my thoughts were occupied by other burdens, which prevented me from listening carefully. Or possibly I enjoyed other things more than the music: the comfortable chair or the paintings on the ceiling. The absence of pleasure, then, indicates precisely that the activity was not brought to perfection.

The objection would be fitting only if it implied that pleasure is the *token* that the activity indeed was brought to perfection: I know that an activity is perfectly performed precisely because I feel pleasure. In other words, if indeed the absence of pleasure does not suffice to indicate that the activity is imperfectly performed, could we not reverse the argument and say that the presence of pleasure suffices to indicate the perfection of the activity? But, if so, pleasure becomes the criterion for the perfection of an activity. However, this seems to be

---

our nature were simple, then the same activity would always yield pleasure (*NE* VII 14, 1154 b 20-25). A few lines further on (1154 b 28-31), the longing for variation is said to be due to the presence of 'some badness' (πονηρία τις) in us, which cannot but mean the changeable material component of our nature. But it is hardly understandable (1) why the activity of the physical element in us would by its nature run counter to the activity of thought (the immobile activity); (2) why this physical element is labelled 'bad'; and (3) how this scheme would explain the absence of pleasure in a perfectly performed activity that is repeated too many times (taking for granted, which Aristotle seems to admit, that the perfection of the performance of the activity is not affected by the repetition): if it is taken as an explanation for this fact, then the very definition of pleasure seems to be implicitly revoked.

impossible, since, as we have seen, Aristotle makes a distinction between pleasure and activity. This presupposes, on our view, that the activity has its own finality and does not need pleasure to be performed perfectly. The perfection of pleasure can only be an additional one[98]. If this is true, then it should be possible for an activity to be perfectly performed even without yielding pleasure. But to hold this is to dismiss the immediate link between pleasure and a perfect activity, which is to imply that the perfection of an activity as such is not enough to secure our pleasure. Even if all circumstances are perfectly arranged, and the activity perfectly performed, pleasure is not guaranteed. This escape from our control is not an accidental quality of pleasure, dependent on the circumstances, but is rather a characteristic of the very essence of pleasure.

On the other hand, it is not clear why only a perfectly performed activity can yield pleasure. Pleasure can have the opposite effect: it can bring (short) relief from the impediments that prevent a perfect performance of an activity. My activity of listening does not have to be perfect in order for me to be able to enjoy music. Even if my ear is affected by a serious disease and I can hardly hear, I can still enjoy music. In such a case, pleasure should be understood as the super-venient perfection of an activity that in itself is not perfect. Contrary to what Aristotle maintains, the perfection of an activity does not seem to be a distinctive element in establishing a definition of pleasure. The class of perfectly performed activities is not coextensive with the class of activities that yield pleasure, although they do coincide in many cases.

The main shortcoming of Aristotle's theory of pleasure, then, is that it does not indicate the exact relation between a perfect activity and the additional perfection yielded by pleasure. How does pleasure occur? If Aristotle's answer is that the link is necessary, we cannot agree: pleasure is by no means guaranteed. And in the other direction, too, the relation does not seem to be the one suggested by Aristotle: pleasure does not necessarily wait until our activity is perfect. It can have a healing function, producing a perfection that the activity itself was not capable of attaining.

3. Finally, Aristotle's rejection of the inherently excessive character of pleasure seems to be undue. According to him, all excesses stem from

---

[98] Cf. the puzzle of Hardie 1968, 411.

a perversion of our desire, not from pleasure itself. But as we have indicated already, the Platonic account seems to be the more correct one. The norm or mitigation imposed on pleasure always is external to pleasure itself. Aristotle recognises this: the measurement resides in the activity that yields the pleasure and is imposed by the temperance of the subject. Hence it is transferred to the proper pleasure of this activity. But Aristotle fails to see that this implies that pleasure in itself does not posses measurement and that it always tends to excess. The danger ascribed to pleasure by both anti-hedonists and hedonists[99] alike is that it always wants to break through its barriers, so that a high degree of self-control is needed to avoid one's being overcome by pleasure.

These criticisms must not, however, conceal the general merits of Aristotle's account of pleasure. It remains a highly nuanced examination, as well as a step forward in comparison with the Platonic account. By linking pleasure to an activity, instead of to the repletion of a lack, Aristotle unambiguously proves the existence of higher forms of pleasure, thereby saving pleasure from the depreciation that followed from the physiological scheme that lies at the foundation of the Platonic definition. In particular, the notion of a pleasure at rest must be welcomed: true and pure pleasure is no longer regarded as the repletion of a lack, but rather as the highest development of our highest activity, a rest yielded by the perfect functioning of our faculties. This took the debate on pleasure into a new direction. Not only was Epicurus to make use of these new insights, but the Neoplatonists were also to take over the Aristotelian scheme — despite their unconditional allegiance to Plato — in order to sustain the absolute desirability of higher reality by claiming that it yields an absolutely desirable kind of pleasure.

---

[99] See, e.g., Aristippus' thesis that pleasure must be mitigated in order to keep self-control, Diog. Laërt. II 75: τὸ κρατεῖν καὶ μὴ ἡττᾶσθαι ἡδονῶν ἄριστον, οὐ τὸ μὴ χρῆσθαι.

EXCURSUS: EPICUREANS AND STOICS

Although the Neoplatonic doctrine of pleasure is basically a combination of Platonic and Aristotelian elements, one must not neglect the importance of the Stoics, and, to a lesser extent, of Epicurus. These thinkers have kept alive the debate on pleasure for centuries, and their theories provided the Neoplatonists with terminology and doctrinal frameworks (such as the bipartition of lower pleasure and higher joy) that could easily be put at the service of the elaboration of the Neoplatonists' proper views.

We do not intend to offer an exhaustive survey of the Epicurean and Stoic doctrines of pleasure. This 'excursus' should rather provide the main arguments and the basic ideas that have played a role in the later discussions.

In what we will present later on as the 'standard Neoplatonic doctrine' (established by Plotinus and Proclus) the main influence of the Stoics lay in the idea that the good life does not produce pleasure (ἡδονή), but rather 'joy' (χαρά). Epicurus, on the other hand, was the opponent against whom Plotinus and Proclus directed their anti-hedonistic arguments. Damascius contradicted this standard view by rejecting the difference in kind between intellectual joy and physical pleasure, thus taking the side of Epicurus rather than of the Stoics.

I. EPICURUS

Epicurus' hedonistic starting point is that our natural impulse to pursue pleasure and avoid pain makes it sufficiently clear that every pleasure as such is good, and every pain as such is bad: pleasure and pain are the irrational, or pre-rational[1], criteria that direct our sensations, indicating immediately what is in accordance with or contrary to our nature (Cic., *De fin.* I 30). Of course, we will have to choose

---

[1] Epic., *Ep. ad Menoec.* 129; Diog. Laërt. X 137. Some Epicureans seem to have given a more rationalistic account, reducing the immediate judgment that is inherent in sensation to an innate preconception in our mind (*notio*, πρόληψις, meaning a self-evident notion: cf. Diog. Laërt. X 33): *De fin.* I 31.

between different pleasures, and sometimes we will prefer a specific pain to a particular pleasure, if this promises to yield a greater or longer-lasting pleasure afterwards (Epic., *Ep. ad Menoec.* 129). But this does not contradict the thesis that every pleasure *qua* pleasure is good and every pain *qua* pain bad. The choice for a particular pain in certain circumstances can only be instrumental, i.e., subordinate to our overall aim of striving for pleasure as the good. Accordingly, Epicurus states that 'pleasure is the beginning and the end of the blessed life'[2].

Although this 'pleasure' can be either physical or psychic, Epicurus explicitly prefers the pleasure of the body, the paradigm being the pleasure of the stomach[3]. Epicurus has a good reason for this: natural needs of the body are clearly limited. The stomach as such is never insatiable: 'What is insatiable is not the stomach, as people say, but the false opinion concerning its unlimited filling' (Epic., *SV* 59). The needs of the body have a much greater chance of being met than do the soul's longings, and so physical pleasures take pride of place (cf. Diog. Laërt. X 137), although some mental pleasures and pains may be much greater than those of the body (Cic., *De fin.* I 55). However, the reduction of all pleasure to the model of the satisfaction of a physical need entails a typical conflation of 'needs' and 'desires', which has already been criticised by Cicero[4].

These claims are complemented by two further statements. First, there is no intermediary between pleasure and pain, since every sensation produces either the one or the other. This entails the rejection of what Plato calls the 'neutral state'. And, second, our sense-experience (which results in either pleasure or pain) is always true, although we can, of course, form false opinions on the basis of our impressions. Hence, Epicurus rejects Plato's acceptance of 'false pleasures'.

One of the main issues of Epicurus' doctrine is the distinction between pleasure in movement (kinetic pleasure), which consists in the ongoing removal of pain, and pleasure at rest (katastematic pleasure), which is defined as the state of contentment or satisfaction that is attained once a pain is remedied (Cic., *De fin.* II 9; Diog. Laërt. X 136). This reiterates a distinction that was already present in Aristotle's

---

[2] *Ep. ad Menoec.* 128-129: καὶ διὰ τοῦτο τὴν ἡδονὴν ἀρχὴν καὶ τέλος λέγομεν εἶναι τοῦ μακαρίως ζῆν.

[3] Usener 409, 70; Long-Sedley 21M.

[4] Cic., *De fin.* II 27. Cf. Mitsis 1988, 36-39.

theory, but the Epicurean view is slightly less complicated than that presented by Aristotle.

Aristotle's notion of pleasure in movement was a corollary to the general theory that, if pleasure is a supervenient element in the perfect performance of an activity, then it is hard to understand how pleasure can occur in the replenishment of a lack, where by definition the activity is tending towards its natural condition and is thus not perfectly performed. As we have seen, Aristotle offers a solution to this problem: the pleasure we take in the replenishment of a lack (i.e., the pleasure in movement) is yielded by the perfect functioning, not of the organ that undergoes the lack, but of a different organ, that which provides the fulfilment (e.g., the nutritive or vegetative function of the soul that gives the body the impulse to quench its thirst). Thus, Aristotle does away with the problem, though at the cost of introducing a complication to the theory: so-called 'incidental pleasure' (cf. supra).

Epicurus' account provides a simpler model, without, however, solving all the difficulties. In the first place, it is not entirely clear how Epicurus conceives the exact relation between the kinetic and the katastematic pleasure[5]. Once a need is remedied, Epicurus says, the pleasure of the flesh cannot be intensified (ἐπαύξεται) but only varied (ποικίλλεται)[6]. According to Cicero's Epicurean interlocutor in the *De finibus*, this variation of pleasure in the state of contentment is kinetic pleasure. Kinetic pleasure, he says, consists either in the replenishment of a lack or in the variation of a katastematic pleasure (Cic., *De fin.* II 10; cf. *ibid.* II 75). Cicero's authority in these matters is not unquestioned, but in this passage he seems to take the correct view of the matter. The idea can be explained in the following way[7]: if, for instance, one is thirsty, then quenching the thirst will give a pleasure in movement. Kinetic pleasure thus consists in the replenishment itself[8].

---

[5] Cf. the puzzle of Cicero, expressed at *De fin.* II 9-10.

[6] Epic., *RS* 18; Cic., *De fin.* I 38. Mitsis 1988, 47, argues that 'the various kinetic states that occur in satisfying genuine needs do not affect our overall satisfaction; they are mere variants [...]', thus suggesting that the variation concerns the way in which we attain the satisfaction, e.g., the choice for brown or white bread to satisfy our hunger (Mitsis' example). However, the text of *RS* 18 clearly indicates that the variation concerns the attained state of satisfaction itself: ...ἐπειδὰν ἅπαξ τὸ κατ'ἔνδειαν ἀλγοῦν ἐξαιρεθῇ.

[7] Cf. Long-Sedley 1987 I, 122.

[8] Epicurus thus holds that the replenishment automatically yields pleasure, just as Plato does; cf. Mitsis 1988, 47.

Once the thirst has disappeared, the absence of it causes a very specific pleasure: the state of satisfaction or contentment, which is the katastematic pleasure. Kinetic pleasure taken in this sense is the movement towards an end. This has been the view of pleasure in replenishment ever since Plato, and it probably predates even him. Epicurus is in no way innovative in this respect. Moreover, he takes over the traditional view that the end consists in the attainment of the natural condition, where all needs have been met. He agrees with Aristotle that this natural condition is truly attainable — indeed, it is the most desirable of all states. The point added by Cicero's Epicurean interlocutor is that kinetic pleasure can also serve to vary the state of contentment (i.e., to feel pleasures other than the state of contentment) without apparently giving up the state of contentment itself. In other words, the kinetic pleasures in this case do not stem from a lack. For example, it remains possible to go on and drink after having quenched the thirst: one can take pleasure in sipping at a glass of wine without feeling any need to drink. If, then, as Cicero holds, this pleasure is kinetic, then one should admit — Long and Sedley, whose line of interpretation we are following here, do not do so explicitly — that kinetic pleasure is not confined to the strict movement towards the satisfaction of a need. Apparently, the state of contentment does not necessarily prevent one from continuing to perform the activity that led to the satisfaction: one can drink (and enjoy drinking) without being thirsty at all. This has important consequences for the nature of kinetic pleasure in this case. After having replenished the lack, it is only the activity (drinking) that remains unaltered, whereas its conditions have changed: we are no longer enjoying the replenishment of a lack but rather the continuation of the act that caused the replenishment, which goes beyond the actual replenishment. Thus, the acceptance of Cicero's authority entails the acceptance of a larger meaning of the term 'kinetic pleasure': in those cases where this pleasure is only the variation of katastematic pleasure, it cannot be attendant on the replenishment of a lack, as was kinetic pleasure in the strict sense. This means, then, that happiness (or life that has attained the highest good, viz. katastematic pleasure) also contains certain kinetic pleasures[9].

---

[9] Cf. Diog. Laërt. X 121: τὴν εὐδαιμονίαν διχῇ νοεῖσθαι, τήν τε ἀκροτάτην, οἵα ἐστὶ περὶ τὸν θεόν, ἐπίτασιν οὐκ ἔχουσαν, καὶ τὴν ⟨κατὰ τὴν⟩ προσθήκην καὶ ἀφαίρεσιν ἡδονῶν. This formulation suggests that within the attained condition of katastematic pleasure (i.e., the εὐδαιμονία) an addition and subtraction of pleasures remains possible. The latter must be *kinetic* pleasure, then, since katastematic pleasure does

They do not lead to a greater amount of happiness, but they might help to vary it, as well as to avoid pain: we might eat before we are hungry. Thus, it is not so much that we do not replenish a lack, as that we simply prevent it, and thus perpetuate the contentment.

Concerning katastematic pleasure, the question has been raised why this state, which was always described in exclusively negative terms[10], as the absence of trouble on the physical (ἀπονία) as well as on the psychic level (ἀταραξία), should be the highest good. Epicurus explicitly says that katastematic pleasure does not allow of degrees: rather, the state of contentment is either present or absent, and it will not be increased or diminished either by its duration or by any other factor. Why, then, is this state preferable to kinetic pleasure, which clearly allows of intensification and which, accordingly, is more likely to give us a greater pleasure? Apparently Epicurus held the view that the satisfaction will not be greater just because the pleasure leading towards it has been more intense. He must have agreed with Plato that a more intense pleasure presupposes a more intense pain that needed to be remedied: those who want an intense pleasure will have to endure an intense pain. Kinetic pleasure (at least in the strict sense) can only be valued as the path leading towards satisfaction, and its intensity reveals a greater contamination by pain, which could hardly be preferable.

This brings us to another candidate for the good life. Would not kinetic pleasure in the broader sense (the variation of katastematic pleasure) be preferable to the mere absence of pain? Again, Epicurus' answer is negative. In this case there is no lack to be remedied. We

---

not allow of degrees.

[10] We do not agree with Gosling-Taylor 1982, 365-396, who claim that the notion of katastematic pleasure cannot be purely negative. According to them, *aponia* is not so much the absence of pain as the 'condition of having sensory pleasures but with no accompanying pain, and *ataraxia* is a state of confidence that one may acquire such sensory pleasures with complete absence of pain. This confidence is itself a positive state ... for *ataraxia* more than the absence of false beliefs is needed: they have to be replaced by true ones' (Gosling-Taylor 1982, 371 [19.1.2]). Thus, according to Gosling and Taylor, katastematic pleasure consists in positive sensations, called χαρά by Diog. Laërt. X 22. However, there is no reason to believe that this would be the case. All the sources are unanimous in claiming that katastematic pleasure is nothing but the absence of pain. Diogenes Laërtius' use of the term 'χαρά' does not add anything more than does the qualification of this state as a 'pleasure'. This means, of course, that this state is choiceworthy; it does not imply, however, that it is more than the contentment that consists in the absence of pain.

have attained the natural condition (of a certain organ), and the pain is dissolved. This pleasure, Epicurus claims, is limited in magnitude by the attained satisfaction (Epic., *RS* 3; Cic., *De fin.* II 9). So this kind of kinetic pleasure can never be intense. Moreover, its existence is completely dependent on the presence of the state of contentment. Thus, katastematic pleasure is absolutely primordial: katastematic pleasure modifies the nature of kinetic pleasure from being a movement towards replenishment into the quiet variation of a state of satisfaction. The core of happiness, then, must be katastematic pleasure. In other words, the happy life is a state with no unfulfilled desires, with quiet motions of body and soul, and limited pleasures attendant upon them[11].

Thus, Epicurus displays much more sympathy to moderation, and even frugality, than his opponents want us to believe[12]. The imposition of a limit, or a measure, is accomplished by the operation of prudence, which allows us to deliberate and to weigh the different pleasures and pains:

> What produces the pleasant life is not continuous drinking and parties or pederasty or womanizing or the enjoyment of fish and the other dishes of an expensive table, but *sober reasoning* which tracks down the causes of every choice and avoidance, and which banishes the opinions that beset souls with the greatest confusion. *Of all this the beginning and the greatest good is prudence.* (*Ep. ad Menoec.* 132, trans. Long-Sedley, our italics; cf. *ibid.* 130)

That is, (kinetic) pleasure is not limited *in se*. Any measure comes from the outside and is imposed by sound reasoning and prudence. Desires that are not measured in this way are said to issue from empty, or vain, opinions (κεναὶ δόξαι, *RS* 30). Thus, excessive pleasures are (kinetic) pleasures that will never attain fulfilment, because they stem from a wrong (i.e., unlimited) desire of our soul.

The basic issue, then, is to find the proper limit to pleasure. This preoccupation with limitedness is also evident in Epicurus' elaborate analysis of desire. He divides desires into three groups, in order to decide which of them are likely to lead to satisfaction and, accordingly, are preferable in view of the good life. The desires belonging to the

---

[11]   This elicits Cicero's irony: *Quam parvo est contentus !* (*Tusc.* V 32, 89).

[12]   The criticism is as old as Epicurus' doctrines: the author himself complains that his ideas are misrepresented, as if he would advocate licentiousness: see Epic., *Ep. ad Menoec.* 131.

first group are natural and necessary (such as drinking when thirsty); the second are natural but non-necessary (such as somptuous dinners); and the third are neither natural nor necessary (such as the awarding of crowns and the erection of statues, i.e., public honours; *RS* 29. The examples are taken from a scholion on this text).

The limitation of desires is naturally followed by a limitation of pleasure. It seems that precisely this requirement to pursue limited pleasures explains Epicurus' preference for katastematic pleasure. This state is limited in itself, as it involves no further lack or need, or, indeed, any excess. Therefore, it is most likely to secure the happy mean between lack and excess. This katastematic pleasure is described in purely negative terms. In doing so, Epicurus avoids any unequivocal definition of the contents of happiness (or pleasure), which, as we saw earlier, would be problematic in any case: it would suggest that we know exactly what to do in order to attain happiness, which obviously is not the case.

The fact that one cannot have more or less katastematic pleasure but can only vary it (by means of kinetic pleasure) means that the pleasure in the state of contentment following upon a sober meal is identical with the pleasure in the contentment after a somptuous dinner. The difference resides exclusively in the means by which the contentment is reached. Consequently, there is no reason to prefer the latter means, which, moreover, contains a greater risk of being frustrated, as it is the result of a natural, but not necessary, desire.

As indicated already, this account clearly implies the rejection of the possibility of a neutral state between pleasure and pain (Cic., *De fin.* I 38). Does this mean, then, that Epicurus assumes that we are always consciously experiencing either pleasure or pain? This is not necessarily the consequence of the analysis. The view that any conscious state will be either pleasurable or painful, i.e., that there is no intermediary state, does not preclude the possibility of a state in which we experience neither pleasure nor pain, i.e., a state without introspection. This might even be the state in which we find ourselves most of the time regarding most of the parts of our body. Epicurus could easily accept this statement without jeopardizing the logic of his system. For it is well possible to affirm that our sensation always consists in either pleasure or pain, and at the same time to acknowledge that we are not always consciously experiencing every affection. In other words, what Epicurus has in mind seems to be that *if we experience anything*, then it is either pleasurable or painful. This is

confirmed by a remark of Cicero: 'a man who is conscious of his
condition at all must necessarily feel either pleasure or pain'[13]. Indeed
it is possible, for example, that our finger hurts and that a few
moments later we notice that our pain has gone away. At that
moment, the (experienced) absence of pain can be — and, according
to Epicurus, it must be — identified with pleasure. But during the time
between our awareness of the pain and our noticing the absence of it
we have had no experience at all regarding our finger. There has been
a lapse of time without any awareness and, in this sense, without any
pleasure or pain. Apparently, this absence of perception can occur
always and everywhere, but its extension is always limited: we never
attain a state without any awareness (except, of course, in death). We
are always conscious in a certain respect, which means that we are
always experiencing a certain pleasure or pain. The absence of
awareness occurs intermittently in the different organs, but never in
the organism as a whole.

This contains a reminder of Plato's assertion that not every
affection is intense enough to be actually sensed. So Epicurus' disagreement with Plato would not concern this point: he could agree
with Plato that sometimes we experience neither pleasure nor pain.
The point at stake is Plato's denial that any sensed affection has to be
either pleasure or pain. The 'neutral state' that Epicurus rejects, then,
is not the absence of awareness, but the possibility of experiencing
anything that is not pleasure or pain. Thus, adapting the terms of the
Platonic definition to the Epicurean, one must say that according to
the latter the perceived absence of pain always is the perfect realization
of the restoration of the natural condition, whereas according to the
former the natural condition *in se* is inaccessible (cf. supra). Logically,
then, the thesis of the real possibility of attaining the natural condition
must be complemented by the thesis that this condition is the most
pleasurable of all[14].

Finally, it was Epicurus' explicit intention to offer a therapy for the
soul. He saw himself — and the Epicurean tradition reinforced this
image — as a doctor providing the medicine that allows one to attain
happiness. Later Epicureans organised their master's teaching in the

---

[13] Cic., *De fin.* I 38: *quisquis enim sentit quemadmodum sit affectus, eum necesse est aut in voluptate esse aut in dolore* (trans. Rackham).

[14] The same issue dominates Aristotle's reaction against the Platonic theory of pleasure; cf. supra.

famous 'fourfold medicine' (τετραφάρμακος)[15]. Philosophy helps us to attain happiness in that it teaches us (1) not to fear the gods, (2) not to fear death, (3) how to deal with pain, and (4) that it is possible to attain happiness. First, fear of the gods is absurd, since they do not intervene in this world. They do not want their eternal blessedness and joy to be disturbed by the imperfections and sorrows of our world (*RS* 1). Second, fear of death is equally senseless, since death has no relation whatsoever with life: it exists when we cease to exist. Moreover, since good and evil are situated in perception[16], a condition without perception cannot be either good or bad (*Ep. ad Menoec*. 125). Death is indifferent, and so it is counterproductive to strive for immortality, particularly since a prolonged life will not yield more intense pleasures (*RS* 19-20; cf. *Ep. ad Menoec*. 124-127). Third, pain can be overcome through the recognition that intense pain will not last for a long time and that long-lasting pain will never be intense (*RS* 4). Moreover, pain can be regarded as a means of attaining pleasure. The fourth medicine, the knowledge that happiness is within our reach, comes down to Epicurus' advice to limit our desires (and, accordingly, our pleasures). This, no doubt, is the core of Epicurus' teaching: if we successfully control our desires, then we shall not fail to attain happiness.

II. The Stoics

The moral theory of the Stoics rests on a very elaborate analysis of the way in which a moral action is brought about[17]. The key terms of their doctrine are 'impulse' and 'assent'. An impulse consists in a specific reaction to a mental impression or presentation (φαντασία) that is brought about by sense-perception (Stob., *Ecl*. 2.86 [= *SVF* 3.169]). In rational beings (i.e., adult persons), this presentation is, as it were, translated into a proposition (a specific kind of the so-called 'sayables', λεκτά), presenting an object or an action either as good (i.e., to be taken) or as bad (i.e., to be avoided). Reason, then, assesses this

---

[15] Long-Sedley 25J; Salem 1989, 18 n.4 indicates that this τετραφάρμακος parallels Epicurus' teachings in *RS* 1-4, and underlies the structure of the *Ep. ad Menoec*.

[16] *Ep. ad Menoec*. 124: πᾶν ἀγαθὸν καὶ κακὸν ἐν αἰσθήσει. Cf. Erler 1994, 155.

[17] For a concise survey of the Stoic doctrine of the mental process leading to action, see Price 1995, 145-152.

proposition. To explain how this rational evaluation takes place, and thus how the reaction to the presentation is brought under our responsibility (*SVF* 2.91), the Stoics introduce the notion of 'assent' (συγκατάθεσις). This term indicates the practical judgment of reason that occurs when a mental impression presents itself. Reason can either agree or disagree, and on this judgment of reason depends the eventual performance of an action. A given assent results in an impulse (ὁρμή), which is defined as a 'motion of thought toward something or away from something'[18]. The first and most important impulse of living beings is the striving for self-preservation, which is directed towards that which is most proper, and thus most appropriate (οἰκεῖον), to them[19]. If there are no external obstructions, then the action follows automatically and immediately upon the impulse (Sen., *Ep.* 113.18 [=*SVF* 3.169]). Thus, for example, the propositions corresponding to the impressions 'I am cold' and 'here is my coat' will result in the proposition 'I should wear my coat'. If reason agrees with this proposition, then the result will automatically be that I reach out my hand and take the coat. If, on the other hand, assent is not given, then I will not perform the action.

This sophisticated scheme allows the Stoics to explain how it is possible that sometimes we go counter to what is appropriate in a given situation: we may be misled by our senses, which brings about a wrong proposition. This proposition, however, does not yet have moral value. It is the result of a merely factual process, and thus it is not under our control. It remains morally indifferent as long as it is not judged by reason. In other words: Stoic ethics starts with reason's assent to a presentation. Hence, of course, animals and children, who are deprived of reason, are a-moral[20].

Although at first sight this might appear to be a survey of the chronological succession of the various steps that lead to an action, one must bear in mind that the scheme does not involve temporal succession. It only offers logically, or theoretically, different aspects of a procedure that happens all at once. This implies that in practice the distinction between the various aspects will not be very clear (see, e.g.,

---

[18] *SVF* 3.92.4-5; Price 1995, 146.

[19] *SVF* 3.178-189; Long-Sedley 57D. This is a reaction against the Epicureans, who fostered the idea that the pursuit of pleasure and the avoidance of pain are the original impulses of all living beings.

[20] Galen, *Plac.* 5.1.10. Cf. Price 1995, 150; Inwood 1985, 72.

Stob., *Ecl.* 2.88, and Galen, *Plac.* 4.3.7). On the theoretical level, however, the distinction is very important, in that it indicates that the moral value of an action is not determined by the impression that awakens it but rather by reason's approval or disapproval of a certain impression.

The assent always has one of three moral qualifications: it can be in accordance with nature, contrary to nature, or indifferent — 'nature' being identical with 'right reason' or 'happiness'[21]. (1) When indifferent, the action will evidently not affect our happiness. States or actions of this kind include health, beauty, wealth, walking, speaking, asking questions, etc. (Diog. Laërt. VII 101-105; Stob., *Ecl.* 2.79-80; 2.96 [= *SVF* 3.501]) (2) If the assent is in accordance with nature, then we are performing the actions of a wise person. Our lives are ruled by reason, and nothing will harm or jeopardise our happiness. (3) If, on the other hand, the assent is contrary to nature, then we are bound to meet the most dangerous enemies of Stoic happiness: the *affections* or *passions* (πάθη)[22]. They are impulses whose existence is the result of an assent that mistakenly considers things 'good' whereas in fact they are bad or indifferent, or vice versa. Although there are many affections, they can all be reduced to four main kinds: appetite (ἐπιθυμία), fear (φόβος), pleasure (ἡδονή), and pain (λύπη). These four are not equal: appetite and fear are said to be primordial (προηγοῦνται), whereas pleasure and pain are secondary, or attendant on the others (ἐπιγίγνονται). Thus, all the affections are assembled under two headings: appetite and fear. The former is a perversion of desire (ὄρεξις), i.e., the natural impulse to acquire the appropriate good, and the latter is a perversion of ἔκκλισις, the natural impulse to avoid the bad (Stob., *Ecl.* 2.88-90 [= Long-Sedley 65A, *SVF* 3.378, 389]). Pleasure and pain, then, are subsequent to these two perverted impulses: pleasure occurs when we attain the object of our appetite or escape what we wanted to avoid, and pain comes about when we either fail to acquire the object of our appetite or encounter what we fear (Stob., *Ecl.* 2.88-89). They consist in specific irrational physiological reactions of the soul (contraction, συστολή, in the case of pain, and expansion, διάχυσις or ἔπαρσις, in the case of pleasure; Galen, *Plac.* 4.2.5; *SVF* 3.391), again based on a

---

[21]   The most important Stoic maxim is that happiness consists in life according to nature, and nature is reason. (see Long-Sedley 63A-M). This 'accordance with nature' is the standard for moral evaluation: cf. Stob., *Ecl.* 2.83 (=*SVF* 3.124).

[22]   For an elaborate survey of the Stoics' theory of the passions, or affections, see Inwood 1985, 127-181; Rist 1969, 37-53.

judgment, namely, that it is appropriate to have this contraction or expansion in the present situation (Stob., *Ecl.* 2.90). This judgment is called a 'fresh opinion' (πρόσφατος δόξα), i.e., an opinion that arises at the moment at which the judged situation or object is actually present. In other words, it is a sudden, implicit and immediate evaluation that immediately gives rise to pleasure or pain.

Affections are called both 'irrational' (Stob., *Ecl.* 2.89) and 'excessive impulses' (*SVF* 1.205, 3.92.5, 92.11 [= Long-Sedley 65A1]). Anthony Price gives an explanation that combines the two accounts: 'The impulse is "carried away and disobedient to reason" (*SVF* 3.92.6) in that it disregards right reason from the first, and soon escapes recall by any reason'[23]. This means (at least, in orthodox Stoicism) that an affection is not a kind of force that runs counter to reason; it is rather reason itself going astray by its own inappropriate decision. Whereas right reason normally (i.e., when the judgment is correct) sets limits and imposes a right proportion on the impulse, the affections consist in improper impulses that disregard the right proportion, and thus eventually escape all rational control.

In sum, then, affections are disturbances of our natural impulses, caused by a wrong judgment of our reason. Since pleasure belongs to these affections, which obstruct the attainment of well-being[24] and do harm to our natural condition (i.e., life according to the λόγος)[25], one should not even try to mitigate pleasure: it should be totally eradicated (*SVF* 3.443-455).

Returning to the assents (impulses, and actions) that are in accordance with right reason, we find three rational pendants of the four principal affections: pleasure stands in opposition to 'joy' (χαρά), fear to 'carefulness' (εὐλάβεια), and appetite to 'will' (βούλησις)[26]. The latter, called the 'good affections' (εὐπάθειαι), are the additional effects (ἐπιγεννήματα) of the correct judgment of a good thing being good, guided by virtue and reason[27].

---

[23] Price 1995, 149. See also Long-Sedley 1987, I 420, referred to below (n.32).

[24] *SVF* 3.95 and 431-442; cf. Steinmetz 1994, 633 and 640; Gosling-Taylor 1982, 415-427.

[25] *SVF* 3.377-420 (in particular 405); cf. Gosling-Taylor 1982, 417.

[26] It should not surprise one that there is no rational counterpart to pain, since the wise person never fails to acquire the object of his rational will nor runs into the things that he cautiously avoids.

[27] Diog. Laërt. VII 94; they are called εὔλογοι in Diog. Laërt. VII 116 (=*SVF* 3.431).

Many authors have emphasised that εὐπάθεια primarily consists in
ἀπάθεια. Indeed, the wise person's life is the result of a successful
eradication of all affections. But this does not mean that there is a
complete identity between εὐπάθεια and ἀπάθεια. The 'good affections' contain a desirable surplus that overreaches the mere 'absence of
affections'. Joy is explicitly presented not only as 'good' (*SVF* 3.85; 95;
106; 111), but also as an expansion of the soul (Cic., *Tusc.* IV 12-14;
Sen., *Ep.* 59.2). This indicates that it is not simply the absence of
pleasure, but the presence of a positive excitement, a physiological
reaction similar to that of pleasure, with the difference that in this case
the expansion is not vain, i.e., based on a wrong judgment.

It is important to note that Stoic joy is explicitly said to be 'in
movement' (ἐν κινήσει: Stob., *Ecl.* 2.73 [=*SVF* 3.111]). Thus, clearly,
the notion of a pleasure 'at rest' does not exist in Stoic philosophy, not
even with regard to rational joy[28].

Of course, this analysis does not mean that the wise person will
never feel pleasure or pain, nor that his pleasures will always be
transformed into χαραί. Hitherto, the presentation of pleasure might
suggest that pleasure is a κακόν *tout court* and that, accordingly, it
should be absent from the good life. In that case, indeed, the wise
person would never feel pleasure. However, one should take into
account the sources where pleasure is said to be indifferent (ἀδιάφορον:
cf., e.g., *SVF* 3.117 and 155). This does not contradict the statement
that it is something bad. The qualification depends on the person's
being or not being overcome by pleasure. It appears to be possible,
then, to feel pleasure without loosing the proper rational control over
one's deeds, i.e., without allowing this pleasure to become an affection.
Indeed, some pleasures are unavoidable, even in the life of the sage:
he, too, must at the very least eat, drink, and have sexual intercourse.
The difference with pleasure as a κακόν lies in the fact that the sage is
not at all affected by these pleasures: to him they are indifferent
(whereas the ordinary man is overpowered by their excessive violence);
the sage does not pursue them. Pleasures are said to be neither
preferable nor dispreferable[29], but when they occur they do not at all
disturb him. Their occurrence is the result of the wise man's correct

---

[28]   This does not prevent the Neoplatonists from combining the Stoic notion of
'joy' with Aristotle's (and Epicurus') idea of a pleasure at rest; cf. infra.
[29]   The preferable and dispreferable are subdivisions of the indifferent: see *SVF*
3.136.

judgment about an indifferent as indifferent. On the other hand, this indifferent pleasure must not be identified with the χαρά: the latter is ἀγαθόν, as we saw, and not indifferent. One should establish, then, not a twofold scheme (ἡδονή — χαρά), but a threefold one: pleasure as a κακόν, pleasure as ἀδιάφορον, and χαρά[30].

Unlike the theories of Plato, Aristotle, and Epicurus, which do not draw any distinction between ἡδονή and χαρά, the Stoics' theory of pleasure hinges on the difference between the two. However, there is no complete agreement within the school concerning the question of the exact difference between them. Are they different in kind or only in quantity (πάθος being an excess, whereas εὐπάθεια is controlled and limited by reason)? Apparently, these two answers have been defended by various Stoic philosophers. Until now, we have generally presented the Stoics as forming a monolithic block, as if there were no disagreements or discussions in the school. What we have expounded are mainly the ideas of Chrysippus, the 'second founder of the Stoa'. There is some justification for this: without neglecting the differences of opinion on minor points[31], one may state that the doctrine of the affections and their rational counterparts is consistently held throughout the development of Stoic philosophy. However, concerning the relation between χαρά and ἡδονή there seems to be a discrepancy that we should not fail to mention here. Apparently, Chrysippus holds that joy and pleasure stem from the same impulse, which, in the case of pleasure, becomes 'excessive', thus going beyond rational proportion[32]. In this case, then, there is no difference in kind between

---

[30] Cf. Long-Sedley 1987, I 421, who qualify the indifferent pleasures as the 'entirely unvoluntary or unavoidable by-products of natural human behaviour'. The problem with this account is that there is no reason to call this judgment about an indifferent as indifferent a 'pleasure' (although the quoted sources do make this inference). Perhaps this 'pleasant sensation' is to be understood as a mere presentation of a present good without any assent to the presentation. In this case, it does not lead to a judgment, and so there is neither a πάθος nor a εὐπάθεια. It simply remains a 'shock' (πληγή, or *ictus*). I owe this idea to R. Sorabji (personal communication). In this case, then, the indifferent pleasure could perhaps be considered a kind of 'preliminary affection' (προπάθεια), which is an 'unchosen bodily reaction to which even the sage remains liable' (as defined by Price 1995, 162).

[31] See, e.g., the difference of opinion between Chrysippus and Zeno concerning the relation between judgment and affection: Zeno loosely speaks of affections as attendant upon a judgment; Chrysippus holds that they are identical. Cf. Inwood 1985, 130-131.

[32] Galen, *Plac.* 4.2.10-18 (Long-Sedley 65J; *SVF* 3.462). The example given by Long-Sedley 1987, I 420, is illuminating: they compare right rational proportion to

pleasure and joy. The only difference is that pleasure exceeds the limits set by rational choice, as explained above. Posidonius, however, strongly disagrees. He rejects Chrysippus' unitary view of the soul, and returns to the Platonic, threefold division of the psyche. He thus draws an opposition between reason and the irrational parts of the soul[33]. This has important repercussions for the theory of pleasure. For one can now maintain that an impulse is brought along either by reason or by the irrational part of the soul. In the former case, the impulse leads to εὐπάθεια (or joy in particular), whereas in the latter it results in affection (viz., pleasure). This entails a difference in kind between pleasure and joy, corresponding to the difference between the faculties from which they originate.

The importance of this modification of Stoic psychology should not be underestimated. Although the overall rejection of affections as such is very much welcomed by the Neoplatonists, the explicit grounding of the difference between ἡδονή and χαρά on the Platonic account of the soul allows the Stoic doctrine to exercise a tremendous influence on the Neoplatonists' theory of pleasure.

---

the setting of a speed limit. What is below the limit is in accordance with reason; what goes beyond it is excessive and passionate.

[33] Galen takes over this view, using Posidonius to criticise Chrysippus; cf. Long-Sedley 1987, 422-423.

CHAPTER TWO

THE STANDARD NEOPLATONIC THEORY:
PLOTINUS AND PROCLUS

I. Plotinus

1. *Plotinus' Definition of Pleasure*

Plotinus' theory of pleasure cannot be considered apart from his overall analysis of the soul and its vital functions. The central assumption
of Plotinian psychology is that there is a certain bipartition in the soul.
The 'higher' part remains steadily in the intelligible world, whereas the
'lower soul' descends into sensible reality:

> Our soul does not altogether come down [i.e., into sensible reality],
> but there is always something of it in the intelligible ... Every soul has
> something of what is below, in the direction of the body, and of what is
> above, in the direction of Intellect.[1]

This does not mean, however, that Plotinus pluralises the soul. For, in
general, he rejects any division of it, pointing out that in its true nature
it is one and indivisible. This 'unity of the soul in its true nature' refers
to what is called 'the higher soul' throughout. The lower, i.e., embodied, soul relates to the higher as its 'image' (εἴδωλον or ἴνδαλμα) or
'trace' (ἴχνος)[2], mirroring the true nature of the (non-incarnate) soul.

In contradistinction to the higher soul, the lower can be divided in
parts, on the basis of the different functions it performs in the body[3].
Or rather, these divisions in the lower soul are not so much 'parts of
the soul' as characteristics of the ensouled *body*, i.e., their division does

---

[1] *Enn.* IV 8, 8.2-3 and 12-13, trans. Armstrong (which will be used throughout).
See also I 1, 3.23-24 and II 9, 2.4-18 (which, however, presents the λόγος as a 'μέσον'
between lower and higher soul; see Steel 1978, 35 and Blumenthal 1971, 105).

[2] ἴχνος: IV 4, 28.10-11; 16-17; 20-21; (particularly) 55-59 and 74-77; ἴνδαλμα: V
9, 6.19; εἴδωλον: I 1, 8.15-18. We agree with Blumenthal (1971, 15 and 65 n.46) that
the difference between 'lower soul' and 'trace of the soul' is a purely terminological
one.

[3] The terms 'ἴχνος', 'εἴδωλον', or 'ἴνδαλμα' can, then, be used to indicate either
the entire lower soul or its different functions.

not affect the essence of the soul (*Enn.* I 1, 4.1-13). For these functions, Plotinus does not use an unequivocal vocabulary. He employs both the Platonic and the Aristotelian division[4], although in practice he seems to prefer the Aristotelian account, making a distinction between the following psychic functions: φυτικόν (also called αὐξητικόν) — αἰσθητι-κόν — διανοητικόν (also λογιζόμενον or λόγος)[5], transcended by the higher soul, which is permanently present in the νοῦς[6].

Within this framework, Plotinus repeatedly discusses the question of whether 'affections' (πάθη, viz. pleasure, distress, desire, etc.) naturally belong to the body or to the soul. The question is raised at *Enn.* I 1, and returns as one of the 'Difficulties about the soul' treated at IV 4[7].

Plotinus' answer is that the soul must be completely 'ἀπαθής'. The seat of affections is the body, but not taken as such: a body in itself would never be able to experience any affection. It must be the body insofar as it is alive and ensouled, or 'the body that wants to be not only body' (IV 4, 20.5-6: ὃ σῶμα μέν ἐστιν, ἐθέλει δὲ μὴ μόνον σῶμα εἶναι). This body resembles 'hot air': it partakes in life (like air partakes in heat), which originates from elsewhere and by which it is essentially modified (IV 4, 18.4-9).

This body, Plotinus continues, belongs to 'us', but it does not determine our essence. Our soul uses it as an instrument (I 1, 3.3-4: Χρωμένη μὲν οὖν σώματι οἷα ὀργάνῳ). 'We' are first and foremost 'the highest part of ourselves' (i.e., the part of the soul that does not descend into the body), although the body does depend on this part.

---

[4] Blumenthal 1971, 21: 'How Plotinus conceived this division is not immediately clear, since we find both Platonic and Peripatetic doctrines, apparently left in more or less haphazard juxtaposition.'

[5] For a more detailed account, see Blumenthal 1971, 44, who also demonstrates (1971, 100-105) that there is no difference between διάνοια and λογιστικόν or λόγος: all these terms indicate discursive reason, which is 'part' of the incarnate soul.

[6] This 'higher soul', in turn, is to be distinguished from the διανοητικόν in the 'lower' one, although Plotinus does not always draw a clear distinction between them. What is at stake is the distinction between intuitive intellect (the immediate contemplation of the intelligible) and discursive reasoning, in which the soul always makes use of external sensible impulses (which are, however, interiorised). Hence, the possibility of errors (and thus also of evil) cannot be excluded at this level, whereas the higher soul always contemplates truth and the Good; cf. III 6, 2.22-32; see Steel 1978, 34-38; Blumenthal 1971, 103-104; Rist 1967[b], 416.

[7] See Also *Enn.* III 6 'On the impassibility of things without body' (Περὶ τῆς ἀπαθείας τῶν ἀσωμάτων), and IV 8 'On the descent of the soul into bodies' (Περὶ τῆς εἰς τὰ σώματα καθόδου τῆς ψυχῆς).

We here find the free adaptation of an Aristotelian idea, which is important for Plotinus' theory of pleasure: the highest attainable state for a being constitutes its 'natural condition'. It is the good proper to this being, and all its parts aspire to this good[8]. Thus, our 'we' is our natural condition, the aim towards which we are directed and through which we participate in the ultimate Good. Although we cannot say that 'we' are devoid of corporeality, our body plays only a subordinate role and does not at all affect our essence. 'We', then, is a technical term, indicating the human soul in its highest realization (the 'higher' part of the soul which is its plenitude). All other human attributes are not 'we', but 'ours': they all depend in their proper way on this upper part[9].

The affections can, then, be situated only in the ensouled body, the combination (τὸ συναμφότερον[10]) of lower soul and body. At *Enn.* I 8, Plotinus states that the soul can only be associated with the body when it descends into 'lower nature' (χείρων φύσις): only in this case can fear, desire, distress, and passions (θυμοί) come to be. They all reveal a certain condition of the combination (σύνθετον, or σύστασις) body-soul: fear that the combination will be resolved, distress when it is resolved, etc. (I 8, 15.14-18).

Although in this passage pleasure is not included under the affections, it completely fits the analysis of the σύνθετον. Plotinus' definition of pleasure makes this clear:

> Pain is consciousness of withdrawal of a body which is being deprived of the image of soul, and pleasure is the knowledge of a living being that the image of soul is again fitting itself back in the body. (IV 4, 19.2-4)

Two elements are essential in this definition: (1) the idea of a resolution and restoration of the harmony between soul and body, and (2) the statement that pleasure is a kind of 'knowledge'.

1. In the first place, pleasure and distress are seen as a movement in which the body is deprived of (or re-harmonised with) the 'image of soul'. Needless to say, the strictly Platonic scheme of lack and re-plenishment is taken over, and pleasure clearly is seen as a 'movement'

---

[8]   This idea is advanced explicitly at I 7, 1.
[9]   IV 4, 18.10-36; cf. I 1, 7.14-18.
[10]   Cf. Plato, *Alc.* 130 a 9.

or 'genesis'[11]. More difficult is the question of the nature of lack and replenishment in this case. As we have seen, the 'image of soul' is the lower soul (thus, from the beginning, pleasure is confined to the lower vital functions). How can the body be deprived of this (embodied) soul, as Plotinus maintains in his definition? Henry Blumenthal indicates the problem and provides an answer in the following way: 'The explanation is probably to be found in his view that all things receive as much of soul, or of the intelligible in general, as they are fit to receive (cf., e.g., VI 4, 15.3-6). If the body is injured or hurt it could be considered less fit to be a receptacle for soul'[12]. This explanation is too vague as it stands. Moreover, it gives the impression that the combination soul-body is a very loose relation, the character of which changes along with the disposition of the body: when the integrity of the body is threatened, the soul would seem to withdraw from this receptacle, which it finds less fit to undergo its vital functions. However, this is not likely to be the case. On the contrary, according to their nature the vital functions of the lower soul (the 'image of soul') do care for an injured body, as well as try to restore the original harmony. An indication that this indeed is the case can be found in Plotinus' description of the way in which bodily impulses are taken up by the soul: the primary impulses take place in the body and are taken over 'as by a mother' by the soul (in the first place by the φύσις, which here is used as synonymous with vegetative soul, τὸ φυτικόν); the vegetative soul tries to fulfil the needs of the body (IV 4, 20.25-36). When the condition of the body runs counter to the natural harmony between body and (the image of) soul, the affections of distress, passion (θυμός), fear, desire, and (when the situation is restored) pleasure come to be[13]. Thus, that the body is 'deprived of the image of soul' does not mean that the combination of body and soul is resolved. This would entail the impossibility of experiencing pleasure, distress, or whatsoever, since perception is one of the psychic functions[14]. It means rather that the combination is threatened and that the body is about to lose the image of soul. The harm done to the integrity of the body (which causes pain) is radically opposed to the natural function of the vegetative soul, whose task it is to nourish, to cure, and to save the

---

[11] Cf. Moreau 1970, 158.
[12] Blumenthal 1971, 60.
[13] Cf. I 8, 15.14-18, referred to above.
[14] Cf. IV 4, 28.22-58.

body. According to this analysis, pain is the awareness of the broken harmony between the actual condition of the body and the natural aim of the function of the soul; pleasure is the consciousness of the restoration of this harmony. The same holds, *mutatis mutandis*, for the other affections, such as passion, fear, and desire.

2. Pleasure and distress are presented here unequivocally as forms of 'knowledge' (γνῶσις). Bodily affection cannot reach the (embodied) soul except in a modified form: the soul consciously perceives the affection, without, however, being affected itself[15]. To be sure, in the soul there can be no question of 'affections'. Plotinus clearly indicates that perception (the sensitive soul) is to be distinguished from affections: the former consists in 'activities *concerning* the affections', which are more precisely termed 'judgments' (κρίσεις), i.e., evaluations of the affections by a faculty of a different nature. For it would be impossible for the soul to be affected in the same way as the body[16].

Thus, the entire soul, and *a fortiori* 'we' (in the technical sense of the word) are completely unaffected: the affections of the body cannot penetrate the soul except as a kind of 'knowledge' (or 'consciousness'):

> For us, the pain of this body and the pleasure of this kind result in an unaffected knowledge. (IV 4, 18.9-10)[17]

Plotinus corroborates this claim with the following argument: if indeed the soul were affected by the pain, then our entire body would suffer. That a wound in our finger, for example, hurts only in this specific place shows, Plotinus says, that only the body (and more precisely this particular member) is affected. If the opposite were the case, i.e., if the soul were to undergo the pain, then the entire body would hurt, since the soul is omnipresent in the body. Instead, the soul merely cognitively recognises the affection as 'pain', without undergoing pain itself[18].

All affections are transmitted in a gradual movement: first to sensitive knowledge, which is situated closest to the body, and then to 'that faculty in which perceptions cease', i.e., discursively-rational

---

[15] IV 4, 18.12-13: Πᾶσα δὲ ᾔσθετο τὸ ἐκεῖ πάθος οὐκ αὐτὴ παθοῦσα. See also III 6, 3.17-19: Καὶ τῆς ἡδονῆς δὲ τὸ τῆς διαχύσεως τοῦτο καὶ εἰς αἴσθησιν ἧκον περὶ τὸ σῶμα, τὸ δὲ περὶ τὴν ψυχὴν οὐκέτι πάθος.

[16] III 6, 1.1-7; cf. Blumenthal 1971, 70.

[17] Cf. III 6, 3.1-7; 16-19; 4.7-8.

[18] IV 4, 19.12-29; see Blumenthal 1971, 46-47; Gerson 1994, 151 n.54 [p.272].

soul[19]. In this way, Plotinus is able to introduce a distinction between two kinds of 'knowledge' (or judgment): the knowledge 'that this particular thing is pleasant' (i.e., sensitive knowledge) and the knowledge 'that this corresponds to the Good' (i.e., knowledge of discursive reason)[20]. They both play a role in the concrete perception of pleasure, though transcending pleasure as such[21].

This analysis betrays a clear contempt for the affections, which must be eradicated if one wants to attain the good life. One will have noticed that the radical view of the soul as ἀπαθής clearly rests upon the Stoic doctrine of the 'affections' (or 'passions'), as expounded earlier in this volume. In the experience of the affections the soul is confronted in a radical way with lower (corporeal) reality, which belongs to an entirely different order from that of the soul itself. Of course, the embodied soul could always be influenced by the body, since it stands at a very slight distance of the body. In the affections, however, the case is worse yet: the soul is confronted, not only with the lower realms as such, but with an entirely proper dynamism of the lower realms, which threatens to carry the soul away and to avert it from its inclination towards the Good. Thus, it is the 'moral' duty of the soul to keep its distance from the lower. We should, as Plotinus says, by means of virtue (which by its nature belongs to the higher soul) overpower the 'terrible and inevitable affections' (δεινὰ καὶ ἀναγκαῖα πάθη) in which we are involved (II 3, 9.7-19).

Plotinus thus reaffirms the Stoic ideal of the sage whose happiness is not disturbed by external fortunes or misfortunes (health or sickness, wealth or poverty, physical security or the danger of death, and even sense perception *tout court*)[22]. What this means, on his understanding of the matter, is that we should leave the level of the body behind us and strive after a full realization of our 'higher' soul:

---

[19] IV 4, 19.5-7: Ἐκεῖ μὲν οὖν τὸ πάθος, ἡ δὲ γνῶσις τῆς αἰσθητικῆς ψυχῆς ἐν τῇ γειτονίᾳ αἰσθομένης καὶ ἀπαγγειλάσης τῷ εἰς ὃ λήγουσιν αἱ αἰσθήσεις.

[20] I 4, 2.18-19: δεῖ γνῶναι οὐ μόνον ὅτι ἡδύ, ἀλλ᾽ ὅτι τοῦτο τὸ ἀγαθόν. The judgment 'that this corresponds to the Good' belongs to discursive reason, not to the intuitively contemplating intellect, although the criterion of 'goodness' clearly is transmitted by Intellect. The judgment in question, then, is a reasoning made by the (embodied) soul. Cf. V 3, 3.1-15, where this is stated explicitly. See also Blumenthal 1971, 105-106.

[21] On the basis of this argument Plotinus refutes the hedonists' claim that pleasure is the supreme Good: cf. infra, p.106-107.

[22] See I 4, 3-16.

> So we must 'fly from here' [*Theaet.* 176 a 8 – b 1] and 'separate'
> [*Phaedo* 67 c 6] ourselves from what has been added to us, and not be
> the composite thing, the ensouled body in which the nature of body
> (which has some trace of soul) has the greater power. (II 3, 9.20-23)

This does not mean that our bodily existence is altogether bad[23]. It
should be added, however, that our care for the body does reduce the
zest with which we strive after the higher[24]. The exhortation to adhere
to the 'higher' and more preferable likewise applies to pleasure (since it
is one of the affections)[25]. Many commentators emphasise that this
negative judgment only holds as regards bodily pleasure[26]. And this is
indeed correct; but, as we will see, there is no pleasure except bodily
pleasure. From the beginning, 'pleasure' has been identified without
qualifications as an affection. Given this definition, no space remains
for a higher pleasure in the strict sense of the term. If one can speak of
'affections' that surpass the level of the body — and Plotinus does use
the term in this sense, defining 'ὄρεξις τοῦ ἀγαθοῦ' as a 'πάθημα τῆς
ψυχῆς' (I 1, 5.27-28) — then this cannot be taken in a literal sense.

Although Plotinus does speak of a kind of pleasure that is 'higher'
than the corporeal one, he can only use the word 'pleasure' in a
metaphorical sense. Therefore, Plotinus prefers a different term to
denote the 'joy' of the higher realms. This is discussed in detail below.
But the general idea may be stated here: the 'pleasure' in the good life
cannot be (genuine) pleasure. Thus, affections (including pleasure)
clearly cannot play any role in the good life. But what, then, about
Plato's central claim in the *Philebus* that the good life must be a
combination of intellect and pleasure?

2. *Plotinus' Refutation of Hedonism*

At *Enn.* VI 7, ch. 24-30, Plotinus presents nine aporiae concerning the
effect of the Good on 'our' particular existence ('Ημᾶς δέ, τί ποιεῖ; –
24.1). One of the essential issues in this context is the relation between
the Good and pleasure. In general, the problem comes down to the
following: if all reality aims at the Good, should not pleasure play an

---

[23] This is affirmed at IV 8, 6-7.
[24] See, e.g., III 6, 5.1-10.
[25] Cf. also Plotinus' discussion of the extent of the purification (κάθαρσις) of the
soul at I 2, 5.
[26] Bréhier IV, 39; Blumenthal 1971, 46-47.

important role in a (partial) fulfilment of this desire? Or even, is not pleasure, or the anticipation of pleasure, the essential stimulus for such a desire? This question is treated in the final chapter (ch. 30) of the passage, which will be discussed at length in the next section. But the answer Plotinus provides there is prepared by a refutation in the previous chapters of the hedonists' claim. We will examine this issue before considering the details of the Plotinian view of the relation between pleasure and the Good.

In the first place, Plotinus discusses the 'desirability' (τὸ ἐφετόν)[27] of the Good[28], and complements this with a discussion of the role reserved to 'joy' (τὸ χαίρειν)[29]: is the desirable the object of desire because it gives us something or because it is enjoyed? And if it gives something, what does it give? If one enjoys it, why precisely this, rather than anything else?

In the passage containing the solution (VI 7, 26.1-24), the question is taken up in a slightly different way: how do we know that we have attained the Good when our desire is fulfilled ? A being endowed with sense perception will recognise the good when it comes to him (εἰ ἥκοι αὐτῷ τὸ ἀγαθόν). But what if he is mistaken ? (τί οὖν εἰ ἠπάτηται;) The answer is rather obvious: the cause of such a mistake is an apparent similarity with the true good. After all, Plotinus infers, the *true* Good remains the ultimate aim.

That every being has its proper relation to the good is evidenced by the very existence of desire and the 'travail' (ὠδίς, i.e., the distress caused by the — provisional — absence of the Good, a metaphor that will become very successful in later Neoplatonism). It is this desire and travail that make a being strive after the Good. But how do we know when we have attained the Good? Plotinus provides four criteria: when we become better, when we do not change our minds any longer (ὅταν ἀμετανόητον ᾖ), when we are fulfilled, and when we remain with the good and do not seek anything else. These Plotinian criteria complement the opinion of Plato: the Good is no longer confined to what is 'perfect', 'desirable', and 'sufficient'[30]. These elements are present in the criteria introduced by Plotinus (i.e., the last one corresponds to what is called 'sufficiency' by Plato; 'desirability' has been discussed

---

[27] Cf. Plato, *Phil.* 20 b – 21 e, and Aristotle, *NE* I 7, 1097 b 1-7; 16-21.
[28] Aporiae 1 and 2, presented at VI 7, 24.4-9 and solved at 25.16-32.
[29] Aporiae 3 and 4, stated at VI 7, 24.10-12, solved at 26.1-24.
[30] Cf. *Phil.* 20 b – 21 e.

earlier). But the series is extended: attainment of the Good must make
us 'better'; we must no longer have doubts as to whether we actually
attained the Good; and it must fulfil us. Here are three 'new' touch-
stones that primarily describe our condition when we have attained
the Good[31].

Just as in the *Philebus*, these criteria are used to test pleasure, and
just as in the *Philebus*, pleasure is found wanting: 'Therefore pleasure
is not sufficient: one is not satisfied with the same thing' (VI 7, 26.
14-15). It always seeks new paths, since it languishes when it lacks
variation. By nature pleasure does not tolerate rest. It is always in
movement. This precludes the occurrence of pleasure in the state of
rest that is reached in the attainment of the Good. A possible objection
against this idea is immediately rejected: is it not so that pleasure as
such is always stable, while its object is ever changing? In this case
there would be a certain 'permanent' pleasure that consists in the
subsequent pleasurable experiences of different objects. Plotinus cannot accept this: it is impossible to speak of 'permanent' pleasure when
it would be caused by different objects (VI 7, 26.15-16: οὐ γὰρ ὅτι
ἡδονὴ πάλιν, ταὐτόν· ἄλλο γὰρ ἀεὶ τὸ ἐφ'ᾧ ἥδεται). This short remark,
which takes up the idea that pleasure cannot be identical *qua* pleasure,
will be important in what follows: it is not possible to detach pleasure
from the pleasurable object.

Following these considerations, Plotinus answers the question: one
cannot reduce the Good to the affection of the being that has attained
it (τὸ πάθος τὸ ἐπὶ τῷ τυχόντι): this πάθος refers to something outside
itself. If one takes this affection to be the Good, one actually remains
empty (κενός); nobody would content himself with the presence of an
affection only, without in fact attaining the object itself by which the
affection is produced:

> This is the reason why one would not find acceptable the affection
> produced by something one has not got; for instance, one would not
> delight in the fact that a boy was present when he was not present; nor
> do I think that those who find the good in bodily satisfaction would
> feel pleasure as if they were eating when they were not eating or as if

---

[31]   Plotinus' view of the possibility of the identification with god differs from that
of Plato and Aristotle. Whereas they presented the ideal of 'deification *as far as
possible*' (see, e.g., Plato, *Theaet.* 176 b 1; Arist., *NE* X 7, 1177 b 34; cf. supra, p.71
n.89), Plotinus unreservedly speaks of a 'deification' (e.g., I 4, 16.12: ἐκείνῳ
ὁμοιοῦσθαι); cf. Beierwaltes 1979, 294-305.

they were enjoying sex when they were not with the one they wanted to be with, or in general when they were not making love. (VI 7, 26.19-24)

In fairly vague terms, Plotinus here adopts the notion of 'unreal' pleasure caused by an erroneous estimation of the pleasurable object, which figures in the *Philebus*. Nobody would prefer this unfounded pleasure. What we strive after is not the affection, but the real attainment of the object of our desire.

This assessment also has consequences for the pleasure that is not 'unfounded': this pleasure, too, cannot be considered as the Good, for it is inferior to that which is enjoyed. What matters is that we attain the object of our desire, not that this produces pleasure. Thus, one can understand Plotinus' claim that pleasure is not 'sufficient', a statement that refers back to the *Philebus* but changes the viewpoint. In the *Philebus* the insufficiency of pleasure was derived from the necessary presence of intellectual faculties: without consciousness it is impossible to feel pleasure. One could neither recall earlier pleasures, nor acknowledge present pleasure, nor anticipate a future one: 'this would not be a human life at all, but a jelly-fish existence, or the life of one of those sea-things that live in shells'. No one would find such a life acceptable[32].

Whereas Plato uses this argument to demonstrate the need for intellect in order to have pleasure (a fact Plotinus explicitly agrees upon[33]), Plotinus radicalises the argument by deriving it from the nature of pleasure itself. For pleasure depends for its existence upon a pleasurable object (in the broadest sense of the word[34]), which by itself jeopardises the autonomy of pleasure.

These remarks lead Plotinus to a firm refutation of hedonism. The discussion is opened in the following way:

> And we must not leave out the following remarks which some cantankerous person might make, 'Really, you people, why do you use this pompous language up and down and all around, saying life is good, and intellect is good, and something transcending these? For

---

[32] *Phil.* 21 c-d.

[33] Cf. supra, p.98-99.

[34] Although Plotinus does not say so explicitly, one can infer that his statement also counts for pleasure in memory or in anticipation (cf. *Phil.* 32 b 9 – c 5 and 33 c 5 – 36 c 2). Here, too, pleasure is dependent on the activity of anticipating or recalling, and/or on the pleasurable object that is anticipated or recalled.

why should intellect be good ? Or what good could the thinker of the
Forms have as he contemplates each of them ? If he takes a deceptive
pleasure in them he might perhaps say intellect was good, and life,
because it was pleasant; but if he is stuck in a pleasureless state, why
should he say they are good ? Is it because he exists ? What then would
he gain from existence ? What difference would there be in existing or
altogether not existing, unless one makes self-love the reason for all
this ? In that case it would be this natural deception and the fear of
dissolution which would account for the acceptance of the supposition
of goods'. (VI 7, 24.17-30)

Pleasure is assigned a central place here in the objection of the
'cantankerous person' (δυσχεραντικός), a lively demur against Plotinus
and his pupils (ὑμεῖς). This formal technique derives directly from the
Philebus (44 c-d), although its content is inverted. Plato had presented
someone opposed to Philebus, someone who stated that pleasure does
not exist, that the term only indicates the absence of distress. Plotinus,
on the contrary, presents the cantankerous person as a partisan of
pleasure, opposed to the ideas of Plotinus himself, asking why intellect,
life, and the transcendent Good should be 'good'. It is quite possible
that some people, like Plotinus, take a deceptive pleasure in life and
the intellect, and so claim that they are good. Thus, even for them
pleasure is the ultimate criterion of the good. But what if we do not
take pleasure in the intellect ? How can the Good be good if it does
not necessarily produce pleasure ? For only pleasure or its anticipation
allows us to qualify something as 'good'. Life and intellect in themselves are not good. It is only by self-love (πρὸς αὐτὸν φιλία, a 'natural'
deception — ἀπατὴ φυσικὴ οὖσα and fear of dissolution (φόβος τῆς
φθορᾶς) that one can infer that life and intellect are good without
taking into account the pleasure they produce.

The importance of this question must not be underestimated. This
is not a kind of cheap, uncritical hedonism: the morose objection
implicitly denies transcendence, or the optimistic belief in the inherent
goodness of the cosmos. Together with the scornful remarks about fear
of dissolution, this rejection of supernatural principles allows us to
identify the opponent as a follower of Epicurus, who held that, since
good and evil are situated in perception (i.e., in pleasure and pain),
there is no need to transpose the good to a transcendent principle.
Moreover, he indicated that our longing for immortality stems from
our fear of death, adding that this fear is absurd (cf. supra, p.79-87).

Plotinus recognises the seriousness of this objection. In his solution (ch. 29) he first discusses the relation between pleasure and the Good. Although this theme will be treated extensively in the next aporia (ch. 25, solved in ch. 30), Plotinus here gives a first sketch of his solution: the Good does not necessarily provide pleasure. Even if one consciously experiences the presence of the Good, this need not lead to pleasure. For one must not confuse the awareness of the presence of the Good with the taking of pleasure in this awareness (VI 7, 29.5-7). In other words: pleasure plays only a subordinate role and cannot count as a criterion by which to evaluate the presence of the Good.

Plotinus also restates an essential element of his definition of pleasure: pleasure occurs only when a lack is restored. The less a being desires the Good, the less it will experience pleasure when it attains its end. In other words, a being that stands at a higher level of reality, and thus partakes more in the Good, will experience less pleasure. One has to acknowledge, then, that at the level of the Good itself, all pleasure will have disappeared (VI 7, 29.7-10).

Moreover, Plotinus defends the transcendence of the Good by refuting the presuppositions of his cantankerous opponent. Whoever states that life according to intellect is not good because it does not convey pleasure has a precise idea of the Good, and *a fortiori* recognises its existence. In every case, he asks 'what profit could I make from this situation?'[35] This question reduces the Good to the product of a calculus of the amount of anticipated pleasure. When his opponent states that intellect is not compatible with this idea of the Good (since intellect does not *per se* furnish pleasure), he accepts the transcendence of the Good (pleasure) with respect to intellect. But this statement, Plotinus argues, leads to a paradox: for it is precisely thought (the calculation of the amount of pleasure) that lies at the basis of this construction. Thus, nobody can despise intellect without falling into a desperate contradiction (VI 7, 29.17-25): intellect is subordinate to the Good (pleasure), and yet experiencing pleasure is subordinate to intellect; indeed, even recognizing pleasure as the Good is an act of intellect. Exactly as in his general definition of pleasure (and in accordance with Plato in the *Philebus*), Plotinus considers intellect to be the necessary condition for feeling pleasure, and as a cognitive grasping of good and evil. Without this faculty of cognition it would be impossible

---

[35]   VI 7, 29.10-17 (a repetition of 24.25-26): ἀπορεῖ τί ἂν καρπώσαιτο.

to develop a calculus of pleasure. So pleasure *in se* is inferior to intellect. Plotinus makes yet another observation: perception (including the experience of pleasure) tends to become 'knowledge' (εἴδησις), i.e., it wants to provide knowledge about the perceived objects. So the experience of pleasure prepares the operation of intellect. Now, if the νοῦς is desirable, then what about the Good, which has brought this intellect into existence ! (VI 7, 29.25-28).

Plotinus adds two general criticisms of his opponent's view. In the first place, he points out that his opponent contradicts himself when he despises life and being. For a lack of esteem for life implies that one discredits all affections inherent in this life, and thus also pleasure. Secondly, Plotinus remarks that to despise the life that is mixed up with death does not automatically entail a contempt for 'true' life (τὸ ἀληθῶς ζῆν: VI 7, 29.28-31). This conclusion parallels the analysis offered at *Enn.* I 4, where Plotinus states that every form of life is to a certain degree an 'image of true life'. The 'true' characteristics of life are eminently present in this genuine life, which is life according to intellect. Now if one despises certain aspects of a particular form of life, this does not mean that one despises life *as such*.

It is a mistake, according to Plotinus, to make the good life dependent exclusively on sense perception, as does Epicurus. If one accepts the latter's view, one fails to see that an additional faculty is needed in order to experience pleasure: a faculty for discerning that the object perceived either does or does not correspond to the Good. Dwelling on this idea, Plotinus states at I 4, 2.21-31 that if one draws a strict correspondence between the good life and perception, eventually no being at all will attain the good life. For perception as such would be completely blind, and unable to judge good and evil.

Plotinus' statement at I 4, 2.21-25 is pertinent here:

> So the good life will not belong to those who feel pleasure but to the being which is able to know that pleasure is the good. Then the cause of living well will not be pleasure, but the power of judging that pleasure is good.

This formula again refers to a central claim in the definition of pleasure: the corporeal affection can only be experienced if it is taken up by the soul in a modified way, i.e., first as a sensitive 'judgment', and then as a discursively rational cognition[36]. In the quoted passage

---

[36] Cf. supra, p.98-99.

this analysis is used to refute hedonism: since pleasure pertains to that which is judged, it can never stand at a 'higher' level than cognition (I 4, 2.25-31).

3. 'Pleasure' in the Good Life

At *Enn.* VI 7, 25, the discussion of pleasure culminates in an analysis of Plato's definition of the good life as a 'mixture' of pleasure and intellect:

> Plato, then, mixes pleasure into the end-object and does not posit the good as simple or in intellect alone, as it is written in the *Philebus*. (VI 7, 25.1-3)

Plotinus here intimates the difference between Plato's and Aristotle's accounts of the Good: whereas Aristotle situates the good in the activity of man's highest faculty (i.e., intellect), Plato in the *Philebus* presents it as a mixture of pleasure and intellect. At the same time Plotinus indicates that the *Philebus* does not fully correspond to his own opinion that the Good always (and thus also in the good life) must be simple and unitary. Thus Plotinus shows that the central idea of the *Philebus* troubles him. Why does Plato feel obliged to regard the good as a combination of pleasure and intellect? Or, to use the words with which Plotinus introduces his solution in chapter 30:

> But whether pleasure must be mixed with the good and life is not perfect, if someone contemplates the divine things and above all their principle, is a question which it is in every way appropriate to keep in sight now that we are getting into touch with the Good. (VI 7, 30.1-3)

Why is pleasure needed in order to qualify as 'good' a life according to intellect, or a life devoted to the contemplation of the divine? Does the general definition of pleasure not entail that pleasure, as an affection, cannot play any role in the definition of the nature of the good life?

The question is made more difficult still by Plotinus' (essentially Aristotelian) account of the good life as the attained natural condition, the perfect performance of the highest activities, of the soul. Starting from the Platonic definition of pleasure, however, it is impossible to attribute pleasure to this condition, as it transcends all lack. Besides, Plotinus himself states that pleasure decreases along with the increasing attainment of the object of desire. It is, then, a difficult task to associate pleasure with this good life, as Plato does in the *Philebus*. But the truth of his words cannot be questioned.

In sum, this is the problem that Plotinus faces in interpreting the overall idea of the *Philebus*. Three apparently contradictory positions have to be reconciled: (1) the (Platonic) definition of pleasure as the movement towards the natural condition, with the corollary that pleasure is impossible when the movement comes to its end, i.e., when the natural condition is attained; (2) the (Aristotelian) account of the good life as the attained natural condition; (3) Plato's claim that the good life requires pleasure and intellect alike. How can Plato maintain that there is pleasure in this state, notwithstanding the fact that all lack and replenishment (and thus pleasure) are left behind?

The key to his interpretation is an original combination of the Platonic and the Aristotelian accounts via the mediation of the Stoic analysis of pleasure and its function in the good life.

Immediately after having stated the aporia, Plotinus presents two possible solutions, neither of which, however, completely satisfies him. Yet despite their rejection, each explanation provides some elements of his eventual answer.

Perhaps, Plotinus says, it is Plato's awareness of the difficulty of a hedonistic equation of the good with pleasure that prevents him from placing the good altogether in the pleasant — and in this he is right — but neither does he think that he ought to posit intellect without pleasure as the good, since he does not see what is desirable in this (VI 7, 25.3-6). Another reason could be that he thinks that the object of desire is necessarily delightful when it is attained, so that anyone who does not have joy (χαίρειν) does not possess the good. This is not unreasonable, Plotinus adds, since Plato himself here is not looking for the First Good, but for 'our good' (τὸ ἡμῶν). For it follows from the discussion of the objection of the cantankerous person that joy is only possible for those beings that partake only partially in the Good, and thus have desire. The Good in itself does not have desire: it is the Good itself, in 'another, greater way' (VI 7, 25.6-16). This first alternative is not a real solution of the problem. It rather restates it by paraphrasing *Phil.* 20 e – 21 e, where it is argued that neither pleasure nor intellect in itself could render a life desirable.

In the second alternative, an initial step is taken towards the final interpretation: the *Philebus* discusses the 'good for us', the good as it is experienced in our concrete existence. In the case of this good (as opposed to the transcendent Good[37]), 'joy' is a necessary element, keeping our desire for the Good going. In this passage, Plotinus avoids the term 'pleasure' (ἡδονή), replacing it with 'joy' (τὸ χαίρειν). In doing so, he is in full agreement with the terminology of the Stoics[38]. Moreover, he indicates that joy, as opposed to pleasure, is possible when the object of desire is attained. Plotinus finds in this Stoic analysis a way to 'reconcile' the Aristotelian and Platonic perspective on the good life.

In his solution of the aporia (at VI 7, 30), Plotinus again provides different explanations for Plato's position. The two solutions he presents here are left in juxtaposition without any evaluation, but it is clear that they constitute a gradation, culminating in a definitive answer encompassing the elements provided by the previous answer.

1. Intellect is the underlying reality (ὑποκείμενον), whereas joy is the affection of the soul (πάθος τῆς ψυχῆς) that thinks. In this case, the Good is situated not in the combination (τὸ συναμφότερον), but rather exclusively in the intellect. Our joy stems from the possession of the Good (χαίροντες τῷ τὸ ἀγαθὸν ἔχειν: VI 7, 30.4-9).

This solution highlights the fact that the *Philebus* discusses '*our* good': pleasure is the affection with which we (our souls) experience the good. But the good in itself transcends this pleasure. The statement presented here is essentially Aristotelian: the good for us consists in the substantial activity of intellect, and subsequent upon this activity is a specific pleasure.

As we saw already, the formula 'πάθος τῆς ψυχῆς' can only have a derived meaning, since the soul is devoid of any affection. For this reason, Plotinus again adopts the Stoic terminology: there is no (genuine) pleasure, but rather 'joy'. Thus, the strict correlation between pleasure and (bodily) affection is maintained, without jeopardizing the acceptance of a 'higher pleasure' that occurs as an 'affection of the soul' when the good life (the natural condition, viz. life according

---

[37]   The distinction between the good of the 'good life' and the transcendent Good is found also at *Enn.* I 4, 3.31-33 and 4.19-20.

[38]   This tendency of combining the Stoic and the Platonic theory of pleasure was present already in Middle Platonism: Alcinous, *Didasc.* 185.24-187.7 establishes a close relation between the Stoic definition of pleasure as πάθος and the Platonic theory of pleasure as a movement.

to intellect) is attained. In this way, the Aristotelian answer is restated in Stoic terms, thus anticipating Plotinus' definitive answer, which follows.

2. From the combination intellect-pleasure (here termed ἡδονή anew) there results a new entity, which is the underlying reality in which the good consists. For it is impossible that 'what is isolated and single'[39] would come to be, or would be chosen, as the Good. But the question remains: what kind of pleasure is meant here? In any case, it cannot be bodily pleasure; but neither can it be, Plotinus adds, the irrational joys of the soul (ἄλογοι χαραὶ τῆς ψυχῆς: VI 7, 30.9-18).

Plotinus then presents his own interpretation in a very abstract and condensed way:

> Every activity and disposition and life must be followed upon and accompanied by the element which is diffused over it (τὸ ἐπιθέον)[40], so that to one of them going its natural way there will be a hindrance and something of its opposite mixed into it, which does not allow the life to be independent, while for another the result of the activity (ἐνέργημα)[41] will be pure and unmixed[42] and its life will be a state of luminous clarity (ἐν διαθέσει φαιδρᾷ). (VI 7, 30.18-24)

---

[39] VI 7, 30.12-14: τὸ ἔρημον καὶ μόνον οὔτε γενέσθαι οὔτε αἱρετὸν εἶναι δυνατὸν ὡς ἀγαθόν. Cf. *Phil.* 63 b 7 – c 1: (in a prosopopoeia pleasures themselves say that they do not want to stay alone: they request a combination with intellect) Τὸ μόνον καὶ ἔρημον εἰλικρινὲς εἶναί τι γένος οὔτε πάνυ τι δυνατὸν οὔτ᾽ὠφέλιμον.

[40] I would defend the reading of the manuscripts, τὸ ἐπιθέον, as opposed to, among others, Hadot (1988, 160 n.258 and n.259), who renders it 'τι ἐπίθετον' (H-S¹ has 'τι ἐπιθέον', following Sleeman, who based this conjecture on the Latin translation of Ficino: *aliquid superfusum*): (1) τό (mss.) is justified, if one considers that this 'element' does have a certain determination: every activity (life, disposition) has its own ἐπιθέον. The article, then, distributes this ἐπιθέον over the different activities, lives, and dispositions. (2) The emendation ἐπιθέον into ἐπίθετον is erroneous. The verb ἐπιθέω (to be diffused over something) is used elsewhere by Plotinus, in a very similar context. See I 6, 5.12-17; also V 8, 10.17. Cf. Sleeman-Pollet 1980, s.v. ἐπιθεῖν.

[41] ἐνέργημα is the result of an ἐνέργεια: cf. VI 8, 16.16-18; see Hadot 1988, 161 n.162.

[42] καθαρὸν καὶ εἰλικρινές: cf. *Phil.* 52 d 6-7, where the formula is used to indicate 'pure pleasure'. However, this is not merely a loose borrowing of a formula: in the *Philebus*, the different kinds of intellectual activity are structured according to their degree of purity and precision, and the highest intellectual activity (Dialectics) is qualified 'τὸ καθαρὸν νοῦ τε καὶ φρονήσεως' (*Phil.* 58 d 6-7). This allows Plotinus to make a link between, on the one hand, the 'pure and unmixed' performance of an activity and, on the other, intellect as the highest actualization of human faculties.

Much is left implicit in this final resolution of the aporia. Moreover, the passage does not completely fit the previous analyses, although they have prepared the ground for this answer. Plotinus here treats the question of the *Philebus* from a different perspective: he regards pleasure (from an Aristotelian viewpoint) as an element that by its nature 'is diffused over' a certain activity. This scheme is initially presented *in abstracto*: every activity, disposition, or life has its own pleasure.

Thus, Plotinus refers to the hierarchy of 'life' as it is discussed at *Enn.* I 4, 3: if the 'good life' is to be found in life itself, then all living beings must be capable of attaining the good life. But the term 'life' is equivocal:

> it is used in one way of plants, in another of irrational animals, in various ways of things distinguished from each other by the clarity or dimness (τρανότητι καὶ ἀμυδρότητι) of their life. (I 4, 3.21-22)[43]

A lower form of life is merely the image (εἴδωλον) of the higher. As a consequence, then, there are just as many stages of the 'good' life as there are different lives. In this case, too, the lower is the image of the higher. The 'truly' good life is to be found in the being that possesses the plenitude of life (ὅτῳ ἄγαν ὑπάρχει τὸ ζῆν), which means, Plotinus adds, that which is in no way deficient in life (I 4, 3.23-28). The perfection of this life entails that its goodness cannot be brought in from the outside[44]. Plotinus immediately adds a qualification: the 'good' is to be understood as the immanent good (τὸ ἐνυπάρχον), not as the transcendent cause[45]. This intrinsic good that renders life perfect is the 'intellective nature' (νοερὰ φύσις). All other kinds of life are an image of this primal life; they are not perfect and pure, and are no more life than its opposite (3.35-37). In sum:

> as long as all living things proceed from a single origin, but have not life to the same degree as it, the origin must be the first and most perfect life. (I 4, 3.38-40)

In reality, then, all life is structured hierarchically, and headed by 'true' life, which is life according to intellect[46].

---

[43] The same idea is expressed at III 8, 8.12-20: the different levels of 'thought' (νόησις or θεωρία) correspond to different levels of life; for every life is a kind of thought, the one clearer, the other dimmer. The clearest life is the 'first νοῦς.

[44] Plotinus here takes up the Stoic doctrine of οἰκείωσις: the good resides in that which is most proper to our nature.

[45] I 4, 3.31-33. This idea accords with Plotinus' statement that the *Philebus* does not discuss the transcendent good, but the good 'for us' (cf. supra).

[46] At I 4, 4, Plotinus argues that all men possess this life either potentially or

In the passage quoted from VI 7, 30, Plotinus provides an essential supplement to this scheme: at every level of reality, the 'good life' is accompanied by a certain 'additional element'. This element can be in full accordance with the activity that is typical for that level: the resulting condition is a 'luminous clarity'. In this first case, the designated pleasure is one that uniquely provides an additional perfection to the activity in its natural condition. On the other hand, the element can also be a hindrance to perfect performance: the activity is then alienated from itself (it 'loses its independence') because it is brought into a preternatural condition. In this case, Plotinus suggests, the additional element leads to pain or distress[47].

Given this abstract presentation, we can adapt the scheme to all kinds of life, indicating the kind of pleasure that is typical for each kind of activity. This step is prepared in the immediately preceding lines, where Plotinus intimates a hierarchical order of corporeal pleasure and the pleasure of the lower parts of the soul (the so-called 'irrational joys of the soul'). Thus, the hierarchy of the different kinds of pleasure suggested at the beginning of this explanation is not absent in the final answer. Nor, however, is it further elaborated. No mention is made, for example, of the pleasure that occurs in the (discursively) *rational* activity of the soul. Strictly speaking, this activity, too, should lead to a specific pleasure. Plotinus, however, opts for another procedure. He immediately puts his new analysis at the service of a normative viewpoint. He wants to indicate the nature of 'truly desirable' pleasure, thus replacing the question 'what is pleasure?' with 'what is the highest pleasure?'. Of course this is, after all, what is at stake in the *Philebus* passage, and Plotinus concentrates on this issue. But it leads him to skip some steps in the argument.

Accordingly, Plotinus goes on to discuss the highest disposition, life, or activity: namely, the 'good life', or 'life according to intellect', which is the highest performance of our natural condition. 'We' are brought here to ourselves, since we coincide with that which is intrinsically most proper to us. The 'pleasure' that occurs here is a state of luminous clarity, which is not a genuine pleasure, as is shown in the following:

---

actually; on this, see Rist 1967[a], 146-150.

[47] Cf. I 4, 5.1-2: Ἀλγηδόνες δ'ἔτι καὶ νόσοι καὶ τὰ ὅλως κωλύοντα ἐνεργεῖν [*sc.* τὸν εὐδαίμονα].

assuming that such a state of intellect is most pleasing and acceptable, they[48] say that it is mixed with pleasure because they cannot find an appropriate way of speaking about it, just as what the other words which we are fond of do metaphorically, like 'drunk with the nectar' and 'to feast and entertainment', and what the poets[49] say, 'the father smiled', and thousands of others. (VI 7, 30.24-29)

To understand the statement that 'pleasure' in the good life can only have a metaphorical meaning, one can again consider the hierarchical structure of the different forms of pleasure suggested here by Plotinus. He combines the Platonic, Aristotelian, and Stoic view of the qualitative distinctions between the different kinds of pleasure, encompassing them in his own hierarchical model. This is witnessed in the first place by the shift in the terminology concerning pleasure in the passage under discussion. Plotinus introduces the term 'ἡδονή' in accordance with the Platonic use (30.1-14), and then wonders (30.14-18) how it is to be understood. The first kind of pleasure that Plotinus considers is *corporeal pleasure* (ἡ σώματος ἡδονή: VI 7, 30.15), which he immediately rejects as a candidate in the mixture intellect-pleasure that is found in the good life. It is important to note that only here is the term ἡδονή used: Plotinus seems to confine its meaning (in accordance with the Stoic terminology) to bodily pleasure, occurring in the replenishment of bodily needs within the combination of body and soul[50]. Genuine pleasure, then, is corporeal pleasure. The next alternative is formed by the 'irrational joys of the soul' (ἄλογοι χαραὶ τῆς ψυχῆς: VI 7, 30.17-18). Using these terms, Plotinus in fact enlarges the Stoic terminology, as the χαρά no longer implies only well-ordered rational activity, but indicates all 'affections' of the soul, whether rational or irrational[51]. As we saw, the rational part of the soul is completely left out of consideration. In the next phase (30.18-29), Plotinus establishes a new terminology, which is broad enough to encompass everything called 'pleasure' in either a genuine or a derived sense. For, although Plotinus discusses only the highest form of activity

---

[48]   One does not expect a plural form here. Clearly, Plato himself is meant in the first place. The plural, however, places the reference in a broader perspective; it may, then, imply the entire Platonic 'school', including Aristotle.

[49]   The plural is again meant to enlarge the scope: only one of the quoted formulas is a reference to a poet (μείδησεν δὲ πατήρ: Homer, *Iliad* V 426, and XV 47). The others are quotations from Plato himself (μεθυσθεὶς ἐπὶ τοῦ νέκταρος: *Symposium* 203 b 5; ἐπὶ δαῖτα: *Phaedrus* 247 a 8).

[50]   Cf. I 6, 6.6-7; IV 4, 18.1-21.

[51]   Also at II 2, 3.12-15 the χαρά is said to pertain to the lower parts of the soul.

and 'pleasure' here, one can adapt the structure to all previous phases: in each case, pleasure is something that is diffused over an activity; it is the result that can be obtained only through the performance of this particular activity. Thus, the hierarchy of pleasure is based upon the hierarchy of activities, lives, and dispositions.

The Plotinian hierarchy goes even further than this stage. The soul can transcend this level of intellect, coming into a union with the One. Here, too, the soul undergoes a certain 'affection': the 'well-being' (εὐπάθεια) that follows upon the ascent of the soul through the stages of 'thinking intellect' (νοῦς ἔμφρων) and 'loving intellect' (νοῦς ἐρῶν). The εὐπάθεια takes the place of the 'drunkenness with the nectar' of the loving intellect[52]. In this way, Plotinus both transcends Aristotelian intellectualism and transposes the Stoic term 'εὐπάθεια' to the 'affection' that accompanies the unification. At VI 7, 34-35, Plotinus describes this 'well-being' as an immediate union, a silence that can be qualified as an 'affection' or 'well-being' only afterwards. It leads the soul to transcend and despise everything that previously provided it pleasure: offices or powers or riches or beauties or sciences — even intelligence itself. It is not afraid of anything that might happen to it; on the contrary, it would be pleased if all the other things around it perished, so that it might be alone with the object of its desire (VI 7, 34.32-35.2).

Although at first sight the general structure (the correlation of disposition and affection) seems to be maintained in this case, this mystical 'top' as such does not fall under the theme of 'pleasure and the good life'. For, apart from the fact that pleasure had already been transcended at the previous level, there is no longer an underlying 'condition or life' in the literal sense here. The εὐπάθεια is a dissolution of all limits and interactions. As such, every kind of desire tends toward such an ultimate moment of unity; nevertheless, it is not possible to speak of a 'disposition' here, since all distinctions are removed. Thus, eventually, the value of this 'well-being' lies in its rarity and

---

[52] VI 7, 35.23-27. Proclus refers to Plotinus' use of the formula 'μεθυσθεὶς τῷ νέκταρι': at *TP* I 14, 66.26-67.2, he writes that, according to Plotinus, intellect has two conditions, as intellect *sensu stricto* (ὡς νοῦς), and as 'drunk with the nectar' (ὡς μεθύων τῷ νέκταρι). He explains this second condition as an ascent of intellect to the 'top' (ἄκρον) of itself, on which it coincides with the One. It is the 'flower of intellect' (ἄνθος τοῦ νοῦ), as discussed in the *Chaldaean Oracles*. Cf. *In Parm.* VI 1047.21-22 and 1080.4-14.

ephemerality. Any contact with the One that would be more than momentary would not lead to a life or disposition, but rather to the destruction of life.

The question remains why the highest affection (to which the scheme was adapted without mentioning the previous phases) can be called 'pleasure' only in a metaphorical sense. In the first place, it is clear that corporeal needs and repletions do not play any role in the good life. Pleasure in this sense is clearly excluded from the good life, as it is in Stoic philosophy. But could one not detach pleasure from any reference to this bodily lack-and-replenishment, claiming instead that the definition of pleasure can be maintained for other kinds of replenishments? In that case, it would be possible after all to situate genuine pleasure in intellectual replenishments (e.g., when we find the answer to a question that has been burdening us). But this solution is rejected by Plotinus. He clearly states that the supreme life cannot be subject to a process of becoming or to a movement[53], as the general definition of pleasure would require. Thus, in *Enn.* I 1, for instance, he observes (completely in accordance with his overall analysis) that pleasure cannot pertain to the soul itself: pleasure only occurs when something is added to the soul. Again, he adopts the Platonic definition of pleasure as the repletion of a lack. But the soul is not susceptible to any addition: it is in fact always fully realised, which precludes the possibility of a pleasure of the soul (I 1, 2.23-25).

A few lines after this statement, however, Plotinus suggests that it is possible after all to ascribe 'pure pleasure' (ἡδονὴ καθαρά) to the soul (I 1, 2.28-30). A further elaboration of this claim is promised, but nowhere provided. The term 'pure pleasure' does figure elsewhere in the *Enneads*, but it is always characterised in negative terms and opposed to 'genuine', bodily pleasure[54]. Whatever it might be (Plotinus does not tell us), 'pure pleasure' can be pleasure only in a derived sense, since it cannot literally correspond to the general definition of pleasure.

---

[53]   VI 7, 30.31-32; cf. also I 4, 6.18-19.
[54]   See I 6, 6.6-8; 5.29; opposed to bodily pleasure: I 2, 5.1-11. At I 6, 4.15-17 and 7.14-16, Plotinus also discusses the πάθη of the soul (including pleasure). The text, however, consists of metaphors borrowed from Plato's myth of the soul. At IV 8, 8.22-24, Plotinus indicates that the higher part of the soul does not enjoy 'momentary pleasures' (πρόσκαιροι ἡδοναί), but again he does not offer any alternative.

So, what is the nature of this 'pleasure' in the good life? At I 4, Plotinus writes the following:

> When people ask about what is pleasant in a life of the sage, they will not suppose that he should enjoy any of the pleasures of the debauchee or of the body — these cannot be present and they are destructive of happiness — or even extreme emotional pleasures of any kind — why should the good man have any? — but only those pleasures which accompany the presence of goods, i.e. pleasures that do not consist in movements or in a process of becoming: for the goods are there already, and the good man is present to himself; his pleasure and cheerfulness are at rest. The good man is always cheerful; his state is tranquil, his disposition contented and undisturbed by any so-called evils — if he is really good. If anyone looks for another kind of pleasure in the life of virtue it is not the life of virtue he is looking for. (I 4, 12.1-12, trans. Rist, combined with Armstrong)

John Rist has noted[55] that the use of the term 'pleasure' is somewhat puzzling in this passage. Having excluded pleasure from the good life in the previous chapters of the present treatise, and having presented his interpretation of the 'mixture of pleasure and intellect'[56], Plotinus now argues that there *is* a kind of pleasure in the good life. Apparently, despite the earlier specifications, his use of terminology here is not rigorous. Plotinus simply takes over the words of his critics and tries to indicate (as they demanded) just what it is that is pleasant in what he conceives to be the good life[57]. But, after all, there is a clear difference between the nature of the pleasure discussed here and the nature of pleasure as outlined in the general definition: Plotinus explains that this peculiar kind of pleasure does not consist in movement or in a process of becoming, thereby avoiding any possible confusion about the meaning of the term 'pleasure' as used here.

This pleasure in the good life comes very close to the 'katastematic' pleasure of Epicurus: the philosopher's condition is 'tranquil' (ἥσυχος),

---

[55] Rist 1967ᵃ, 150: 'As so often, Plotinus goes back on his own language and reintroduces terms — with new meanings — which he has rigorously excluded before.'

[56] *Enn.* I 4 occupies the forty-sixth place in Porphyry's chronological scheme, while VI 7 is the thirty-eighth treatise.

[57] A parallel case is I 5, 4.3-4: 'But pleasure could not be rightly counted in with happiness. But if someone says that pleasure is an unimpeded activity, then he is stating just the conclusion we are seeking' (cf. Rist 1967ᵃ, 151-152). Plotinus suggests that 'pleasure' as used in a different sense is acceptable to him; in this case, the Aristotelian notion of 'unimpeded activity' (identical with pleasure) goes well with his own view of happiness.

'cheerful' (ἵλεως), and 'contented' (ἀγαπητή). But it would be going too far to say that Plotinus takes over the ideas of Epicurus: for, as we have seen, the Epicurean view of the ideal life is rejected in *Enn.* I 4, 2 and VI 7, 29. For that reason, a straightforward acceptance of Epicurus' account of 'higher' pleasure is hardly possible. In the first place, Plotinus would reject the identification of the good life with pleasure (even pleasure at rest); but, more importantly, he would deny the need for sense experience in the good life — which is essential to Epicurus' katastematic pleasure.

As John Bussanich has indicated[58], the essentials of this scheme derive from the Platonic account of the static eternity of the Forms, as well as from the Aristotelian theme of divine immobility. To this one could add that this description of the contemplative life as a state of rest is complemented by the acceptance of a concomitant 'pleasure', a kind of 'contentment' that consists in the absence both of distress and, Plotinus adds, of genuine pleasure. In this way, Plotinus appropriates the Platonic notion of a 'neutral state' (i.e., an escape from distress and corporeal, or genuine, pleasure), identifying it with the 'natural condition'.

4. *Conclusion*

'If one were to look at Aristotle's definition of pleasure with the eyes of a Platonist, one would be approaching the position of Plotinus'[59]. This statement by John Rist succinctly indicates the essence of Plotinus' theory of pleasure — although one should not underestimate the importance of the contribution of the Stoics. Generally speaking, however, Plotinus' theory of pleasure indeed consists in a combination of the views of Plato and Aristotle, with an indisputable preference for the former.

Plotinus never challenges the Platonic definition of pleasure. Pleasure, being the awareness of the restoration of the harmonious relation between body and soul, always remains a 'movement' and the 'replenishment of a lack'. These two notions play a central role in the Platonic account. Within the general lines of Plotinus' psychology, the experience of pleasure is presented as the combination of a corporeal

---

[58]   Bussanich 1990, 171, esp. n.47.
[59]   Rist 1967ª, 151.

'affection' and a judgment (of both the sensitive and the discursively rational soul).

However, at a crucial point, in his discussion of the role of pleasure in the good life, Plotinus appropriates the terms used in the Aristotelian definition of pleasure: every perfect activity, life, or disposition yields a typical supervenient element. This Aristotelian scheme is then adapted to the hierarchy of lives and activities. Plotinus, in other words, bases the qualitative distinction between the different kinds of pleasure on the hierarchical structure of reality. The highest or 'true' life is the life of intellect, which constitutes the true nature of the human soul. This also reflects the Aristotelian doctrine that the natural condition of man is the unimpeded performance of his most elevated activity. Thus, the 'natural condition' is presented as an attainable ideal.

But this a priori modified doctrine of the natural condition and the good life makes a literal reproduction of the Platonic theory very difficult. Plato had pointed out that the natural condition is the full repletion of all lack. But since our lives are a continuous flux of lack and replenishment, this natural condition is an unattainable state. So if one accepts a different interpretation of the 'natural condition', insisting that it is an attainable state, and even that it coincides with the good life, it is impossible to find a place for pleasure (defined as the replenishment of a lack) in this condition.

Things are made worse for Plotinus by his acceptance of the Stoic understanding of pleasure as an 'affection' that must be eradicated to attain the good life. Pleasure, then, has no role to play in εὐδαιμονία.

Moreover, in the Plotinian system, intellect is self-sufficient: if it is directed towards the Good, it does not require anything else, and it may develop its own good life (which is the 'paradigm of good life') without any addition. As a consequence, Plato's claim that pleasure is required in the good life is entirely dismissed.

Hence, Plato's thesis that the good life is a 'mixture' of pleasure and intellect introduces a problem that affects the very core of Plotinus' view of pleasure and the good life. If one accepts the Plotinian analyses, then how can one agree with Plato that pleasure is a necessary component of the good life?

In solving this difficulty, the theory of the Stoics proves very helpful. Their distinction between pleasure (ἡδονή) as an 'affection' and the 'joy' (χαρά) of correct reason is used by Plotinus to maintain the original meaning of the Platonic notion of pleasure. This notion is opposed to that of a 'higher affection', which Plato also calls 'pleasure' because he cannot find an appropriate term for it. Yet the terminology of the Stoics is not entirely adequate either. Unlike the Stoics, Plotinus applies the term 'χαρά' to the 'irrational affections' of the soul. For when corporeal pleasure is left behind, there is no longer any lack or replenishment: the soul is always perfect and complete. As a consequence, the 'affection' on this level must be something different from pleasure.

Nor can the highest 'pleasure', which Plato envisages when he discusses the good life as a 'mixture of pleasure and intellect', be identified with pleasure. It might be a kind of χαρά (as opposed to the irrational joy of the soul), but Plotinus prefers either to speak of a 'state of luminous clarity' or to use such poetic metaphors as 'drunk with nectar', and the like. But all of these are only suggestions. Essentially what he has in mind is to indicate the state of intellectual 'rest'.

This interpretation comes very close to the *katastematic pleasure* of Epicurus: the highest pleasure is a condition of rest that is reached when all desires have been fulfilled. In Platonic terms, this state is the 'neutral condition' discussed in the *Republic* and the *Philebus*, combined with the notion of the 'natural condition': it is a state of rest consisting in the complete repletion of all lack. The problem for Plato, then, is that this neutral condition is by definition the absence of all pleasure (and distress). Plotinus does acknowledge this. The very difference between his position and that of Epicurus is that on Plotinus' view this higher condition does not yield (genuine) pleasure.

This has important consequences for the term 'pure pleasure'. Although Plotinus uses the term, he clearly establishes an opposition between 'pure' pleasure and genuine (corporeal) pleasure. He cannot adopt the Platonic understanding of 'pure pleasure', as this implies the replenishment of a lack (not a perceived lack, to be sure). This cannot possibly exist in what Plotinus conceives as the 'good life'. The Aristotelian sense of the term, on the other hand, does apply. Aristotle maintains that pleasure has greater purity the further it is removed from matter. In this sense, pleasure in the good life is the most pure pleasure (cf. supra, p.70-71). This is wholly, and even *a priori*, in harmony with Plotinus' dualistic view. Even then, however, there remains a problem: for the term suggests that pleasure in the good life is after all a genuine pleasure (as it is for Aristotle). This could explain the reservation with which Plotinus uses the term.

In one way, the Plotinian account can be seen to be a step backward vis-à-vis the Aristotelian. Plotinus' concern to remain true to Plato's vision led him away from the Aristotelian scheme, although initially he had used it in a very interesting fashion, holding that every life, disposition, and activity possesses its own 'supervenient element'. Eventually, though, he comes to reject the view that all of these 'elements' can be called 'pleasure'. Pleasure is refused access to the good life, since the perfectly performed activity of intellect does not yield *pleasure*. In the end, Plotinus' analysis of the good life is developed separately from his theory of pleasure.

This raises new problems. On what basis can higher 'pleasure' be regarded as a metaphor? Does this not mean, at the very least, that there is some kind of 'additional effect' of intellectual activity that bears some resemblance to genuine (corporeal) pleasure? In other words, does not Plotinus exaggerate the gap between corporeal and intellectual pleasure?

Despite these shortcomings Plotinus makes an important contribution to the analysis of pleasure. He attempts to surmount the limitations of the Platonic definition of pleasure without wholly rejecting it as insufficient (as Aristotle does). He thereby enlarges the Platonic theory of pleasure, paving the way for his successors.

II. Proclus

In the extant works of Proclus, no analysis of the *Philebus* theory of pleasure is given, let alone an all-embracing analysis of pleasure. There are, however, scattered references that allow us to reconstruct to some degree Proclus' views of pleasure.

Proclus' ideas on this subject correspond closely to the analysis made by Plotinus. For the latter, pleasure is to be situated exclusively in the replenishment of a bodily lack. It results from the combination of a corporeal affection and the judging faculty of the sensitive soul. On the other hand, pleasure in the good life, which accompanies the perfect performance of the activity of intellect, cannot be called 'pleasure' except in a metaphorical sense. Although it is a supervenient element, which 'is diffused over the activity' (ἐπιθέον), it cannot be an 'affection' (and thus neither a pleasure) because the soul always remains unaffected.

Apart from some nuances, Proclus adopts this same scheme. He accepts that 'pleasure' in the good life (in the natural condition) is a supervenient element but not a real 'affection'[60]. As opposed to Plotinus, however, who does not use an exact term for this 'pleasure' (he speaks loosely of a 'state of luminous clarity'), Proclus consistently uses the terms εὐπάθεια and εὐφροσύνη. In doing so, he restores Stoic terminology to its original form, as opposed to Plotinus, who uses the term εὐπάθεια for the mystical experience of union with the One (cf. supra).

1. *Proclus' Definition of Pleasure*

The first issue to be discussed concerning Proclus' theory of pleasure is the use he makes (*à la* Plotinus) of the Aristotelian definition of pleasure as the supervenient element of the unimpeded performance of an activity. Proclus states this in the following way:

> All life that easily performs its activity receives a pleasure that is paired with it. (Procl., *Chald. Philos.* 207.15-17 Des Places)

Apart from this, Proclus adopts the Platonic definition of the *Philebus* to describe corporeal pleasure. As he says in his *Commentary on Plato's Timaeus*:

> Concerning the body, the way to the preternatural state and the privation of life produce pain, whereas the return to the natural condition and the adaptation to life produce pleasure. (*In Tim.* III 287.17-20)[61]

This is a modification of the definition of pleasure given by Plotinus, who describes pain as the 'consciousness of the withdrawal of the body when it is deprived of the image of soul', and pleasure as the re-establishment of the original harmony (cf. supra). Proclus replaces this with, respectively, a 'privation of life' and 'the way towards the natural condition', apparently to employ the wording of the Platonic definition. The idea, then, is made clearer than it is in Plotinus: pain occurs as the result of a certain degree of disintegration, of a decline of life in which the body participates. But precisely this use of the notion of 'life' signifies that the theory of Plotinus remains unchanged, for the body does not partake in life except through the soul (in Plotinus, 'the

---

[60] For Proclus, too, the soul is ἀπαθής: cf. Steel 1978, 70-71.
[61] Cf. *In Remp.* I 226.22-227.27; 208.11-209.2.

image of the soul'). Thus, the disintegration (or re-establishment) of life implies exactly a disturbance of (or return to) the natural harmony of body and soul.

This corporeal pleasure, Proclus maintains, is experienced in the faculty of appetition (τὸ ἐπιθυμητικόν), that part of the soul which, through its contact with sense-experience[62], is primordially linked with the body[63].

The relation between desire and pleasure is elaborated in another passage. In his commentary on the *Republic*, after having recapitulated the thesis that the appetitive part of the soul is 'φιλοσώματον' (*In Remp.* I 225.22-226.22), Proclus discusses the two forms in which appetition manifests itself: the desire of pleasure and of possession[64]. In the first case, the desire is oriented towards the body itself in which it is situated; it strives to bring this body to its natural condition — and thereby, Proclus paraphrases the *Republic*, it becomes a lover of pleasure (φιλήδονος), 'because every pleasure is an evolution towards the natural condition' (*In Remp.* I 226.26-27: καὶ κατ᾽ αὐτὴν γίνεται φιλήδονον, πάσης ἡδονῆς εἰς φύσιν οὔσης ἀγωγῆς). The second form of desire is directed towards that which secures the preservation of the body. To meet the needs of the body, the appetitive faculty strives after external goods (226.27-227.3). Normally, these desires (for the natural condition and for external goods) should co-exist in an harmonious way. But their relation is disturbed when they are directed to a wrong end: the first form of desire starts to strive after the supervenient effect (pleasure) in itself, neglecting the natural condition — a neglection that causes terrible harm to the body. The second is only interested in external goods for their own sake, not for the sake of self-preservation. Thus a conflict arises between the two desires, in which they try to annihilate each other. The uninhibited desire for pleasure, for

---

[62] Contrary to Plotinus' practice, Proclus prefers the Platonic scheme to the Aristotelian division of the psychic faculties. Likewise with regard to the relation αἴσθησις-ἐπιθυμία Proclus follows Plato: compare *In Tim.* I 286.2-287.10 with *Phil.* 33 c 5 – 36 c 2.

[63] *In Tim.* I 287.20-23. This combination of ἐπιθυμία and pleasure stems from Plato: cf. *Phil.* 34 e 10 – 35 e 6. At 288.9-27 Proclus links the hierarchy thus established between the different parts of the soul to the growth of the body: first, the faculty of perception is developed, followed by the appetitive faculty, which leads to the experience of pain and pleasure; then follows the passionate spirit (θυμούμενον) and, finally, the faculty that safeguards the body, makes it move, and measures it under the influence of reason.

[64] Plato, *Rep.* IX 580 e 5 – 581 a 10.

instance, obliges one to spend much money — because, Proclus says, this striving after pleasure requires the addition of other bodies, which can only be procured by spending ones resources — and on the other hand, the acquisition of possessions requires thrift in the expenses that produce corporeal pleasure (227.3-19).

Proclus does not explain whether the perversion of desires is unavoidable or due to an accidental circumstance. His terminology seems to imply that a possible perversion is the result of a disturbed relation between the different parts of the soul, i.e., that the ἐπιθυμητικόν follows a fully proper dynamic when it is no longer governed by λόγος. In doing so, he would simply take over Plato's analysis in the *Republic*.

The relation between appetition and body is not negative *per se*: the striving after pleasure (without further specifications) is the natural task (ἔργον) of desire. What matters is to allow the appetitive faculty to perform this task without impediments. This requires that our desires be maintained in their natural place, i.e., that they remain subordinate to the rational faculty of the soul (*In Remp.* I 208.11-209.2). In the same way Proclus states elsewhere that the striving after pleasure, which in itself is unlimited (ἀπέραντος), should be governed by λόγος[65].

Although Proclus' objections against the dynamic of the striving after pleasure are almost painstakingly anti-hedonistic, his view of pleasure is not purely negative. An examination of §19 of Damascius' *In Philebum* illustrates this. Damascius here presents the doctrine of Proclus, whose answer to the question of why the Ancients did not accept a deity called 'Pleasure'[66] runs as follows:

> Why did the ancients not give the name of Pleasure to any deity? Proclus' answer is: because it is neither a primary good nor bad in itself nor intermediate and therefore indifferent; for how can its magic be indifferent? (Dam., *In Phil.* 19.1-3)[67]

---

[65] *In Remp.* I 129.9-11; 132.1-7: οὐ γὰρ θέμις ἐν εὐδαιμόνων πόλει τὴν ἀπέραντον κρατεῖν ἡδονὴν καὶ τὸν τοῖς γαστριμάργοις προσήκοντα βίον. II 176.8; *In Alc.* 58.21-59.6.

[66] The question itself is put forward by Proclus.

[67] Damascius' own answer is that the ancients *did* accept a deity called 'Pleasure': μία γὰρ τῶν Χαρίτων ἡ Εὐφροσύνη (19.4-5), which clearly implies that according to Damascius εὐφροσύνη (used by Proclus to indicate the highest affection, and not pleasure) *is* a kind of pleasure. The formula recurs in Proclus, *In Tim.* III 119.9-10: ... τὴν δὲ Εὐφροσύνην τῶν Χαρίτων ὡς ἑκάστοις ἐνδιδοῦσαν ῥᾳστώνην τῆς κατὰ φύσιν ἐνεργείας. So Proclus defines Εὐφροσύνη in exactly the same way, without, however,

According to this presentation, Proclus would have given three arguments to exclude the existence of a deity named 'Pleasure': (1) pleasure
is not a primary good; (2) nor is it bad as such; (3) nor is it indifferent.
But despite Damascius' presentation, only the first really counts as an
argument. For how could the existence of a deity called 'Pleasure' be
excluded by pointing out that pleasure is not bad in itself, nor
indifferent to good and evil: rather, these arguments seem to support
the contrary statement, namely, that there can be such a deity after
all.

There is no problem with the statement that a deity should be a
'primary good' (προηγούμενον ἀγαθόν). In his *Elements of Theology*,
Proclus characterises the henads (i.e., the gods) as προηγούμεναι αἰτίαι,
each of which heads a proper series and transmits his own
characteristic to it (*ET* 156, 136.33-34). A προηγούμενον ἀγαθόν, then,
is a deity that, through its own characteristic, transmits the Good to
the lower realms. Pleasure, Proclus argues, does not correspond to this
feature (we will have to return to the question why it does not), and so
it cannot be a deity. This settles the question. But Proclus goes further.
Apparently, he has been tempted to dwell upon the nature of pleasure,
and an echo of this digression is found — as so often — in the
commentary of Damascius. That the existence of a goddess 'Pleasure'
is impossible need not lead to the conclusion that pleasure is bad in
itself; and on the basis of the two previous theses one need not
conclude that pleasure would be indifferent to good and evil. The only
possible conclusion is the implicit one that pleasure is good in some
respect. A hint in this direction is the 'magic' that pleasure causes:
pleasure, Proclus suggests, attracts us at least, and that which is
attractive must be good in some respect. This conclusion is supported
by *In Phil.* 22.4, where Damascius refers to the statement of Proclus
(φησίν) that 'pleasure bears in it a trace of the good' (ὅτι ἴχνος τι
ἀγαθοῦ ἀποφέρεται).

In what sense does pleasure bear a 'trace' of the good? In his
Alcibiades commentary, 153.13-154.3, Proclus clarifies this with a
reference to the 'elements' of the Good as discussed by Plato in the

---

considering it a kind of pleasure (cf. Westerink 1959, *ad* 19.4-5: 'There is a connection with pleasure, but no identification as proposed here by Dam.'). This issue is
important in the context of Damascius' new theory of pleasure: the existence of a
deity named 'Pleasure' implies that pleasure really (and not as a metaphor) exists in
the highest realms. Cf. infra.

Philebus: the Good is desirable, perfect, and sufficient, these three being inseparably linked together. Proclus adds:

> The many[68] have only a partial grasp of the good, and some, seeing only its desirability, pursue pleasure, which is but a shadow of the object of desire in the world of reality. (*In Alc.* 153.18-21, trans. O'Neill)

Similarly, some are only interested in perfection, and strive after possession, which is an image of the self-sufficiency (αὐτάρκεια) of the Good[69]. Still others are fascinated by sufficiency: they want power, which is a representation (φάντασμα) of the ἱκανότης of the Good[70].

Plainly, then, pleasure is akin to the Good: it is an image (εἴδωλον) of the desirable in the Good. But an image is defective: pleasure cannot be a primary good (προηγούμενον ἀγαθόν), because it participates only at a lower level and in just one aspect of the Good. It is not a productive principle that transmits the Good. On the contrary: those who strive after only pleasure, or the pleasurable, have only bad experiences. They do what 'οἱ πολλοί'[71] do, namely, they turn themselves toward lower reality and imprison themselves by means of their affections[72]. It is the task of education to turn us away from pleasure (where we waste our time in the partial images of the Good) and towards the higher (*In Alc.* 153.25-154.3).

This entire analysis implies the rejection of the general idea behind the Stoic theory of pleasure. Not only does Proclus deny the thesis that pleasure is bad, he even holds the view that it is good — at least in a

---

[68]   οἱ πολλοί: the personal form indicates that, in the first place, this term has the Platonic (ethical) meaning of 'the many', in contradistinction to the 'philosophers', who are able to withdraw from the thoughtless behaviour of the 'many'. The term does have the additional metaphysical connotation of 'the multiple', over against the unity of the higher realms. This means that the 'characteristics' of the good, which are present in the Good in a unitary way, are captured by the inferior only as a multiplicity. The translation of Segonds ('les êtres multiples') puts a one-sided emphasis on this connotation.

[69]   Striving after possessions is the second modus of ἐπιθυμία, apart from longing for pleasure; cf. supra, p.122.

[70]   *Ibid.* 21-25. Striving after power is a perversion of the θυμοειδές in the soul: cf. Plato, *Rep.* IX, 581 a 9 – b 7.

[71]   Cf. *In Alc.* 152.10-11: τὰ γὰρ εἴδωλα πανταχοῦ τὰς ἑαυτῶν ἀρχὰς ὑποδυόμενα περισπᾷ τὰς ἀνοήτους τῶν ψυχῶν.

[72]   Cf. *In Alc.* 95.5-8: [Socrates is able to judge the way of life of Alcibiades] ... πότερον ἀποδέχεται τὰ τῆς ἀρετῆς ἐπιτηδεύματα, τὰ δὲ τῆς κακίας ἀποστρέφεται, ἢ τῷ φιληδόνῳ τῆς ψυχῆς ἐνδίδωσι καὶ ῥέπει πρὸς τὸ χεῖρον καὶ ὑπὸ τῶν παθῶν ἀνδραποδίζεται.

certain respect. Apparently, then, and notwithstanding his general
agreement with Plotinus on the matter, Proclus does not follow him in
his acceptance of the Stoic idea that pleasure (a πάθος) should be
eradicated in order to make the good life attainable. He even rejects
the Stoic view that pleasure could be indifferent. To be sure, Proclus
does agree with the Stoics and Plotinus that pleasure does not play a
role in the good life, but the reason for his contempt differs from
theirs: pleasure simply is not worthwhile. Being but an image of the
Good, it should elevate us towards the 'true' Good. Moreover, if it is
no longer regarded as a mere image, it will have its proper dynamism,
which causes great harm to our soul.

2. 'Pleasure' in the Good Life

The 'higher reality' towards which education should orient us is the
activity of the rational faculty and intellect within us[73]. Those who
manage to perform this activity in a pure way reach a condition
beyond pleasure and pain, as well as beyond their mixture:

> Philosophers, and all those who perform their activity in a pure way
> experience neither pleasure nor pain, nor their mixtures [...] for they
> set themselves apart from the affections that are material and generate
> becoming. (*In Remp.* I 124.5-7)[74]

This text takes up the Aristotelian idea of an 'unimpeded activity'. The
'purity' with which we perform our (intellectual) activity is linked here
to a renouncing of the material world. The possible impediment of our
highest activity must be due, then, to matter[75] — or rather to our
attachment to matter in the ἐπιθυμητικόν.

   Moreover, Proclus draws an important distinction between pleasure
(which always occurs in correlation with pain, because it is *per
definitionem* the repletion of a lack), and the condition that one reaches
when leaving behind the material world. There is no pleasure in this

---

[73] Cf. *In Alc.* 104.21-105.3.
[74] The philosophers are opposed here to those whose activities are guided by the
affections, and thus who find themselves in the company of pleasure and pain, and
the like (*In Remp.* I 124.11-14).
[75] *TP* I 15, 74.24-25 [life of the gods is without burdens or distress] πάντες δὲ οἱ
πόνοι καὶ τὰ τῆς ὀχλήσεως ἐκ τῶν τῆς ὕλης ἐμποδίων. *In Alc.* 144.7-10: ὅτι τὸ χωρισθῆ-
ναι τοῦ σώματος τὴν ψυχὴν ἀπαλλάττει τῆς ἐν τῷ θνητῷ τόπῳ δυσχερείας καὶ τῶν
ἐμποδίων τῶν ἐνταῦθα παραγινομένων εἰς τὴν τεῦξιν τοῦ προσήκοντος τέλους.

condition. For, although one can also speak in this context of an unimpeded 'activity', there definitely is no 'return to the natural condition', which makes it impossible to talk about 'pleasure' at this level.

The term Proclus uses for this attained natural condition (the unimpeded activity of the νοῦς) is θεία ῥαστώνη[76]. Normally this term is used to describe the activity of the gods, an activity that is situated more precisely at two levels: their carefree providence and the 'unburdenedness' (ἀπονία) of their transmitting the Good to lower realms. This is the natural condition of the gods: the 'easy life' (ῥαστώνη) that they live[77].

This condition of ῥαστώνη is not, however, the exclusive privilege of the divine: it is transferred to the non-incarnate souls, which are able to contemplate the highest[78]. Moreover, it is recognised in human life as well[79], viz. when people manage to transcend material impediments and thereby to reach the 'good life' or the life according to their nature[80]. In this Proclus follows Plato, who in his *Republic* mentions the ῥαστώνη of the soul when it renounces the world of becoming and directs itself towards truth and being[81]. In short: this condition always

[76] For the term ῥαστώνη: cf. Plato, *Rep.* VII 525 c 5-6; *Laws* X 903 e 3 – 905 c 4. The term is modeled upon Homer, 'ῥεῖα ζώοντες' (*Il.* VI 138; *Od.* IV 805; V 122) and also Hesiod, *Erga*, 5-7 (about Zeus); cf. Plot., *Enn.* V 8, 4.1; Proclus, *In Alc.* 127.16; *In Crat.* 81.14-15; *De mal. subsist.* 12.1-3; *In Parm.* I 667.14 (texts referred to by Segonds 1985-86, 105 n.6 [n. compl. 198]).

[77] *TP* I 15, 76.1-5: [after having shown that the natural condition never is ἐπίπονον, at no level of reality, Proclus adapts this idea to the gods] Ὥστ᾽εἰ μὲν κατὰ φύσιν τοῖς θεοῖς ἡ τοῦ ἀγαθοῦ μετάδοσις καὶ ἡ πρόνοια κατὰ φύσιν, καὶ ταῦτα μετὰ ῥαστώνης καὶ αὐτῷ τῷ εἶναι μόνον παρὰ τῶν θεῶν ἐπιτελεῖσθαι φήσομεν. See also Segonds 1985-86, n.c. 198.6: 'Chez les néoplatoniciens θεία ῥαστώνη exprime que la production et la providence ne coûtent aucune peine aux dieux: c'est évidemment une pointe anti-épicurienne.' The notion of ῥαστώνη is also linked etymologically to the 'superabundance' of the gift of the higher reality: [the name of the deity 'Ρέα can be explained] διὰ τὸ ἐπιρρεῖν ἀεὶ τὰ ἀγαθὰ καὶ διὰ τὸ αἰτίαν εἶναι τῆς θείας ῥαστώνης, θεοὶ ῥεῖα ζώοντες (*In Crat.* 143.15-17).

[78] *In Remp.* II 350.1; *TP* V 7, 28.13-14.

[79] *In Tim.* I 158.5-6: καὶ περὶ τὸν βίον τὸν ἀνθρώπινον ὑπῆρχέ τις ῥαστώνη. Cf. *In Parm.* I 667.11-32. In *De mal. subsist.* 12.1-3 Proclus states that the *intelligentiae indeflexae* partake in the *affluentia* of the gods.

[80] *In Alc.* 127.11-17: τοῦτο δὲ [i.e., the pleasure Alcibiades feels in being together with Socrates, as opposed to the boring contact with the rest of his lovers] ἐνδείκνυταί που τὴν μὲν εἰς ὕλην ῥέπουσαν ζωὴν ἀσχάλλειν καὶ λυπεῖσθαι διὰ τὰ ἐκεῖθεν ἐμπόδια, τὴν δὲ εἰς νοῦν ἀναγομένην εὐφροσύνης πληροῦσθαι· τὰ μὲν γὰρ ἐμπόδια τῆς ζωῆς ἐκ τῆς ὕλης ἐφήκει ταῖς ψυχαῖς, ἡ δὲ ῥαστώνη καὶ τὸ εὔλυτον ἀπὸ νοῦ καὶ θεῶν· ἐκεῖ γάρ ἐστι τὸ ῥεῖα ζῆν, παρὰ τοῖς θεοῖς.

[81] *Rep.* VII 525 c 5-6: αὐτῆς τῆς ψυχῆς ῥαστώνης μεταστροφῆς ἀπὸ γενέσεως

occurs when an activity is performed according to nature. As Proclus himself puts it:

> All those things of which the acts are according to their essence act with ease.[82]

Proclus nearly always describes this condition in negative terms: it is an ἀταραξία or ἀπονία, an absence of burden, trouble, sorrow, pain, and all impediments of the activity (*TP* I 15, 74.21-25). When he does offer a more positive account, he mentions 'peace' (εἰρήνη: *In Remp.* I 87.15-19), 'mildness' (πραότης) or 'intellective rest' (γαλήνη νοερά)[83].

Once again, this analysis follows very closely the opinions of Plotinus, who himself follows the Stoics and Epicurus (although he rejects the latter's overall views) in speaking of the 'rest' of intellectual activity. Moreover, Proclus refers explicitly in this context to Plotinus' description of this condition as 'drunk with nectar'[84].

With regard to the definition of this 'affection', however, Proclus' opinion is slightly different from that of Plotinus. For Proclus calls this affection a 'well-being' (εὐπάθεια or εὐφροσύνη)[85] and states that it accompanies the unimpeded performance of the activity according to nature, at the different levels on which ῥᾳστώνη occurs[86]. This activity

---

ἐπ'ἀλήθειάν τε καὶ οὐσίαν. Cf. *Laws* X 903 e 3 – 905 c 4.

[82] *In Tim.* II 281.15-16: πᾶν τὸ κατ'οὐσίαν ποιοῦν ἃ ποιεῖ μετὰ ῥᾳστώνης ποιεῖ. Cf. III 119.9-10: [the Orphics considered Εὐφροσύνη to be one of the Graces,] ὡς ἑκάστοις ἐνδιδοῦσαν ῥᾳστώνην τῆς κατὰ φύσιν ἐνεργείας.

[83] *In Crat.* 178.14-19: [the name of Λητώ can be explained] διά τε τὸ λεῖον τοῦ ἤθους πορίζειν ταῖς ψυχαῖς καὶ τὸ τῆς ἑκουσίου ζωῆς παρεκτικὸν καὶ τῆς θείας ῥᾳστώνης χορηγόν. ταῦτα γὰρ ἐνδίδωσι τοῖς εἰς αὐτὴν ἀνατεινομένοις ἄφατον ἐνέργειαν ⟨καὶ⟩ ζωὴν ἀπήμονα καὶ πραότητα καὶ ἀταραξίαν καὶ γαλήνην νοεράν.

[84] *In Parm.* V 1037.36-1038.3: θεῖόν ἐστι τοῦτο τὸ μετὰ ῥᾳστώνης ἐνεργεῖν· τὸ γὰρ ἄκμητον παρ' ἐκείνοις, οἷς Ἥβη τὸ νέκταρ ἐπινάει, καὶ ἡ πρόνοια μετὰ τὴν πόσιν τοῦ νέκταρος, ἄφετος οὖσα καὶ ἀνεμπόδιστος. Cf. also *In Remp.* I 166.17-20.

[85] The terms θεία ῥᾳστώνη, εὐπάθεια, and εὐφροσύνη are combined in Dam., *DP* I 58.5-12 (quoted below, p.148-149).

[86] [ῥᾳστώνη, εὐπάθεια and/or εὐφροσύνη at the level of the gods] *In Remp.* I 127. 19; 166.17-20; II 151.26; *TP* I 24, 107.3-10. [On the soul] *In Remp.* II 160.3; 168.17; 171.19; 186.30; 327.18; *In Parm.* I 679.17-18; *De mal. subsist.* 12.7-11; Proclus alludes to the myth of the soul in Plato's *Phaedrus*, particularly 247 c 3 – e 6 (247 d 1-4: ἅτ' οὖν θεοῦ διάνοια νῷ τε καὶ ἐπιστήμῃ ἀκηράτῳ τρεφομένη, καὶ ἁπάσης ψυχῆς ὅσῃ ἂν μέλῃ τὸ προσῆκον δέξασθαι, ἰδοῦσα διὰ χρόνου τὸ ὂν ἀγαπᾷ τε καὶ θεωροῦσα τἀληθῆ τρέφεται καὶ εὐπαθεῖ). [Generally, as an element attendant upon every unimpeded activity] *In Parm.* I 667.2-32; *In Remp.* II 303.1-4: τὸ δὲ 'λεῖον καὶ οὐράνιον' (σημαίνει) τὴν εὐπα-θείας μέτοχον καὶ εὐμοιρίας (ζωήν). πᾶσα γὰρ τραχύτης ἐμποδών ἐστι ταῖς κινήσεσιν, οὐκ ἐῶσα ῥᾳστώνης μετέχειν, πᾶσα δὲ λειότης ἀπαραπόδιστον παρέχει τοῖς πορευομένοις τὴν διέξοδον. Cf. *In Remp.* I 97.10-17.

consists, in the first place, in contemplation (θέα)[87], as well as in the transmission of the good to the lower realms: the lower receives this good according to the measure of its εὐδαιμονία[88].

In his commentary on the *Republic*, Proclus intimates that this affection is comparable with what is called 'pleasure' in the lower realms:

> The wisest man among the Greeks [i.e., Homer] did not consider pleasure worthy of ruling good constitutions, whereas well-being was. From Plato we have learnt the difference between those two. (*In Remp.* I 131.14-16)[89]

'Well-being' is therefore seen as a transposition of affections to a higher, intellectual level. In this sense, however, there is always an irreducible difference between well-being and 'pleasure', although they are both the 'accompanying element' of an activity.

Proclus' interpretation of the 'mixture of pleasure and intellect' is unknown to us, but he most likely adopts the Aristotelian scheme, together with the Plotinian nuance that the accompanying element of the activity of intellect cannot really be pleasure. As opposed to Plotinus, however, Proclus re-establishes the Stoic terminology in its original form. As we have seen, the Stoics uses the term εὐπάθεια to denote the accompanying element (ἐπιγέννημα) of correct judgments of reason, whereas Plotinus relates it to the mystical experience of union with the One. Here, it is impossible to speak of any 'condition' or 'affection' whatsoever. By relating εὐπάθεια to the 'accompanying element of the natural condition', Proclus opts for a return to the original meaning.

Although Proclus carefully avoids any possible confusion between this higher affection and (corporeal) pleasure, he does follow Plotinus in relating this higher affection to what Plato calls 'pure' pleasure. In *In Alc.* he explicitly states this: having insisted that we should renounce

---

[87] Procl., *Chald. Philos.* 207.9-15 Des Places: [attendant upon the separation from matter and becoming is] θέα τῆς πατρικῆς μονάδος, εὐφροσύνη δὲ ἄχραντος ἐπ'αὐτήν, εὐστάθειά τε ἀπὸ τῆς νοερᾶς ταύτης περιωπῆς· ἀφ'ὧν δῆλον ὡς μικτὸν ἡμῶν τὸ ἀγαθόν, ἔκ τε κινήσεως καὶ τῆς συμφυοῦς εὐφροσύνης. For an analysis of this text: cf. infra.

[88] *TP* V 7, 28.4-6. This transmission of the good to lower reality gives rise to an εὐφροσύνη, which also exists in the higher realms; see *TP* I 24, 108.11-12: (on the Beautiful) διότι μετ'εὐφροσύνης καὶ τῆς θείας ῥᾳστώνης ἐπορέγει τοῖς δευτέροις ⟨τὰς⟩ ἀφ'ἑαυτοῦ πληρώσεις.

[89] Cf. Plato, *Tim.* 80 b 5-8; also Procl., *In Alc.* 127.11-17 (quoted above).

the lower realms and ascend towards the true and really existing things
(τὰ ἀληθῆ καὶ ὄντως ὄντα: *In Alc.* 152.12-13), he observes that this is
precisely the pedagogic method used by Socrates:

> ... to elevate each individual to his appropriate object of desire, and to
> show the lover of pleasure where pure pleasure, unmixed with pain,
> exists (clearly this is preferable to the pursuer of pleasure, instead of
> pleasure mixed up with its opposite). (*In Alc.* 152.14-18, trans. O'Neill)

Pure pleasure lies in the natural condition itself, precisely because in
this state pleasure is fully devoid of its contrary, distress[90]. Proclus goes
even one step further:

> Now power, self-sufficiency and pleasure are not concerned with
> things involved in matter; matter is weakness and poverty and cause of
> decay and pain, and it is clear that, if anywhere, the former exist in
> what is immaterial and separable. (*In Alc.* 152.25-153.1, trans. O'Neill)

Proclus separates pleasure (i.e., 'true' pleasure) from the material world
and situates it exclusively in higher reality, on the basis of the argument that matter can bring forth only perishing and pain. Pure pleasure, then, is the well-being we experience in the activity of the natural
condition.

   Just as in Plotinus, this terminology of 'pure pleasure' does not
apply except in the Aristotelian sense, meaning that pleasure which is
the furthest remote from matter (cf. supra). Certainly, this thesis rests
upon a Platonic basis, taking for granted that true (or real) pleasure is a
pleasure without previous pain and that the natural condition is by
definition detached from all lack and pain. Still, Proclus' interpretation
ultimately differs from the Platonic theory of pleasure, and actually
destroys its consistency. For, from the very beginning, Proclus situates
pleasure — wholly in accordance with Plato's definition — in the
ἐπιθυμητικόν, that part of the soul which by its nature is nearest to the
body. Pleasure is the supervenient affection of the movement towards
the natural condition. In the discussion of pure pleasure, however, this
scheme is recanted: the two most important criteria of the Proclean
definition (i.e., the relation with the body and the restoration of the
natural condition) are vitiated. Detached from matter, pure pleasure
occurs within the natural state itself, no longer in the movement that
leads to it. Pure pleasure as understood by Proclus no longer fits the
general definition of pleasure; in other words, pure pleasure is no

---

[90] Cf. *In Remp.* II 82.17-83.2.

'genuine' pleasure. As with Plotinus, Proclus too is forced to admit that true pleasure cannot be called 'pleasure' except in a metaphorical sense — although this acknowledgement is not explicitly made in Proclus' extant works. It is clear, however, that Proclus normally chooses terms other than 'pleasure' to denote this highest affection. In point of fact, the term 'true pleasure' is used very rarely, which suggests that Proclus wishes to avoid it — just as Plotinus does.

So pleasure in the strict sense is confined to bodily pleasure; this is the affection that occurs in the movement towards the natural condition. This 'lower' affection is, then, contrasted with the element that accompanies the activity (movement) of the natural condition itself: εὐπάθεια or εὐφροσύνη. The Aristotelian definition is taken over here, although it is detached, in a certain sense, from the strict notion of pleasure. Exactly as in Plotinus, the Aristotelian 'additional element of an activity' is applied to all kinds of psychic activity, although apparently only at the lower levels can this additional element be properly termed 'pleasure'. Εὐπάθεια or εὐφροσύνη, on the contrary, are not pleasure, as their nature cannot be reconciled with the Platonic definition.

3. *Conclusion*

To conclude this survey, we quote a text in which Proclus, as it were, resumes his theory of pleasure. In his *Chaldaean Philosophy*, Proclus notes the following:

> 'Depth of soul'[91] means the threefold cognitive faculties of the soul: the intellective, the discursive, and the opining, whereas 'all eyes' are its threefold act of cognition. For the eye is the symbol of cognition, and life is the symbol of desire, both of them being tripartite. The 'earth', whence one should 'lighten the heart', intimates all material and diverse things drifting in becoming, and every corporeal imprint. Upon this [i.e., upon 'lightening the heart'] follows the contemplation of the paternal monad, and the immaculate joy attendant upon it, a well-being resulting from this intellective vision. Hence it is clear that

---

[91]   *Or. Chald.* fr. 112 Des Places: 'May the immortal depth of the soul open itself. May all the eyes dilate aloft.' (Οἰγνύσθω ψυχῆς βάθος ἄμβροτον· ὄμματα πάντα / ἄρδην ἐκπέτασον ἄνω). Given the context of Proclus' quotation, the verse must also have contained a reference to 'life' (8: ζωή, to be interpreted as 'ὄρεξις'), as well as an exhortation to 'lighten the heart, moving away from earth' (cf. 9-10: Γῆ δὲ ἀφ᾽ ἧς δεῖ κουφίζειν τὴν καρδίαν...).

our good is mixed, consisting of movement and the conatural joy. For all life that easily performs its activity receives a pleasure that is paired with it. (*Chald. Philos.* 207.5-17 Des Places)

'The good for us', Proclus says, 'is mixed', consisting in a movement and the joy that is conatural (συμφυής) with it. He explains this by pointing to the relation between a perfectly performed activity and its accompanying 'pleasure', which means that the Aristotelian definition is adopted here. But the Platonic scheme is restored by stating that joy occurs in the activity of the intellect, whereas 'pleasure' is situated in the realm of the body, the 'earth whence one should lighten the heart'.

Strikingly, Proclus introduces the discussion of pleasure by noting the difference between cognition (γνῶσις) and desire (ὄρεξις), which later plays a major role in Damascius' theory of pleasure. We cannot determine whether Proclus also adapts this distinction to the mixture of the *Philebus* (as Damascius does at *In Phil.* 13), but the presence of this distinction in the immediate neighbourhood of the theory of pleasure seems to indicate that this is indeed the case.

Agreement had already been reached on the identification of 'intellect' (in the mixture of the *Philebus*) with γνῶσις. We saw that Plotinus had already made this point, regarding pleasure as a combination of bodily affections and sensitive cognition. Additionally, Damascius, *In Phil.* 10, indicates that Iamblichus, too, had already interpreted 'intellect' this way. According to Iamblichus, Damascius says, the *Philebus* speaks of pleasure that by its nature accompanies intellect, in which 'intellect' is to be understood as the 'γνωστικὴ ἰδιότης'[92].

The identification of 'pleasure' in the mixture with 'desire' is, however, something new; it will, moreover, be of great importance in the context of Damascius' interpretation. The reason why Proclus introduces this innovation is not immediately clear. Of course, Proclus situates pleasure in the ἐπιθυμητικόν, which readily allows for the extension of the meaning of 'pleasure' to 'desire'. But this does not explain the fundamental reason behind his making this extension. Possibly he needs the broader range of the term 'desire' to explain away the difficulties of the Platonic statement that there is 'pleasure' involved in the good life. The Platonic statement implies a characterization of the good life as a combination of intellectual activity and genuine pleasure (i.e., pleasure that consists in the restoration of the

---

[92] Dam., *In Phil.* 10.4-5; Damascius approves this: οὕτω μέντοι καὶ Πλάτων (10.5).

natural condition). Since this pleasure is generally considered to be 'corporeal', and thus cannot play a role in the good life (the attained natural condition, the life according to intellect), one can no longer maintain that Plato means 'pleasure' in a literal sense. The object must be something more general, which can be combined with 'cognition' in the 'lower' as well as in the 'higher' life. This might be the reason why Proclus chooses the term 'desire'.

As we will see, Damascius takes over this reformulation, but in his theory it has fundamentally different implications. He uses it to point out that in the 'higher' life as well as in the 'lower' a genuine and literal pleasure occurs.

This general survey of the traces of Proclus' theory of pleasure leads to the following conclusion. Just like Plotinus, Proclus identifies himself as a Platonist by adopting the Platonic definition: pleasure is the 'restoration of the natural condition'. This leads him to the same conclusion that Plotinus had already reached: no pleasure is possible in the attained natural condition. The Platonic definition covers only the lower, corporeal kind of pleasure.

Concerning 'pleasure' in the natural condition (the good life) Plotinus and Proclus rely in the first place on Aristotle's definition of pleasure. The perfect performance of an activity by its nature gives rise to a supervenient element ('pleasure'), and this counts a fortiori for the perfect performance of intellectual activity. Despite this application of the Aristotelian definition, however, the influence of Plato prevails, since the supervenient element of the good life is called εὐπάθεια or εὐφροσύνη, and not 'pleasure' — which saves the Platonic definition after all.

CHAPTER THREE

A DIFFERENT VIEW:
DAMASCIUS' COMMENTARY ON THE *PHILEBUS*

1. *Introduction*

We are quite well informed about Damascius' theory of pleasure, which can be extracted from his commentary on Plato's *Philebus*. Although there is evidence of many ancient works devoted to the *Philebus*[1], Damascius' *In Philebum* is the only ancient commentary on this dialogue that has been preserved. As the work of one of the last ancient authors, it has the advantage of encompassing the entire tradition, thus allowing us to get at least a partial picture of the lost works. But this fortunate situation also entails a difficulty: Damascius presents a very condensed version of the tradition. He discusses the views of his predecessors without clarifying the importance of the items discussed. Moreover, he presents his own opinion in such a way that it is extremely difficult to distinguish between traditional issues and his own interpretation. In general, the major difficulty for his readers is that he uses the traditional technical language, but he continuously struggles with this language to express his own original ideas.

The research on this work has not been very intense. Since the publication of the critical edition by L.G. Westerink in 1959[2], only a few studies have been written on this commentary[3]. Nevertheless, it provides a unique gateway to the thought of Damascius, to the

---

[1] Proclus wrote an authoritative commentary on the *Philebus*, as well as a 'Μονόβιβλος' (a work consisting in one book) on the three monads in this dialogue (beauty, proportion, and truth, 64 a – 66 a). His commentary is the text on which Damascius' *In Philebum* is based. Other (Neoplatonic) commentaries are known to have been written by Porphyry, Iamblichus, and Marinus, and probably also by Amelius, Theodore of Asine, and Syrianus; see Dörrie-Baltes III, 198.

[2] L.G. Westerink, *Damascius, Lectures on the Philebus. Wrongly Attributed to Olympiodorus. Text, Translation, Notes and Indices*, Amsterdam (North Holland), 1959. A new critical edition of this text is being prepared for the 'Budé'-collection.

[3] Rare examples are 'Temi delle *Lezioni sul Filebo* di Damascio' by Claudio Moreschini, in Cosenza 1996, 73-92, and 'Epicurus Neoplatonicus' by D. O'Meara, in Fuhrer-Erler 1999, 83-91.

Neoplatonists' interpretation of the *Philebus* in general, and to their theory of pleasure in particular.

By way of introduction, we will first discuss a couple of practical issues: the problem of the identification of the author and the method used in the commentary.

1.1. *Identifying the Author*

The commentary on the *Philebus* under discussion here came down to us together with two closely related commentaries on the *Phaedo*. After the loss of the first sheets of the codex containing the collection, the texts were included in a collection of commentaries by Olympiodorus, a pupil of Damascius who was more of a compiler of texts than an original thinker. For this reason, the texts have been attributed to Olympiodorus, examples of this being the Stallbaum edition[4] and the study of William Norvin[5]. Later scholars have remarked that the criteria used by Norvin in attributing the texts to Olympiodorus are very weak. He based his view on the similarities between the latter's general doctrines and the ideas expounded in the commentaries on the *Philebus* and *Phaedo*. But, as Westerink has noted in his introduction, this method is not reliable when applied to the Neoplatonists, all of whom were keen to take over each other's ideas: 'if, for example, we had only anonymous extracts from Proclus' commentary on the *Alcibiades* instead of the full text, it could be claimed for Olympiodorus on the same line of argument'[6]. New research led R. Beutler[7] to the conclusion that the commentaries on the *Phaedo* stem from the school of Damascius. *In Philebum*, however, continued to be regarded as a work of Olympiodorus, although Beutler did agree that the 'professor' (ὁ ἡμέτερος καθηγεμών) who is omnipresent in the commentary must have been Olympiodorus' master, i.e., Damascius.

Westerink, for his part, indicates that this needlessly complicates the situation: of the three texts added to the corpus of Olympiodorus, the first two (the commentaries on the *Phaedo*) would be regarded as

---

[4] *Platonis Philebus, recensuit, prolegomenis et commentariis illustravit Godofredus Stallbaum*, Lipsiae, 1820.

[5] W. Norvin, *Olympiodorus fra Alexandria og hans commentar til Platons Phaidon*, Kopenhagen, 1915.

[6] Westerink 1959, XV-XVI.

[7] Beutler 1939.

written by Damascius[8], whereas the third one would again be taken as
Olympiodorus' own work. Moreover, the only apparent ground on
which Beutler based his attribution was the title 'Σχόλια εἰς τὸν
Πλάτωνος Φίληβον ἀπὸ φωνῆς Ὀλυμπιοδώρου τοῦ μεγάλου φιλοσόφου'.
This title, however, was a reconstruction by Stallbaum, based on
analogue titles in the corpus[9]. Rather than accepting this fiction, one
should opt for a simple solution: 'ὁ ἡμέτερος καθηγεμών indeed refers
to Damascius; but he is not the master of the one who taught the
course, but rather the teacher himself[10].

1.2. *Method*

The text came to us as a collection of student notes. It is not the result
of a careful redaction. From the structure of the commentary we can
deduce a picture of the method employed in Damascius' course. The
Philebus was read systematically, per lemma, after having established
(at §7) a rough division of the dialogue into three parts: first, Plato
gives a general exposition of the problems at stake, in which he also
indicates the methods (viz. syllogistics and division) he will use (*Phil.* 11
a – 20 b); in the second part, Plato uses a simple method to
demonstrate the obvious thesis that the mixed life is the best life (*Phil.*
20 b – 31 b); in the third part he offers a 'systematical proof' (140.2:
πραγματειώδης ἀπόδειξις) of the same thesis, based on the methods
indicated in the first part (*Phil.* 31 b – 67 b). The *Philebus* was thus seen
as a 'treatise' in which Plato systematically expounds his ideas on the
good life as a mixture of intellect and pleasure. The 'corpus' of the
discourse is found in what is here called the 'third part'; the two
preceding parts deal with preparatory issues concerning methodology
and provide a general outline of the theory.

After having read the lemma (which never figures in the text)
Damascius almost invariably presented the interpretation of 'a'

---

[8] In the introduction to his edition of *In Phil.* Westerink still uses the labels that
Norvin attached to the commentaries: Phaedo B, CI-III en D (Phaedo A being the
proper commentary of Olympiodorus, to which the other commentaries were
added). In his edition of the commentaries of the *Phaedo*, however, Westerink shows
that there are only two different commentaries (Westerink 1976-77, II, 15-17), which
are the lecture notes of two different courses given on the same subject.

[9] In the manuscripts, the *Philebus*-commentary is simply titled Εἰς τὸν Φίληβον,
without any mention of the author's name. Some *recentiores* even have 'Φιλήβου εἰς τὸ
περὶ ἡδονῆς'.

[10] Westerink (1959, XVIII-XX) gives more arguments to corroborate this claim.

commentator (ἐξηγητής), who for the most part remains anonymous (φησι), but who can in the large majority of cases be identified as Proclus[11]. This was sometimes followed by a correction, criticism, or nuance added by the professor himself (ὁ ἡμέτερος καθηγεμών), whose opinion is introduced typically by ἡμεῖς δέ..., μήποτε δέ..., ἄμεινον δέ..., ἢ τό γε ἀληθέστερον..., etc. The general character of these corrections is always a 'return to Plato', in which Damascius pays more attention to the literal wording and nuances of the text[12].

Strangely enough, however, the authority of the 'commentator' is so great, that the text of Plato itself fades into the background[13]. For the questions discussed are not determined primarily by the text of the *Philebus*, but by the issues treated by the ἐξηγητής[14]. Thus, e.g., §17 presents a classification of the different forms of ἀνάγκη, with an explicit reference to Proclus, whose opinion is refuted by the professor. The entire paragraph is supposed to be a comment on *Phil.* 11 c 7, which only contains the remark that Protarchus must *of necessity* take over the role of Philebus. This note, then, offers only a remote reference to the *Philebus*; it is inspired by Proclus' discussion of the lemma. Another example is §19, treating the question of why the Ancients did not have a deity called Ἡδονή — again with an explicit reference to Proclus, as we have seen already. Afterwards, the question itself appears to be mistaken, since Damascius answers that the Ancients did have a deity who was the patroness of pleasure (viz. Euphrosune, one of the Graces). The fact that the question is asked, then, is due to the dominant influence of Proclus, whose answer is quoted first. Likewise §152 departs from the text of the *Philebus*, presenting instead a discussion of Amelius' refutation of pleasure-in-movement.

At times, the author seems unable to distinguish between the texts of Plato and Proclus. At §51 he discusses the term 'νεαροπρεπής, presenting his own interpretation of the word. The term, however, does not figure in the *Philebus*, and must have been taken from the commentator.

---

[11] Cf. Westerink 1959, XVII-XVIII.

[12] Cf. Westerink 1971, 259-260.

[13] The authority of Proclus' *Philebus* commentary was proverbial: Damascius reports in his *Vita Isidori* (66.8-14 and 67.15-23 Zintzen) that Marinus committed his own commentary on the *Philebus* to the flames after Isidorus' remark that Proclus' commentary was sufficient; cf. Westerink 1959, XX-XXI.

[14] Cf. Westerink 1971, 254: 'dans la composition et dans la position des problèmes, l'initiative est laissée partout à Proclus'.

The conclusion must be, then, that the *Philebus* itself was not as prominently present on the students' desks as was the commentary of Proclus. Apparently, the text of Plato was 'supposedly known', and Damascius assumed that his students had in front of them a copy of the commentary of Proclus[15]. Modern readers, deprived of this privilege, find themselves faced with enormous difficulties when trying to understand Damascius' commentary.

In this context, a peculiar position is taken up in §206. The formula, 'ἤ, τό γε ἀληθέστερον', by means of which Damascius introduces his correction of the quoted authority, is used here to refute *Plato himself.* Damascius puts forward the view that there *is* pleasure in the neutral life and that this pleasure does not follow from a previous lack. This mistreatment of the primary text might be explained by supposing that the author (or his pupil) did not know that the refutation concerns the thesis of Plato himself. He might have thought that this was a passage from a commentary, with which one could freely disagree[16]. But this case is different. For this departure from Plato is *essential* to Damascius' theory of pleasure, and it is highly improbable that Damascius would not have been aware of this[17] (we will return to this). Damascius' own doctrine, however innovative, is 'disguised' here (as it is very often) in the form of a critique of details or an incidental remark to correct other people's views. The motive for this peculiar strategy might have been the permanent external threat to which the ever-decreasing Neoplatonic circles were exposed, and which compelled them to avoid open disagreements[18].

Given the above, our reading of Damascius' commentary on the *Philebus* will have to be nuanced. His commentary is not a mere paraphrase of Proclus' teaching. Under the surface (i.e., the language of the tradition and the reliance upon Proclus' commentary) lies a

---

[15] Cf. the remark on Damascius' commentary on the *Parmenides*, Steel 1978, 80.

[16] Thus Westerink 1959, *ad* 206.9.

[17] Of course it remains possible that the note-taking student did not recognise the dissension from Plato, and that the confusion is due to his misunderstanding. Still, even on this assumption, it is an indication that Damascius refrained from explicitly mentioning his departure from tradition.

[18] The remark of L.G. Westerink is particularly pertinent: '...c'était devenu une nécessité vitale pour l'école et pour la petite communauté païenne qu'elle représentait, de souligner la continuité de la tradition proclienne. (...) Même si Damascius était capable d'une révolution philosophique, les circonstances la rendaient impossible. De propos délibéré, il opta pour le système proclien, tout en accentuant son indépendance par une critique minutieuse des détails' (Westerink 1971, 255).

profound disagreement with his predecessors. Certainly, it is true that 'in the lectures on the *Phaedo* and the *Philebus* Proclus' contribution considerably outweighs that of Damascius himself.'[19] But one has to take into account the subtle game that leads Damascius to depart (albeit implicitly) from his precursors on crucial points. His theory of pleasure constitutes a good example of this typical procedure.

2. *The Central Theme (σκοπός) of the Dialogue*

2.1. *Introduction*

In his Commentary on the *Philebus*, Damascius follows the common practice of later Neoplatonism: one of the first questions he raises concerns the central theme, the σκοπός of this dialogue. In answering it, he first offers a short survey of the opinions of his predecessors and then discusses successively the characterization of the *Philebus* as a treatise 'On pleasure' (§1), and 'On intellect' (§3), both of which are immediately followed by a refutation (resp. §2 and §4).

Damascius addresses the opinion that the theme of the *Philebus* can be entirely reduced to that of pleasure, a view which is supported by two arguments. First, one can take the 'sub-title' (ἐπιγραφή) as an argument: 'Περὶ ἡδονῆς' ('On Pleasure'). And second, one can argue that Socrates' own investigations show the importance of pleasure in this dialogue:

> he proposes pleasure as the subject of the conversation, then proceeds to discuss it, and, thirdly, ends with the explicit conclusion that pleasure is not the goal of life. (*In Phil.* 1.2-4)

On this view, then, the main aim of the dialogue is to show how pleasure ought to be conceived, as well as what role it ought to play in the good life. Damascius refutes this opinion, however, by the argument that positing pleasure as the central theme cannot account for the many digressions that clearly depart from this main theme (§2).

Peisitheos (a pupil of Theodorus of Asine, otherwise unknown) proposes intellect as the central theme of the *Philebus*. The 'mixed life' mentioned in the text is life according to the intellect, since the

---

[19] Westerink 1976-77, II, 11. This is very typical for Damascius' method, and was used by Westerink as an argument in favour of attributing the text to Damascius: Westerink 1959, XIX; cf. 1971, 253-254.

intellect itself is the first 'mixed', immediately below the One Good
(§3). This position, too, Damascius refutes. Since the 'mixed', which is
a central issue in the *Philebus*, is presented explicitly as a mixture of
intellect and pleasure, there is no reason to think that the dialogue is
about intellect rather than about pleasure (§4).

2.2. *Damascius' Own View*

Thus, it is clear that the central theme of the *Philebus* certainly must be
sought in the direction of the 'mixture' of pleasure and intellect. This
more nuanced opinion, which better suits the text of Plato, is treated at
§5 and §6. We find ourselves here exclusively in the company of
Athenian Neoplatonists (Iamblichus, Syrianus, and Proclus at §5,
Damascius himself at §6).

Iamblichus[20] and the school of Syrianus and Proclus consider the
Philebus to be a dialogue on the final cause of all reality. This is not,
Damascius points out, the transcendent Good, but the Good that
permeates everything: it is manifested in all existing things, as their
goal and end (as opposed to the transcendent Good, which is
unattainable). Hence, Socrates, though promising to investigate the
human good only, takes into account all reality, from the highest
principle down to matter (§5).

In the next paragraph, Damascius contrasts this with his own view:

> Our professor suggests that the subject under discussion is not the
> Good that pervades all things generally, but that which is present in all
> animals, from the divine down to the lowest. For Socrates makes the
> mixed aim of life consist of intellect and pleasure, thereby limiting it to
> beings with appetitive and cognitive faculties; now there is no cogni-
> tion either beyond intellect or below irrational animals (or, if you like,
> plants, since Plato endows these too with sense-perception). And, on
> general grounds, as he is in search of a mixed goal, he can hardly be
> aiming at the good simpliciter, but it must be the mixed good. There
> is, indeed, also a simple good, which is twofold, namely either the tran-
> scendent or the particular; but neither of these can be meant here, the
> former being unattainable, the latter being inferior in quality and
> range to the good that is the object of the search; as, for example,

---

[20]   The inclusion of Iamblichus in this group is not altogether obvious: according
to the anonymous author of *Prolegomena to the Philosophy of Plato*, Iamblichus would
have defended the thesis that the central theme of the *Philebus* is precisely the
transcendent Good (*Proleg.* 26.26-29). This contradiction can, however, be mitigated;
see Van Riel 1997[b].

pleasure or intellection. Of the mixed good there are also two kinds, one restricted to living beings, the other, more perfect kind shared also by non-animals. Socrates' subject is not the latter, because the cognitive character is not apparent in it, but the good that consists of intellect and pleasure, both of which are seen in beings naturally cognitive and appetitive. (*In Phil.* 6.1-15)

This determination of the central theme of the *Philebus* is based upon a double distinction: the good *simpliciter* is distinguished from the mixed good, and each of them has its own subdivisions. This implies the following classification:

1. The simple good that precedes everything and is unattainable for all existing things. The reference to the First, Ineffable Principle is obvious.
2. The 'more perfect' mixed Good, which does not explicitly have the typical characteristic of cognition (6.13: γνωστικὸν ἰδίωμα, 6.11: νοερὸν ἰδίωμα). By this 'mixed Good' Damascius means 'the Unified' (τὸ ἡνωμένον). It is the highest intelligible realm, in which the One and Being are combined in an undivided way. Indeed, this realm does not possess cognition except implicitly, as its cause: the knowing intellect will proceed from this intelligible intellect at a lower level of reality[21].
3. The mixed Good that is confined to living beings: the mixture of pleasure and intellect, which is the goal (6.3: μικτὸν τέλος) of those beings endowed with desire and cognition. These faculties are proper to all living beings, from the divine down to the lowest.
4. The simple good that is partial (ἐν μέρει), e.g., the good of pleasure or of the intellective faculty in itself.

According to Damascius, only the third level of this classification corresponds to the central theme of the *Philebus*: the mixed good that consists in the mixture of pleasure and intellect. Immediately and without further explication, however, this definition is taken up again as a mixture of 'cognition and desire'. We will have to investigate this reformulation below.

---

[21] See esp. *DP* II 88.1-93.9.

That which surpasses this mixture either does not possess cognition (i.e., the second level of the classification) or is simple and cannot be a 'mixed good' at all (i.e., the first level). That which is 'lower' than this mixed good is also simple and unmixed (the fourth level). Thus, the combination of cognition and desire exists neither 'above' intellect (ἐπέκεινα τοῦ νοῦ, 6.4-5, meaning the νοῦς νοερός) nor 'below' the irrational animals (one could possibly add plants here, Damascius says, as it is not obviously impossible that they too are endowed with sense perception)[22]. The subject matter of the *Philebus* is, then, reality from the irrational animals (possibly also plants) through the (knowing) intellect. Here, and only here, is to be situated the 'mixed good' that is the combination of desire and cognition.

3. *Damascius' Account of the Soul as a Basis of his Theory of Pleasure*

The 'mixed good' that is the subject matter of the *Philebus* occupies a middle position between the intelligible world (the νοητόν or ἡνωμένον) and the material world. This middle position is exactly the 'place' of the soul in the Neoplatonic universe. Just as is the Plotinian interpretation, Damascius' interpretation of the *Philebus* is structured by the different realms between which the existence of the soul fluctuates, from the lowest contact with matter to the highest intellective activity: the νοερὸς νοῦς.

After Plotinus, however, Neoplatonic psychology underwent a thorough change. All later Neoplatonists (from Iamblichus onwards) agree that Plotinus' dual scheme of the soul is inadequate. Given that the soul is one and indivisible, it would be absurd to say that one part of the soul remains steadily and eternally in the intellectual realm, whereas another part descends to the material realm. On the contrary, one has to accept that the soul descends entirely, although it retains its stability in this ever-changing world. There is no agreement, however, when it comes to determining the relation between stability and change in the existence of the soul. Proclus defends a 'classical' position, stating that the soul is stable in its substance (οὐσία), whereas its activities are variable[23]. The solution of Iamblichus and Damascius, on the other hand, is revolutionary: they propose the view that the

---

[22] Cf. Plato, *Tim.* 77 b, as indicated by Westerink, *ad loc.*, but also *Theaet.* 167 c.
[23] Steel 1978, 69-73.

change in the soul affects its substance without, however, jeopardizing its numerical identity[24].

This means that the substance of the soul fluctuates according to the manner in which it relates to the external world. Its activities fluctuate along with its substance, as they are the effect of this changing substance. The soul can be substantially determined by irrational impulses, but it can as well be fully rational. The various 'faculties' or 'parts' of the soul that are distinguished in the Plotinian account are now modified into the different realms in which the soul finds its substantial determination and performs its activities[25]. The different 'activities, ways of life, or dispositions' given prominence by Plotinus (who considered them to be the performance of a specific faculty) are now seen as different 'οὐσίαι' of the soul.

This implies that the 'natural condition' of the soul can change. In his commentary on the *Phaedo*, Damascius makes this point clear. He states that the different souls are scattered everywhere in the universe and that they belong to the higher, middle or lower realms according to their substance (κατ'οὐσίαν). Although their lives can be more or less elevated, the state itself in which they perform their vital functions is their natural condition. Some souls, Damascius adds, descend as low as the Tartarus; for others the descent stops in the higher heavenly spheres; still others occupy a middle position[26]. Thus, the natural condition of the soul differs according to the position it occupies; or, more precisely, the natural condition is identical with the substance (οὐσία) of the soul[27].

This opinion, however, does not give rise to relativism. Damascius does not mean that every natural condition of the soul would be equally good. On the contrary: he re-establishes the normative thesis of his predecessors, maintaining that the natural condition on the level of intellect is the most desirable destination for the soul. This opinion, too, is to be found in Damascius' commentary on the *Phaedo*:

> If intellection lifts the soul up to the level of intellect and brings it to its natural condition, while sense perception brings it down to the level of

---

[24] Cf. Steel 1978, 52-69 (Iamblichus) and 102-116 (Damascius).

[25] Steel 1978, 97: 'Damascius observes that these inferior lives are 'substantial' forms and not merely different faculties or activities produced by the same unchanging substance.' Steel refers to *In Parm.*, R. II, 253.23-26; Priscianus, *In De an.*, 219.32-34, and 247.36 (possibly dependent on Iamblichus).

[26] *In Phaed.* II 143.

[27] Cf. *In Phil.* 1 36.10: αὐτὸ γὰρ τὸ κατὰ φύσιν ἡ οὐσία ἐστίν ...

the body and to an abnormal state, there can be no doubt as to the
conclusion. (Dam., *In Phaed.* I 327.1-2, ad *Phaed.* 79 c 2 – e 7)

Damascius presents this thesis in *In Philebum* as well. Although he states
that the soul can occupy different 'natural conditions'[28], he still
adheres to a clearly normative position: the highest 'κατὰ φύσιν' is life
according to intellect. Just as it is for Plotinus and Aristotle, this is the
good life (βίος εὐδαίμων), which yields the highest pleasure[29].

This doctrine of the soul serves as a *Leitmotiv* for the complete theory of
pleasure of Damascius, which we will discuss below. One element of
extraordinary importance in this context, however, should be
mentioned here: Damascius' thesis that the soul cannot be unaffected
(ἀπαθής). The opposite view is defended by Plotinus and Proclus,
according to whom affections (πάθη) belong exclusively to the body.
The role of the soul in the sensation of affections is restricted to a kind
of cognition, namely, the awareness of the presence of a certain πάθος.
The soul itself, however, remains unaffected. If the term 'affections of
the soul' (and thus also 'pleasure of the soul')[30] has a meaning, it can
only be a metaphorical one.

Damascius fiercely rejects this view. The soul, he points out, can
never come under the influence of the body — i.e., it can never lower
its own status through contact with the body — if it is not literally
affected by it[31]. This possibility that the soul could be affected is one of
the arguments Damascius provides to support his psychology: it is the
substance of the soul itself that is affected, and the activities it performs
are congruent with this substance[32].

This thesis is of particular importance for Damascius' theory of
pleasure, since, if the soul is affected in its substance, then pleasure as a
πάθος, i.e., *pleasure in the literal sense of the word*, also belongs to the
substance of the soul. Pleasure, then, is not solely an affection accompanying the movement towards the natural condition; rather, it occurs
a fortiori in the attained natural condition itself[33].

---

[28] Cf. *In Phil.* 136.7-8: τὸ οἰκεῖον κατὰ φύσιν, complemented with the statement
that ἔνεστι καὶ ἐν νῷ τὸ κατὰ φύσιν (136.8); also §155, where the different kinds of
pleasure are linked with the typical κατὰ φύσιν of each level.

[29] Cf. §155.

[30] Used by Plotinus, cf. supra p.109.

[31] *In Parm.* R II 253.5-11; cf. Steel 1978, 96.

[32] *Ibid.* 253.4-5.

[33] Cf. *In Phil.* 155.8, where the pleasure of the natural condition of intellect is

4. *Damascius' Interpretation of the 'Mixture of Pleasure and Intellect'*

In his account of the central theme of the dialogue, Damascius interprets without further ado the 'mixed goal' of pleasure and intellect as the mixture of desire and cognition (ὄρεξις and γνῶσις)[34]. This incidental terminological modification is of profound importance: it serves as the basis on which Damascius' entire interpretation rests. As we have pointed out, this reformulation was already prepared by Proclus, although he did not draw the same conclusions from it as Damascius does.

This reformulation, however, is not without problems. First, one needs to explain how all beings that are covered by the central theme of the *Philebus* do indeed have desire and cognition. And second, one has to make explicit the thoroughgoing consequences of this reformulation.

4.1. *Desire and Cognition in Sense-perception and Intellect*

We turn first to the question of whether the definition of the 'mixed good' as a mixture of desire and cognition holds true for all realms covered by the central theme of the dialogue. Damascius states that the mixture of desire and cognition is proper to all living beings, from those that have perception through (and including) the knowing intellect. If we could see, now, whether these two extremities indeed are a mixture of cognition and desire, then we could perhaps find out if this same feature holds true for all intermediate beings. The first question, then, is: how can Damascius state that perception (the lowest level) and intellect (the highest) are a mixture of desire and cognition?

4.1.1. *Perception as a 'Mixture of Desire and Cognition'*
Concerning perception one may state that Damascius simply takes over the analysis made by Plotinus. Perception, he says, always implies a surplus over the purely passive reception of sensible impulses. It also contains a judgment that allows us to recognise that which is perceived. Perception thus contains a cognitive aspect. Only when this is present can desire arise: the perception of a lack (e.g., thirst and

---

called 'the very paradigm of pleasure' (αὐτο τὸ παράδειγμα τῆς ἡδονῆς); cf. infra.

[34] 6.3-4: εἴπερ ἐκ νοῦ καὶ ἡδονῆς συνίστησι τὸ μικτὸν τέλος, ὅπερ ἐστὶ τοῦ ὀρεκτικοῦ καὶ γιγνώσκοντος.

drought) gives rise to a desire for replenishment. This does not mean, Damascius says, that the soul (the subject of desire) is itself 'emptied' too: rather, it undergoes the affection (or feels the appetite) because it is present together with the idea of moisture, even if this idea is not actually realised in the concrete thing. This 'contact'[35] of the soul with Form, resulting in desire, is due to cognition[36]. Cognition is thus seen as inherent in perception. Damascius explains this view of the matter at §157, where he explicitly asks (*ad Phil.* 33 c 5 – 36 c 2) what Plato might mean by the term 'perception' (αἴσθησις). He answers that cognition is

> a judgment on the identity of anything, evoked by the body alone, i.e., by the bodily process. (157.8-9)

So a cognitive element, a judgment, is required in every perception, even that of irrational animals (and possibly plants). Hence it cannot be identical with the 'reasoning faculty' (τὸ λογιστικόν) of the soul. It is rather a possibility of introspection that is shared by the lower parts of the soul. Despite this distinction, however, there is a certain kinship between cognition and the rational part of the soul. In his *De Principiis*, Damascius says:

> it is obvious that sense-perception intimates (ὑπαγορεύει) the rational soul. (*DP* I 42.21-22)

Perception is, then, akin to the higher faculty of the soul, precisely because of the implicit presence of cognition in it; it contains a weak foreshadowing of that which prevails in a higher realm[37]. This is why Damascius always relates γνῶσις to the highest activity of the soul: life according to intellect. This assessment is prominently put forward at §13. We will return to this feature in our discussion of Damascius' interpretation of the 'mixture of pleasure and intellect'.

---

[35] 'Contact': ἐφάπτομαι, cf. *Phil.* 35 a 6 – c 1. According to the *Philebus*, this contact is only possible on the basis of memory, which is 'a safeguarding of perception'. So Damascius extends the idea: the contact is present already in perception itself; 'memory', too, Damascius argues, is a kind of cognition, i.e., 'a judgment on the sensory image that remains in the soul' (158.5-6: ἀλλ᾽ ἔστιν ἡ μνήμη τοῦ εἴσω μένοντος αἰσθήματος κρίσις).

[36] 160.4-8: τὸ μὲν γὰρ διψῶν [*sc.* σῶμα] κενὸν ὑγροῦ, ψυχὴ δὲ πῶς ἂν κενωθείη; οὐδὲ γὰρ ἂν πληρωθείη· καὶ μὴν πάσχει ἢ ὀρέγεται συνοῦσα τῷ εἴδει τοῦ ὑγροῦ καὶ μὴ παρόντι (...) ἡ δέ γε ψυχὴ τῇ γνώσει ἐφαπτομένη ὀρέγεται. Cf. §161; 86.3 (γνῶσις as a κρίσις).

[37] At *DP* II 153.19-154.6 Damascius even states that every form (even wood, stone etc.) encompasses a certain cognition (γνῶσις) and introspective consciousness (συναίσθησις), albeit in a way hidden to human experience.

Damascius is in no way innovative in advancing this position. As has been said already, it is completely congruent with the theory of Plotinus. He, too, considered perception to be the coincidence of sensitive impulses and a sensitive judgment (αἰσθητικὴ γνῶσις or κρίσις), which by its nature presents the information to a higher judgment situated within discursive reason (cf. supra).

Perception, then, can be called a mixture of cognition and desire. The cognitive element refers to the (sensitive) judgment that allows the soul to recognise a sensitive impulse as such. 'Desire', on the other hand, consists in a modified (i.e., cognitive) representation of the sensitive impulse within the soul, which causes the soul to seek a 'remedy' for this impulse.

4.1.2. *The Desire of the Knowing Intellect*

On the other hand, the realm that is ranked highest under the σκοπός of the *Philebus* should be *per definitionem* a living animal, containing a mixture of cognition and desire. In *De Principiis* Damascius explains the relation between this (νοερὸς) νοῦς and life: as the third phase in the triad οὐσία — ζωή — νοῦς, the intellect combines the characteristics of the first two realms. So it participates in 'being' and 'life', but in a peculiar manner: it is not being or life 'as such' (ἁπλῶς), rather, it is being or life according to the characteristics of its own nature (κατὰ φύσιν), and this nature is cognition (γνωστικὴ φύσις). So the knowing intellect is 'living', the first in reality to participate in life. Life 'as such' transcends this intellect, and thus it cannot partake in cognition[38]. Consequently, 'that which is beyond intellect' (ἐπέκεινα τοῦ νοῦ) is excluded from the σκοπός of the *Philebus*.

However, to be in agreement with the σκοπός, the intellect must also in some way possesses 'desire'. This was already seen by Plotinus[39], and is now restated by Damascius:

> Great is the love of truth [i.e., in the intellect] and the well-being in attaining it. (*In Phil.* 87.1-2, trans. Westerink modified)

In *De Principiis* this statement is repeated from a metaphysical perspective. In a long discussion, Damascius explains the ascent from the lowest realm to the highest, the Ineffable Principle. The leading principle of this ascent is 'need': 'that which does not have need always

---

[38] *DP* III 129.3-11.
[39] Plot., *Enn.* IV 4, 28.71-76; I 6, 7.1-21; I 2, 1.14; cf. Blumenthal 1971, 32-33.

naturally precedes the needy'[40]. One can arrange all forms of need in one line: the lower always desires the higher. After discussing the need of the body, of nature (and vegetative life), of irrational and rational soul, and before discussing the One Being (the νοητόν), the One and the Ineffable, Damascius discusses the need of the νοῦς[41]. What could be lacking to the intellect, which carries everything in itself, and never changes? How can one speak of 'need' in a being that is so complete that Aristotle could consider it the highest principle in reality? Damascius' answer starts from a recapitulation of the second hypothesis of Plato's *Parmenides*: intellect is one and multiple; it is a whole having parts; it has a beginning, middle and end. The lower parts, then, need the higher, but the higher also need the lower, in order to constitute a whole. Moreover, the One of the intellect needs multiplicity, because this one possesses its substance within the multiple (i.e., it is a whole of parts), and keeps the multiple together. So, to begin with, there is a great *internal* need within the intellect: the parts need each other, and the whole needs the parts. But there is also a need for the higher: in order for intellect to know, there must also be a known, intelligible (νοητόν) object. This νοητόν, then, is the 'peculiar object of desire' (οἰκεῖον ἐφετόν) for intellect. Although the need of the intellect is always to some degree fulfilled[42], since it takes itself as its own object of cognition, this does not preclude the existence of a need that pertains to the nature of the intellect[43].

Further on in the text[44], the same point is stated even more explicitly: the νοῦς constitutes a total universe in itself, and contains all lower things, albeit according to its specific way of being. Thus it also possesses the irrational parts of the soul; not only perception, but also a divine imagination (θεοπρεπὴς φαντασία) and desire (ἡ ὀρεκτική). However, passionate spirit (θυμοειδής) and appetite (ἐπιθυμητική), which belong to this desire, exist in a different, 'higher' way in the intellectual than in the sensible world:

> The appetitive faculty experiences comfort in the divine ease and is a
> permanent state of joy of the living being, whereas the passionate spirit

---

[40] *DP* I 27.14-15: Λεγέσθω τοίνυν τὸ ἀνενδεὲς φύσει πάντως εἶναι πρὸ τοῦ ἐνδεοῦς.

[41] *DP* I 34.9-35.13.

[42] 35.10: εἰ καὶ ἡ τεῦξις ἀεὶ τῇ ἐνδείᾳ σύνεστιν.

[43] 35.11-12: ἀλλὰ φύσει γε ὅμως καὶ ἔνδειά τις τῷ νῷ συνουσίωται. Cf. *DP* II 150.19-24.

[44] *DP* I 58.5-12.

enjoys the perfect and sublime transcendence belonging by its nature to a being which is an entire universe. (*DP* I 58.9-12)[45]

Clearly, then, intellect does include desire, albeit completely in accordance with the specific nature of intellect. For the moment it suffices to point out the existence of this desire: it justifies the inclusion of intellect in the σκοπός of the *Philebus*.

4.2. *The 'Mixture of Desire and Cognition'*

The second question to be asked about Damascius' interpretation of the mixture of pleasure and intellect is more fundamental: how can he redefine 'pleasure and intellect' as 'desire and cognition', and what are the consequences of this modification ?

At §13, almost immediately after the discussion of the central theme of the *Philebus*, Damascius explicitly raises the question of how one should understand the 'mixture of pleasure and intellect'. It is the first point raised regarding the content of the dialogue — thus revealing the importance of the issue. Damascius answers that the combination of pleasure and intellect in this dialogue is not to be taken literally. To be precise, he adds two modifications:

> How can intellect be the opposite of pleasure ? In the first place, it is rather desire that is contradistinguished from cognition, and desire and pleasure are not identical; besides, there is also a certain pleasure in cognition. (13.1-3)

Once again, Plato's 'mixture of pleasure and intellect' is changed into 'a mixture of cognition and desire'. As we saw already, all levels of living animals contain a mixture of this kind. In this way, a rather simple scheme is elaborated, in which the internal correlation between ὄρεξις and γνῶσις is established at every single level in the scale of living beings: 'desire' is always accompanied by a certain cognitive aspect.

This simple scheme, however, is made complicated by a very typical hierarchy. The proper 'place' of desire (ὄρεξις) is clearly distinct from the level to which 'cognition' naturally belongs. Despite the statement that desire also pertains to the knowing intellect, desire itself, in the strict sense, is to be situated in appetite (ἐπιθυμία), the part of

---

[45] Cf. also *DP* I 118.5-9. For the meaning of θεία ῥαστώνη, εὐπάθεια and εὐφροσύνη, cf. supra, p.127-129.

the soul that stands closest to the body. An indication of this is that bodily desires are always much more violent and the intensity of desire decreases as the soul ascends[46]. Moreover, we saw that desire is initiated within the sensitive soul: as the result of a combination of sensitive impulse and sensitive judgment, the soul desires to remedy the affection it experienced[47]. Desire in the strict sense is, then, to be situated properly in the lower, irrational parts of the soul.

In the same way the term γνῶσις does not retain the broad sense in which it was used initially. With the second modification in the text quoted above, in which Damascius states that there is also a certain pleasure in cognition (to be read in combination with the statement made in the first modification, namely, that desire and pleasure are not identical), the simple scheme of the first modification is *de facto* recanted. For, clearly, 'cognition' no longer means a vague kind of consciousness within perception, but rather an autonomous, higher faculty, which is *in se* distinct from desire[48] and which for this very reason yields a proper kind of pleasure. 'Cognition' here stands for intellect *tout court* — and so the Platonic terminology is taken literally after all. Indeed, the specific characteristic of cognition (γνωστικὴ ἰδιότης[49]) is to be situated at the level of the νοῦς[50]. The form of 'cognition' that is present in the lower parts of the soul is to be considered a lower, less explicit, and derived form of this proper cognition in the intellect[51]. Thus, Damascius now narrows the meaning of 'γνῶσις' by contrasting it with desire, which lies at the

---

[46]   Cf. 194.3-7; 196.2-5.

[47]   The link between αἴσθησις and ἐπιθυμία, as well as between the latter and pleasure, was established by Plato himself: experiencing a lack leads by itself to the desire of repletion, which in turn gives rise to pleasure (*Phil.* 34 c 10 – 35 e 6). In this way, even 'corporeal pleasure' belongs to the soul: the emptiness of the body is followed by a desire in the soul (cf. §160, quoted above). Proclus, too, adheres to this analysis: cf. supra.

[48]   Cf. Proclus, *In Tim.* I 243.26-244.31, where the γνῶσις is seen as the νόησις typical for the rational soul (esp. 244.16-19); as νόησις it is even to be placed within a large series, departing from νόησις νοητή. So, by its nature, it belongs to higher reality.

[49]   Cf. the terms γνωστικὸν ἰδίωμα, νοερὸν ἰδίωμα in the determination of the σκοπός, 6.11 and 13.

[50]   Cf. *DP* III 129.3-11; cf. supra.

[51]   Cf. Damascius' statement that the judging faculty within sense perception always contains a suggestion of the rational soul (*DP* I 42.21-22; quoted above). See also *In Phil.* 95.2, where Damascius presents intellect as a 'φραστὴρ ὁδοῦ' for desire.

other extreme of the scale covered by the central theme of the *Philebus*[52]. Desire naturally belongs to the lower parts of the soul (the bottom of the 'mixed good'), whereas cognition finds its natural 'place' in intellect (the top).

This thoroughly modifies the scheme that was initially presented. Instead of a combination of desire and cognition on every level, we now have a picture in which desire and cognition are placed at the opposite extremes, with each one — and this is an essential addition — yielding its own pleasure. If desire and pleasure were strictly linked (as they were at the outset), it would be impossible to situate pleasure within cognition. For then, again, pleasure (desire) remains clearly distinct from cognition. That which has attained its goal no longer desires, and so, strictly speaking, it cannot experience pleasure any more. Cognition, i.e., the result of a quest, would be devoid of pleasure, if pleasure were to occur only in the quest. On his analysis, Damascius is able to avoid this deadlock.

By redefining the terms of the 'mixture', Damascius opens up a new perspective on the role of pleasure within the good life. It is no longer seen as a monolithic block loosely combined with (and opposed to) intellect. On the contrary, Damascius accepts within the mixed life (desire and cognition together) an internal link, not between desire and cognition, as might seem to be the case at first sight, but between, on the one hand, desire and the pleasure that is specific to it, and, on the other, cognition and its specific pleasure[53].

The contrast between desire and cognition is further elaborated in lines 13.3-9, where Damascius presents additions to the two previous modifications. To the second, he says, one should add that in cognition, too, there is a kind of pleasure, insofar as cognition partakes in desire. The pleasurable disposition (τὸ διατίθεσθαι ἡδέως) that cognition experiences when it attains its proper object (γνωστόν) is due to the participation of cognition in desire (13.3-5). Here, at first sight, desire (of cognition towards its object) and pleasure are strictly linked again. But upon reflection, we see that the term 'desire' is used here in

---

[52]   In the same way, in *DP* I 32.19-33.11, the ὄρεξις is linked exclusively to the embodied soul (33.8-9: ἐψυχωμένον σῶμα of σωματοειδὴς ψυχή). This is complemented by the subsequent lines of §13, where γνῶσις, too, is said to encompass a certain desire. In this case, too, the distinction at stake is between the ὄρεξις in the strict sense, belonging by its nature to the irrational parts of the soul, and the less marked presence of desire on the realm of the higher faculty of the soul.

[53]   This idea is put forward most explicitly at §257 and 185.1-2; cf. infra.

a very specific way. It should not be taken as a 'way towards
cognition', but as the disposition of cognition *after it has reached its object*.
So, Damascius' statement that cognition yields pleasure because it
partakes in desire must mean that pleasure in this disposition is only
possible thanks to a (previous and now satisfied) desire. What is
designated thereby, then, is the replenishment of a striving that not
only is pleasurable during the replenishment itself but also yields a
pleasurable disposition afterwards. Without the striving this disposition
would not be possible, and so Damascius can state that the participation of cognition in desire is responsible for the pleasurable disposition
that prevails when the cognitive desire is replete[54].

   The first modification in the quoted text (that the distinction
concerns cognition and desire, and that 'pleasure' is not identical with
'desire') is clarified in the following way:

> To meet the first objection we may say that the analogue of the
> appetitive function is the urge to inquiry; for inquiry can be described
> as cognitive desire, being a way to an end, just as desire is directed to
> an end; cognition, however, is attainment of truth, and its analogue is
> attainment of desire. (13.5-9)

Desire here is defined as the 'way to an end', whereas in cognition the
end has already been achieved. Here, too, 'cognition' is no longer
considered (as it was the case in the passage on the definition of the
central theme of the dialogue) to be a cognitive aspect that accompanies desire. On the contrary, cognition starts where desire comes to
an end. Thus, the issue appears to revolve around a distinction
between *process* and *end*, movement and rest[55]. But this is not the whole
story. Cognition is not the end of any desire whatsoever. To the
'hitting of the target' or the 'end' (τεῦξις) in which cognition consists
corresponds a very specific 'movement': inquiry (ζήτησις), or more
precisely, a cognitive desire (γνωστικὴ ὄρεξις, 13.6-7). Thus, desire is
not restricted to irrational striving. Cognition, too, has a proper desire,
to which corresponds a proper end[56]. In this regard Damascius draws
an analogy, on the one hand, between the quest for cognition and the
irrational desire, and, on the other hand, between cognition and the

---

[54]   The same idea, that both the movement towards the end and the attained end
itself are implied in the 'movement', is found also at §136: cf. infra.
[55]   Cf. 14.2-4: cognition causes the movement, whereas the knower is moved; this
movement of the knower, Damascius adds, goes on as long as the knower is
searching (ὅταν ζητῇ), not when it has reached its end (οὐχ ὅταν ἐν τέλει ᾖ).
[56]   Cf. *DP* II 149.16-23.

object of desire (τὸ ὀρεκτόν). Just as an inquiry comes to an end with the attainment of truth, an irrational desire ends when it reaches its object.

Damascius' interpretation of the 'mixture of intellect and pleasure' thus hinges on a double distinction: (1) between process and end (movement and rest); and (2) between the lower and higher functions of the soul, i.e., desire (in the strict sense, belonging to the lowest function of the soul) and to cognition (in the strict sense, belonging to intellect). One can bring this together in the following scheme:

$$
\text{intellect} \left\{
\begin{array}{ccc}
\gamma\nu\hat{\omega}\sigma\iota\varsigma & = \tau\epsilon\hat{\upsilon}\xi\iota\varsigma = & \dot{o}\rho\epsilon\kappa\tau\acute{o}\nu \\
\uparrow & & \uparrow \\
\zeta\acute{\eta}\tau\eta\sigma\iota\varsigma & = \dot{o}\delta\dot{o}\varsigma\ \dot{\epsilon}\pi\acute{\iota}\ \tau\iota\ \tau\acute{\epsilon}\lambda o\varsigma = & \ddot{o}\rho\epsilon\xi\iota\varsigma
\end{array}
\right\} \text{lower soul}
$$

Of these four terms, only two are mentioned in the 'mixture of pleasure and intellect': cognition and desire. Each of these belongs naturally to a specific level in reality (although they can be brought together by using the terms in a broader sense). These are the two extremes: the movement of the lower functions of the soul and the rest of the intellect. Damascius seems to argue that the two other terms (the inquiry of cognition and the attainment of the object of desire), but also all intermediate levels of reality (each of them representing a proper combination of a kind of cognition and a kind of desire), are implied by mentioning the extremes[57].

This double distinction serves as a basis for the definition of pleasure. Pleasure, which has already been explicitly distinguished from desire, will be attributed to every branch of the scheme: it is yielded by the movement towards the end as well as by its attainment. So it occurs in ὄρεξις and ζήτησις, as well as in the attainment of the ὀρεκτόν and the γνῶσις[58]. Damascius says this explicitly at §185,

---

[57] This seems to have been a more general hermeneutical principle of Damascius; cf. 56.4-5: μήποτε δὲ καὶ τὰς ἐν μέσῳ συνείληφεν κατά τε τὸ εἰωθὸς ἐν τοῖς ἄκροις.

[58] On the basis of this statement, Damascius was able to state that pleasure in the mixture stands for 'desire' — 13.1-2.

stating that pleasure occurs 'in some forms of cognition as well as in
some forms of desire'[59]. We will return to this text, which clearly shows
Damascius' intention to situate pleasure at both poles of the mixture
— something which would not be possible using the terminology of
'intellect versus pleasure' in a rigid way.

4.3. 'Essence' and the 'Way towards the Essence'

The main distinction set out in the previous analysis is that between
the movement towards a certain condition (the ὁδὸς ἐπί τι τέλος,
manifested paradigmatically in irrational ὄρεξις) and the attained
condition itself (the τεῦξις, under the paradigm of the attained γνῶσις),
a distinction that holds at all subsequent levels of reality.

This distinction corresponds exactly to that which forms the main
thesis of Damascius' psychology. In this respect, the 'τεῦξις' is the
οὐσία of the soul, whereas the 'ὁδὸς ἐπί τι τέλος' is the way towards this
οὐσία, the activity of the soul that leads to its substantial change. As we
saw, Damascius sometimes calls this 'substance' the 'natural condition'. An 'activity according to nature', then, is an activity that corresponds to the οὐσία of the soul.

Damascius himself establishes this connection between 'οὐσία' and
'τεῦξις of the end' more than once in *In Philebum*. At §136 he states that

> activity is movement towards being, from which it has detached itself
> and to which it is therefore impatient to return. (136.11-12)

So there is a distinction between οὐσία as an end and the activity that
tends towards this end[60]. Indeed, in his psychology, Damascius maintains that the substance of the soul changes according to the activities
of the soul (cf. supra). This presupposes that the soul's activity is not
always congruent with its substance. The activity can 'detach' itself
from the substance and evolve in a different direction, which eventually results in a substantial change[61].

---

[59] On the basis of this statement, Damascius said that in cognition, too, pleasure
is present — 13.2-3.

[60] 215.6-7: καὶ γὰρ πᾶσα ἐνέργεια γένεσίς τε καὶ ἕνεκά του· διὰ γὰρ οὐσίαν καὶ
σπεύδουσα ἐπ'αὐτήν. Cf. 94.3-4 (the end is the οὐσία); §70; cf. *DP* II 81.25-26.

[61] Of course, this does not have to be the result. It remains possible that the
activity, after a 'painful' departure from the οὐσία, returns to it. Precisely this return
furnishes a kind of pleasure, as we will see below.

One of the presuppositions of this theory is the thesis that 'activity' pertains not only to the movement towards substance but also to substance itself, a thesis that Damascius explicitly maintains[62]. So both the natural condition and the way towards it have their proper activities.

This is of central importance for Damascius' theory of pleasure. For it allows him to attribute 'pleasure' to both elements. His basis for doing so is the Aristotelian definition of pleasure, according to which pleasure in all cases is a by-product of unimpeded *activity*. So, Damascius' analysis consists mainly in a 'return to Aristotle', whom he follows in maintaining that, in addition to pleasure in movement, there is pleasure at rest. On this, then, he dissents from the Platonic tradition, which situates pleasure (in the literal meaning of the word) exclusively in the movement towards the natural condition, and not in the natural condition itself.

5. 'Struggling with Tradition'

Damascius' innovative opinion cannot readily be reconciled with the Platonic definition of pleasure, the authority of which was beyond questioning. In a very typical procedure, Damascius tries after all to reconcile his position with the traditional view. In most cases, his starting point is the position of Proclus, a position that he immediately modifies in order to harmonise with his own opinions. These two 'steps' in the interpretation are not actually distinguished in Damascius' own analyses, a fact that seriously hinders one's reading of *In Philebum*. For present purposes, however, we will distinguish them throughout.

---

[62] 145.3-4: ἐπειδὴ δὲ καὶ αὐτὸς [*sc.* ὁ κατὰ φύσιν βίος] κατὰ φύσιν ἐνεργεῖ ... Cf. 190.3: ἀνεμποδίστως ἐνεργούσης τῆς φύσεως. 136.8-11: ἔνεστι γάρ τι ἐν νῷ τὸ κατὰ φύσιν καὶ τὸ πρὸς τοῦτο ὁδεύειν, ἀλλ᾽ ἐν τῷ ὡδευκέναι τὸ εἶναι ἔχον· σύνεστι γὰρ ἡ πεπηγυῖα ἡδονή. αὐτὸ γὰρ τὸ κατὰ φύσιν ἡ οὐσία ἐστὶν ἧς τῇ ἐνεργείᾳ σύνεστιν ἡ ἡδονή. For this text: cf. *infra*, p.163. In *DP* II 80.5-82.15, Damascius shows that οὐσία as well as κίνησις are kinds of ἐνέργεια. He even states that there is a 'passive activity': the activity of undergoing.

5.1. *The Proclean Position*

As we saw, in Plato's definition[63] pleasure is considered to be the restoration of a previous lack. The central issue here is the notion of a 'natural condition': the perfect harmony that is disturbed when we experience lack and pain. Pleasure, then, is enjoyed in the return toward this condition. Although yet another lack always interferes, which implies that we never fully attain the natural condition, this natural condition surely is the final term toward which our pleasure is directed. So, clearly, Plato's definition turns upon the *movement* toward the natural condition.

In Damascius' commentary, this passage is treated at §141-145. According to the author, we are here at the beginning of the third part of the *Philebus*: the systematic discussion of the 'mixed good'[64]. Plato starts this discussion, Damascius says, from the bottom upwards. Plato first speaks about corporeal pleasure[65], and for this category Damascius literally adopts the Platonic wording:

> First comes the cause of pain and pleasure, namely, want or repletion: consequent on this cause there is motion towards the preternatural or the natural condition, not of course simultaneously; after these come pleasure and pain. (143.1-4)

Thus, pleasure is linked with the movement toward the natural condition[66]. Damascius also agrees with Plato concerning the natural condition itself: life κατὰ φύσιν does not imply movement, because it remains constantly in this condition. So *by definition* there is neither pleasure nor pain in this life. At §144, Damascius puts this very clearly:

> In a life in complete accordance with nature, he [Plato] says, there is neither pleasure nor pain; for it is not subject to change, since it never swerves from its natural condition; and because it does not change, it cannot be aware of any 'shock'[67]. (144.1-3, tr. Westerink modified)

---

[63] *Phil.* 32 a 8 – b 4; cf. supra.

[64] This mirrors the division presented at *In Phil.* 7.

[65] 141.1-4.

[66] Damascius complements this definition with an etymology of the terms ἡδονή and λύπη: λύπη is the dissolution (λύειν) of sight (ὀπωπέναι), which serves as the paradigm of sensitive life; hence λυ-όπη. The ἡδονή is the return, the new way (ἠοδονέα) towards τὸ κατὰ φύσιν (142.6-9).

[67] 'Shock' (πληγή) is a Stoic term, indicating a sharp contraction of the soul caused by a mere appearance, which is not yet emotion so long as there is no assent and therefore no judgment, e.g., growing pale, shedding tears, male stiffening (cf. Seneca, *De Ira* 2.1-4, Cic., *Tusc.* III 83). Westerink misses this point by translating it

He dwells on this point at §151. In his discussion of Plato's statements that the neutral life, without pleasure or pain, is the most divine (θειότατος) and that the gods do not know pleasure or pain (*Phil.* 33 b 6-9), Damascius adds the following remark:

> This absence of joy and pain also characterises the vehicles of divine souls, which, because they never deviate toward the preternatural, cannot feel joy[68] on returning to the natural condition. (151.5-7)

In §154 this reasoning is adapted to the intellect:

> As for intellect, here, too, there can hardly be any pain, but only a disposition that transcends both pleasure and activity [...] At every level, then, cognition manifests itself most clearly in the neutral life, because, to be intellect, it does not need pleasure, as pleasure does need intellect if it is to be pleasure. (154.3-8)

In these three cases, we find a clear instance of the claim that whatever does not have a movement to and from its natural condition cannot have pleasure[69].

Although the definition of pleasure implied here is clearly Platonic, a thoroughgoing change has occurred in comparison with the *Philebus*, particularly concerning the 'natural condition'. In the *Philebus*, this condition (the final term that directs our striving for pleasure) was defined only in a negative way, as the 'restoration of all lack'. Since Aristotle, however, the perspective has changed. The natural condition has become an accessible ideal: the perfect performance of a natural ability. And this counts for every single vital function: body, soul, and

---

as 'vehement affliction'. I am very grateful to R. Sorabji for having brought this to my attention.

[68] The term that Damascius uses here is not ἥδεσθαι, but rather the qualitatively superior χαίρειν, thus taking over the Stoic and Plotinian terminology. So the 'pleasure' under discussion is not merely 'corporeal' or 'inferior'; rather, it implies any kind of pleasurable experience. Thus, the question is stated in a still more radical way.

[69] The statement that the natural condition does not entail pleasure is also put forward explicitly in §196: 'When the natural condition has been attained, there is no longer any pleasure, because there is no discomfort now.' (196.5-6: ἐλθοῦσα εἰς τὸ κατὰ φύσιν οὐκέτι ἥδεται ἅτε λύπης οὐκέτι μετέχουσα. It is not clear what is the subject of this sentence. In the given context, it should be 'ἐπιθυμία', but strictly speaking there could be no question about 'desire', once the natural condition is attained. The most probable explanation is that Damascius refers to ψυχή, which is the implicit logical subject). However, this passage is not completely reliable as an expression of Damascius' opinion, since it is only a paraphrase of the *Philebus* passage where Socrates discusses the opinion that pleasure, being only the relief from pain, does not exist — a position with which Socrates does not totally agree (*Phil.* 44 a 12 – d 6).

intellect all have their own natural conditions[70]. Damascius, in accordance with the theories of *eudaemonia* of Aristotle, Plotinus, and Proclus, adds a normative description to this general outline: the natural condition of man is to be found in man's highest faculties, i.e., in the perfect performance of intellectual activity[71].

Although the natural condition does not entail any pleasure, this 'life according to the intellect' must produce a specific supervenient affection, in order to be the object of our desire. At §13 Damascius calls this affection 'well-being' (εὐπάθεια):

> To this [i.e., the attainment of the object of desire], one might, for want of a more appropriate term, apply the word 'well-being'. Plato uses the current word 'pleasure', not, however, in the sense of the pleasure that attends attainment, but that which is coincident with attainment and is prior to pleasure properly so called. It would be illogical in any case to parallel a lower existent with one belonging to a higher order. (13.9-12)

Thus, the pleasure that occurs here cannot be *genuine* pleasure, or 'pleasure in the true sense of the word': it has left behind this pleasure-in-movement. Genuine pleasure is relegated to a lower (ἑπομένη) level of reality. At §210 Damascius readdresses this issue, raising the question of why Plato calls pure pleasure (pleasure without any pain) 'divine'. A possible reason, Damascius says, for Plato to put things this way is that divine beings do not have any pain at all, although they always experience well-being and joy (εὐπαθοῦσιν ἀεὶ καὶ εὐφραινο-μένοις, 210.3-5).

According to this line of argumentation, the higher affection is always regarded as belonging to a rank different from that of 'pleasure', which is confined to lower reality and always associated with previous pain. In taking this position, Damascius is in full agreement with Proclus' theory of pleasure as outlined above. The Platonic definition of pleasure applies here only to the 'lower' (i.e., corporeal) forms of pleasure; for higher 'pleasure', such other terms as εὐπάθεια and εὐφροσύνη are required.

---

[70]   This can be inferred from the survey of the different kinds of pleasure listed in §155 (cf. infra). Cf. also the formula 'τὸ οἰκεῖον κατὰ φύσιν' in 136.7-8.

[71]   Cf. Arist., *NE* X 7, 1177 a 12-18.

5.2. *Damascius' 'Correction' of Proclus' Position*

Like Proclus, Damascius appropriates the definition of Aristotle, according to which pleasure is a supervenient element of the unimpeded (perfect) performance of an activity (ἐνέργεια)[72]. Damascius repeatedly employs this phrase[73], mostly as a premiss in an argument. It appears from this use that the phrase was known to his readers/students and accepted without much ado.

Damascius places more importance on this Aristotelian phrase than does Proclus, even to the extent of eventually replacing the strict terms of the Platonic definition.

As we have seen above, Damascius draws a distinction between activity in movement and activity at rest. The former he considers to be the 'way towards substance', whereas the latter he regards as occurring in the attained 'natural condition' (or substance) itself[74]. This has important repercussions for the theory of pleasure: if one agrees with Aristotle that pleasure occurs in a perfectly performed activity, and if one distinguishes between two forms of activity, as Damascius does, then one has to acknowledge that pleasure occurs both in the way towards the natural state and in the attained natural condition itself.

Proclus avoids this conclusion by stressing the fact that according to the Platonic definition no pleasure can exist in the attained natural condition. Although we perform a certain activity (at rest) in our natural condition, and although a perfectly performed activity produces pleasure, there cannot be (Proclus suggests) any question of pleasure in the literal sense in this case.

So, although at first sight Damascius agrees with the Proclean position, he radically shifts the perspective. He accepts the Aristotelian definition, stating consistently that 'higher' activity, too, produces genuine pleasure. This we find very clearly stated at §136:

> For in intellect, too, there is a natural condition [...] the natural condition is nothing else but the essence, the activity of which is attended by the sensation of pleasure. (136.8-11)

---

[72] Arist., *NE* X 4, 1174 b 14-1175 a 21.

[73] See, e.g., 87.2-3: ὅλως ἀεὶ τῇ ἀνεμποδίστῳ ἐνεργείᾳ κατὰ φύσιν οὔσῃ σύνεστιν ἡδονή. 121.10: ἀεὶ γὰρ τῇ ἀνεμποδίστῳ ἐνεργείᾳ ἕπεται ἡδονή. 150.10: ταῖς δὲ ἐνεργείαις ἕπονται καὶ αἱ ἡδοναί.

[74] Cf. supra, p.154-155.

This change of perspective is also evident in Damascius' interpretation of the strict link established by Plato between 'pleasure' and 'movement'. At §143, Damascius modifies the relation between the two, by stating that they are surely not identical:

> Thus seen, the movements themselves are distinct from the attendant pleasures or pains; but because pleasure and pain are inseparable from the movements, he [Plato] sometimes applies the word 'movement' to these too. (143.6-8)[75]

This modification is less innocuous than it might appear at first sight. By drawing a very clear distinction between pleasure and (perceived) movement (a distinction not made by Plato), Damascius opens the way towards the acceptance of a second kind of pleasure: pleasure at rest.

In doing so, Damascius returns to Aristotle's theory of pleasure in its original form: there is pleasure at rest and pleasure in movement. Eventually, however, he proclaims himself a true Platonist, trying to reconcile this view with the Platonic definition.

Yet, this 'revolutionary' position, by means of which he dissents from Proclus and the entire Platonic tradition, is never presented as an innovation. It strikes the reader as though Damascius formulates his unorthodox opinions hesitantly and, as it were, incidentally. But this does not render the innovation less radical; nor does it preclude one from deducing this position from the details of Damascius' treatment. For the Proclean position that is initially adopted is, throughout the commentary, immediately modified. Thus, for instance, the interpretation of the definition of pleasure at §144, where Damascius clearly takes over Proclus' thesis, is tempered in the immediately following text (§145):

> It is true that the completely natural life does not admit of those pains and those pleasures that are mentioned here, i.e., the kind that attends a change from the preternatural to the natural or conversely; but as such a life, too, has a natural activity of its own, and activities are accompanied by a kind of pain and pleasure that does not come with a shock, but quietly, they must be of a quiet nature in that life. That is why he indirectly hints at them himself, saying that the natural condition is not attended by pleasure and adding that this is to be understood as violent pleasure. (145.1-7, trans. Westerink modified)

---

[75] The same distinction is to be found at 215.3-4: (pleasure is) οὐκ αὐτὸ ὅπερ ἡ γένεσις, ἀλλὰ τὸ ἑπόμενον τῇ κινήσει ἤτοι τὸ ἐπιγιγνόμενον. See also 35.1: Ὅτι ἅμα κινήσει ἡ ἡδονή, παρακολούθημα γάρ.

Unlike the position we can deduce from §144, it appears from this passage that one cannot say that the natural condition does not have any pleasure. For 'he' only means, according to Damascius, that pleasure in this condition is 'quiet' or 'mild', as opposed to the 'violent' pleasure in the movement towards the natural condition.

Contrary to the thesis of L.G. Westerink[76], the notion of a 'quiet pleasure' is not opposed to Plato's theory. Westerink claims that Plato never uses this term in the *Philebus* and that, accordingly, the additions at the end of §145 (put forward in the third person) should be ascribed to Proclus. But, although this term does not occur in the *Philebus*, it clearly has a Platonic basis. One can infer this from Plato's characterization of true pleasure: in this kind of pleasure, the previous lack is imperceptible and does not cause pain. In another passage of the *Philebus* (44 d – 46 b), an absence of pain of this sort is said to result from merely a slight defect in the natural condition, whereas a serious lack results in a violent pain. If one combines the theories found in these two passages, the statement that by definition true pleasure can never be violent appears to be made implicitly by Plato in the *Philebus*. So the notion of a 'quiet' pleasure *in se* is clearly Platonic[77]. One has to admit, then, that the addition 'αὐτὸς ἐνδείκνυται' in 145.6 refers to Plato[78]: indeed, the *Philebus* does not do more than 'hint' at this quiet

---

[76] Westerink 1959, *ad* §145.

[77] The term ἠρεμαία ἡδονή also stems from Plato, though not from the *Philebus*. See, e.g., *Laws* 733 d – 734 d, where Plato states that the pleasurable life is the temperate life: it yields 'soft distresses and joys', as opposed to the licentious life, which yields violent pleasure, violent pain, etc. *Tim.* 64 a – 65 b (quoted above, p.27) presents the same reasoning as the *Philebus*: all lack is not equal; the smaller the lack, the more quiet (ἠρέμα — 64 d 2) the distress and pleasure. Perhaps, then, we ought to interpret the text of §144 in the following way: καὶ ταύτας 'ἠρέμα' εἰπὼν (*sc.* in the *Timaeus*).

[78] Westerink denies that reference is made here to Plato on the ground of two objections. In the first place, he says, 'Plato has not yet brought up the subject of the neutral life at this stage [i.e., *Phil.* 31B2-32B4].' This statement, however, appears to be erroneous, if one takes into account that the condition of 'harmony' in the passage referred to by Westerink is identified by Plato, as well as by Damascius, with what is later on called the 'neutral life'. The second objection starts from the consideration that there is nothing in the *Philebus* 'that could be read as the restriction made at 145.5-7 [i.e. the attribution of 'quiet' pleasure to the natural condition]; on the contrary, Socr. repeatedly says that, unless there is a great physical change, we feel no pleasure or pain whatever (32E5-7; 43C4-6). Consequently ... the αὐτός at 145.6 must refer to Proclus, who is, however, anticipating Plato's conclusions at 32D-33C (42D-43C).' In fact, however, in this objection the problem is distorted. Surely, for Plato the natural condition is completely devoid of pleasure, and

pleasure. Moreover, it is impossible that Damascius would quote
Proclus on this matter, as the latter opposed the view that there would
be any pleasure (even 'quiet' pleasure) in the natural condition. On the
contrary, the statement that this condition does produce pleasure, and
even 'true' pleasure, is exactly the 'revolutionary' position that marks
Damascius' dissent from the entire tradition.

The modification of the definition of pleasure at §145 is not an
isolated case. At §154, Damascius subtly revokes his former formulation, by stating that, although νοῦς does not need pleasure in order to
be νοῦς, it remains inferior to the mixed life (i.e., the good life is, after
all, a mixture of pleasure and intellect), because there is *pleasure* in the
'divine easy life' (θεία ῥᾳστώνη), in the state in which intellect is 'drunk
with nectar'[79]. The supervenient affection of the natural condition,
which before had been opposed to (lower) pleasure, is now explicitly
seen as a genuine form of pleasure.

So, after reflection, it appears that Damascius modifies the consequences of the Platonic definition (pleasure as the movement towards
the natural condition) by stating that there is pleasure in the natural
condition. Or in his own words:

> Great is the love of truth, and so is the joy of attaining it; in general,
> any undisturbed activity in its natural condition is attended by
> pleasure, so that this must be true of cognitive activity too. (87.1-4)

This idea is repeated at §§145 and 190: it is not true that we do not
experience pleasure in the neutral life. For, since the natural condition
is a kind of activity, pleasure must also occur here as a supervenient
element. Apparently, Damascius identifies the 'neutral condition' with
the 'natural condition'[80]. The name 'μηδέτερος βίος', which Plato uses

---

Damascius does indeed deviate from Plato's opinion. But this deviation is not the gist
of the passage under discussion. Rather, it is implied as a presupposition. The
emphasis in §145 lies on the *nature* of the pleasure yielded by the neutral condition,
and here, after all, Damascius takes up Platonic elements. The statement that this
pleasure must be 'quiet' is certainly Platonic, if one assumes, as Damascius does, that
this pleasure is true pleasure. However, the question remains whence Damascius
took over the addition 'καὶ προσθεὶς πληκτικάς': neither πληγή nor πληκτικός is
applied to pleasure by Plato (cf. Brandwood 1976, *s.v.*). A possible solution, suggested
by Westerink, is 'to make Plato the subject by reading 'πρόσθες πληκτικάς'' (Westerink 1959, *ad loc.*).

[79]   154.8-9: ὅτι ἐστί τις ἡδονὴ κατὰ τὴν θείαν ῥᾳστώνην ἐν τῷ 'μεθύειν τῷ νέκταρι'
τὸν νοῦν. For the term 'ῥᾳστώνη': cf. supra; for 'μεθύειν τῷ νέκταρι': see Plato, *Symp.*
203 b 5, and Plotinus, *Enn.* VI 7, 30.23-29 (cf. supra).

[80]   With this identification, Damascius deviates from Plato: in the latter's view,

to indicate a condition fully detached from all pleasure and pain, is given a paradoxical use here: this condition, according to Damascius, is not exempt from pleasure and pain; his aim is precisely to show that there is pleasure in this condition after all.

6. *Two Kinds of Pleasure*

Breaking with the tradition, Damascius maintains that there is pleasure both in the way towards the natural state and in the natural condition itself. The first is 'violent' and in motion; the latter is 'mild' and at rest. This thesis is clearly stated in the following text, extracted from §136:

> For in intellect there also is a natural condition and the progress towards it, but one that is essentially completed progress; the pleasure that attends it is constant. The natural condition, indeed, is nothing other than the essence, the activity of which is attended by the sensation of pleasure, and activity is movement towards being, from which it has detached itself and to which it is therefore impatient to return. (136.8-12)

Damascius clearly says here that the natural condition of intellect is a stable situation and that a stable pleasure is supervenient upon the activity of this situation. Opposed[81] to this is the activity in the movement towards substance. The same idea is elaborated at §94:

> What causes pleasure is either the goal itself or an activity leading to it, so that pleasure is an attendant circumstance. (94.4-5)

This position is the final consequence of the above analysis. Consistent with his theory of the soul, Damascius acknowledges that both the movement towards the end and the attained end itself are a form of 'activity'. Since he takes over Aristotle's definition, stating that an unimpeded activity is always accompanied by pleasure, he cannot but attribute pleasure in a literal sense to both cases.

---

the 'neutral condition' is the absence of all pleasure and pain, because lack and repletion are so small that they cannot be experienced. The 'natural condition', on the other hand, is the absence of all lack — a condition which we never attain in its purity. Cf. supra.

[81] One cannot but state that 136.10-11 presents two *different* kinds of ἐνέργεια: the former is yielded by the natural condition, while the latter (ἡ δὲ) is attached to the movement towards it.

This idea was also foreshadowed both in Damascius' characterization of the central theme of the *Philebus* and in his interpretation of the
mixture of 'pleasure and intellect'. He reduced this distinction to a
difference between desire and cognition, with the corollary that cognition, too, is accompanied by a kind of pleasure. On reflection, one can
see that this interpretation already involved a distinction between
movement and end, and thus that Damascius stated *in nucleo* that both
movement and end cause pleasure. By replacing the terms pleasure
and intellect with 'cognition' and 'desire', he, as it were, unglued the
term 'pleasure' from the strict terminology of the *Philebus*. In this way,
the term can be applied to both desire and cognition. Thus, Damascius' interpretation of the 'mixture' in the *Philebus* is a subtle prepara-
tion for a differentiation within pleasure. In the first case, pleasure is
regarded as a *movement*; in the second it is a *state*[82].

This connection between Damascius' interpretation of the 'mixture'
and his recognition of two forms of pleasure is made explicit:

> If anyone should remark that cognition is also a kind of movement
> towards its object, we could argue that the act of cognition itself is
> distinct from this movement, and so it is again the movement that is
> attended by pleasure. (138.1-3)

Damascius here employs the distinction he drew in §13 between
movement and end. Just as he did there he applies this distinction to
cognition: he allows an imaginary opponent to use the term 'cognition'
for the 'movement' (he himself does not do so; the issue clearly is not a
terminological matter), but he points out that this movement likewise
ends in a state, here called 'knowing' (τὸ γιγνώσκειν). So the underlying
scheme corresponds to the one given in the definition of the central
theme of the dialogue. In some cases Damascius is more explicit,
saying that pleasure is the effect of both desire (the movement) and
cognition (the 'hitting' of the end). So, for example, at §185:

> Pleasures are associated both with certain forms of cognition and with
> certain forms of desire. (185.1-2)

And elsewhere Damascius shows the bipolarity of pleasure:

> consequent on choice and cognition is pleasure, the attainment being
> either actual or anticipated.[83]

---

[82] Cf. the distinction between *kinetic* and *katastematic* pleasure in Epicurus, who is
explicitly referred to further on in the text.
[83] 126.4-5: ...ἕπεται δὲ τούτοις [*sc.* αἱρέσει and γνώσει] ἡ ἡδονή, τῆς τεύξεως ἢ

He also provides some indications of exactly how he understands the difference between the two kinds of pleasure. Lower, bodily pleasure is,
Damascius repeatedly remarks, 'violent'[84]. Higher, intellectual pleasure, on the contrary, is 'mild' and 'quiet'[85]. This might give the impression that the difference is only a *quantitative* one, which would mean that Damascius eventually and implicitly agrees with hedonism. But upon consideration, this quantitative difference is interwoven with a double qualitative distinction:

1. At §207 Damascius links the quantitative difference to a distinction based on the activity or passivity that characterises pleasure:

> Some pleasures are violent and passive, namely those that are coupled with pain; others are purely active, being observed in the animal when in a state of perfection and of activity; in others, again, there is but little passivity. (207.1-3)

Passivity and vehemence are combined here, and, consequently, the quantitative distinction is made co-extensive with a qualitative one. Moreover, Damascius recognises intermediary categories between the two extremes, which makes it possible to establish a certain classification. It should not be surprising that there is also a pleasure characterised as 'passive' (whereas pleasure is defined as the result of an activity), since Damascius explicitly states in his *De Principiis* that 'being affected' is also a kind of activity[86].

2. A second qualitative difference is based on the degree of purity of pleasure. Damascius takes over Plato's thesis that purity characterises that pleasure which is in no way contaminated by pain: it is pleasure without προλύπησις (206.1-5). This pure pleasure, Damascius adds, occurs when a faculty has attained its natural condition (206.3). This implies that every vital function can have a pure pleasure, a kind of pleasure that is not restricted to the highest realms; indeed, Damascius maintains that there is pure pleasure in the body, in the soul, and in

---

παραγιγνομένης ἢ ἐλπιζομένης. Desire (ὄρεξις, *appetitus*) is taken up here as 'choice' (αἴρεσις). The meaning of the two terms is closely related: according to Proclus' definition, αἴρεσις *(electio)* is a ...*potentia rationalis appetitiva bonorum verorumque et apparentium* (*De Provid.* 191.23-25; quoted by Westerink *ad* §126). This is, then, synonymous with what was called ζήτησις in §13: rational desire for knowledge of truth.

[84] 145.1-7; 152.2-3; 190.1-2; 207.1; intimated in 144.2 (translated above, p.156).
[85] 145.1-7; 190.3-6.
[86] Cf. supra, n.62. At §136 this passive activity is called πεπόνθησις; cf. infra.

the combination of the two of them (208.1-5). Thus, the difference based on purity is co-extensive with neither of the two aforementioned distinctions: pure pleasure is not *per se* the highest pleasure; it occurs in the natural condition of any faculty. On the other hand, Damascius applies this distinction to the hierarchy discussed above: he generally considers the 'pure' to be the 'highest', and the impure to be the 'violent' (τὸ σφοδρόν), the latter of which is situated at the lowest level (212.2-6). It is clear, then, that pure pleasure is distinguished from the impure, just as the violent is opposed to the mild. In short, the two classifications can overlap.

Thus, pleasure is clearly characterised and subdivided in a qualitative sense, at least, Damascius says, on the basis of good and evil[87]. It becomes possible, then, to classify the different kinds of pleasure according to their relative degree of participation in the good. We will return on this classification.

7. *An Original Reading of Plato*

In adopting this theory of pleasure, Damascius breaks with the Platonic tradition. Plato himself argues that there can be no pleasure in the natural condition, and this feature becomes well established in the Platonic tradition. Even the change of the perspective discussed above, by which the natural condition is seen as an accessible ideal state, does not rule out the main lines of the Platonic theory. The 'affection' (if affection it is) that occurs in this attained natural condition is considered to be pleasure only in a metaphorical sense.

Aristotle (and his disciples), on the contrary, maintain that the 'higher' pleasure (the pleasure in the good life) is indeed genuine pleasure. But Aristotle starts from a totally different definition of pleasure. And, although some elements of his doctrine (particularly his analysis of the 'natural condition') profoundly influence the Platonic tradition, his definition of pleasure never supersedes the Platonic one.

Damascius, for his part, subscribes to the Aristotelian account. He takes over Aristotle's thesis that pleasure can consist both in movement and in rest, and that both are genuine pleasures: a supervenient element of the perfect performance of an activity.

---

[87]   173.8-9: πεποίωνται ἄρα καὶ αἱ ἡδοναί, εἰ μηδενὶ ἄλλῳ, τῷ ἀγαθῷ καὶ κακῷ.

Thus, even while commenting on Plato, Damascius adheres to the Aristotelian tradition[88]. Nevertheless, he continues to count himself among the 'true Platonists'. He never says *expressis verbis* that he prefers the Aristotelian position to the Platonic one; more importantly, he tries to base his own position on the Platonic definition of pleasure. By presenting his ideas as an original interpretation of Plato, he, as it were, disguises his break with the Platonic tradition.

Concerning pleasure 'in movement' Damascius' position does not cause many difficulties, for he simply takes over the Platonic-Proclean definition. As we saw, however, he adds some elements that allow him to modify Plato's definition.

As regards pleasure 'at rest', on the contrary, Damascius manipulates the Platonic definition in order to bring it in line with his own opinion. In broad outline, there are two steps in his 'manipulation' of Plato. First, he maintains that the notion of 'pleasure at rest' is also implied in the very definition of pleasure. Second, he reduces the nature of pleasure at rest to this definition: just like pleasure in movement, this pleasure is a 'restoration'. Although Damascius himself does not clearly distinguish these two steps, we do so for didactical purposes.

§136 sheds much light on Damascius' first step. Here we find the most succinct exposition of his theory of pleasure in general; many things discussed later in the commentary are implied here. This paragraph is a recapitulation of the theory, and interrupts the analytical commentary[89]. This feature seems to indicate that the chapter is a synthesis given *en marge* of the lectures (maybe as an answer to a direct question of a student); it was inserted here when the notes were assembled.

The text contains close parallels with §13 (discussed above), but it presents the theory from a different perspective. Damascius starts with

---

[88]   The general opinion of the commentators on Aristotle is fairly close to Damascius' reading of the *Philebus*. See, e.g., Philop., *In Cat.* 3.2-4 (CAG 13); Elias (olim David), *Proleg.* 112.8-16 (CAG 18,1); Olympiodorus, *Proleg.* 5.16-18 (CAG 12,1). I thank D. O'Meara for having brought these texts to my attention. One could add Michael, *In Eth. Nic. IX-X passim*; at 530.1-24 and 546.5-9 (CAG 20) he uses the same image as did Philoponus, Elias and Olympiodorus, stating that pleasure is added to a perfect activity just like a shadow accompanies those who are walking in the sun.

[89]   Westerink (1959, *ad loc.*) states that reference is made in this paragraph to *Phil.* 31 a 8-10, where pleasure is said to pertain to the class of the unlimited. This issue, however, is only treated from §137 onwards.

a reference to the distinction between form (εἶδος) and matter. The latter is characterised by a receptivity (ἐπιτηδειότης), an upward movement (προκοπή) through which it presents itself to form. This movement of matter is termed 'πεπόνθησις' by Damascius. In his *De Principiis* and *In Parmenidem*, he uses this term as equivalent to 'μέθεξις', participation[90]. In his *Philebus* commentary[91] he establishes a parallel between this πεπόνθησις and the strained attention (ἔκτασις) of the desiring subject. The process, which characterises matter, is opposed to the form, which 'wholly and at once' imposes itself on matter (ὅλον ὁμοῦ παραγίνεται — 136.1). This is an immediate presence, without evolution, by means of which Damascius makes an allusion to what is called 'τεῦξις' (hit) at §13. The reference to §13 is clearer still insofar as Damascius adds that it is πεπόνθησις, and not pleasure, that is movement towards γνῶσις (136.5-6). So here again we find the distinction between process and result, elaborated in this case through the relation between form and matter. Again we must conclude that Damascius detaches pleasure from the opposition to intellect, which allows him, eventually, to attribute pleasure to intellect itself.

Damascius' discussion of pleasure in this paragraph begins with these distinctions. Pleasure, he says, is a consequence of the strained attention that characterises our desire[92]. This refers to the first kind of pleasure, i.e., the kind that occurs in the movement towards the natural condition. As regards the second kind, the following remarks are of major importance:

> It would even seem that all pleasure, including the invariable kind, has this character of blooming on motion towards the natural condition of anything. For in intellect there is also a natural condition and a

---

[90] Cf. Galpérine 1990, 45: 'Comme chez Platon, le langage de la participation est celui de la passion'. The term πεπόνθησις refers to the Platonic formula τὸ πεπονθὸς τὸ ἕν, *Soph.* 245 a 5 – b 10. The notion is to be linked here to what is called 'passive activity' in *DP* II 81.1-26: receptivity as the act of that whose task (ἔργον) consists in undergoing. Cf. supra, p.154-155.

[91] The use of the term in *In Phil.* is confined to this passage of §136. Nevertheless, Damascius does refer to a previous mentioning of it: 'ἣν πεπόνθησιν ἐκαλοῦμεν' (136.3), and 'τὴν πεπόνθησιν ἣν ἐλέγομεν' (136.5). This can be explained in two ways: either Damascius refers to an earlier use of the term in *In Phil.*, which entails the conclusion that the text is corrupt (this is the view of Westerink 1959, *ad loc.* and *Introd.* p.XXII), or he refers to another work in which he had previously used the term. This solution is not improbable, considering the general and digressive character of the passage.

[92] 136.4-5: ...ἡ τοῦ ὀρεγομένου ἔκτασις, ᾗ ἐπακολουθεῖ ἡ ἡδονή.

progress towards it, but one that is essentially completed progress; the pleasure that attends it is constant.[93]

Damascius starts here from the classical Platonic thesis that all pleasure occurs ('blooms', ἐπανθεῖ) in the movement towards the natural condition. He acknowledges the general validity of this thesis, but gives a very original interpretation of it. For he distinguishes two phases in the 'movement towards the natural condition': the path towards it and the end point of this path, the attained natural condition ('substance'). Pleasure, then, blooms in both of them. In holding such a position, it is possible to recognise pleasure in movement as well as at rest (i.e., the 'invariable' or 'stable' pleasure) without changing the general terms of the Platonic definition.

In such a manner is the first step in the 'manipulation' of the Platonic definition accomplished: Damascius brings the scheme of rest-movement into the definition by subtly suggesting the possibility of a broader interpretation.

In the next, decisive step Damascius identifies 'stable' pleasure with the 'true' pleasure of the *Philebus*. In his interpretation of this notion (§§205-206), Damascius is very opinative. First, he discusses Plato's thesis that pleasure occurs, not only in the dissolution of pain, but also in the restoration of a lack that was not experienced. He gives four arguments in support of this interpretation. (1) Dialectics is concerned with pure forms, which are devoid of everything that does not belong to the essence. This also counts for the notion of 'pleasure'. If it exists, it must exist apart from its counterpart. This means that the existence of the term 'pleasure' implies a real distinction between pleasure and pain. (2) The movement towards the natural condition

---

[93] 136.6-10: καὶ μήποτε πᾶσα ἡδονὴ τοιαύτη, καὶ ἡ ἀμετάβλητος, οἵα ἐπανθεῖν τῇ πρὸς τὸ οἰκεῖον κατὰ φύσιν κινήσει. ἔνεστι γὰρ καί τι ἐν νῷ τὸ κατὰ φύσιν καὶ τὸ πρὸς τοῦτο ὁδεύειν, ἀλλ'ἐν τῷ ὠδευκέναι τὸ εἶναι ἔχον· σύνεστι γὰρ ἡ πεπηγυῖα ἡδονή. The causal relation indicated by the particles requires some explanation. The first 'γάρ' (ἔνεστι γὰρ καί τι...) seems to explain the interjection 'καὶ ἡ ἀμετάβλητος'; thus, the 'constant' pleasure is directly linked to the essence of the intellect. In the second case (σύνεστι γὰρ ἡ πεπηγυῖα ἡδονή) one would expect a consecutive clause (οὖν,...), rather than a causal one, given the context. Damascius' sentence can be understood only if one admits that the notion of 'constant pleasure' has already been fully explained (or at least is supposed to be known), and that it can thereby serve as a premiss from which to deduce the existence of a state of rest in the intellect. This would show, again, that this passage does not wholly fit the given context and that it presupposes the entire Damascian theory of pleasure.

clearly differs from the movement towards a preternatural state. Thus, the form 'pleasure', which goes together with the former movement, must exist apart from the form 'pain', which occurs in the latter. (3) In an opposition, the lower always is the absence (στέρησις) of the higher[94]. Just as 'coldness' is the absence of 'warmth', and passing away the absence of coming to be, so pain is the absence of pleasure. (4) Pleasure gives rise to desire, and pain to aversion. Since aversion is the absence of desire, pain too is the absence of pleasure, rather than vice versa[95].

With the first two of these arguments, Damascius attempts to show that there is a *formal* distinction between pleasure and pain, based upon a double division: in their pure state, they both can be considered apart from their counterpart, and they occur in a totally different movement from their counterpart. We find nothing of this in the *Philebus*. On the contrary, Plato there seems to mean that there is a strict correspondence between the movement towards and the movement away from the natural condition: the greater the lack (and so the pain), the greater the restoration (and so the pleasure). 'True', or 'pure', pleasure can only occur after a minuscule lack[96]. In the third and fourth argument, Damascius starts from the idea that pain is the privation of pleasure. He thus reverses the argument of the 'δυσχερεῖς' in the *Philebus*, who argue that, since pleasure is only the absence of pain, it does not exist[97]. Here, too, we find the double distinction present in both of the previous arguments. Pain is the privation of pleasure, which also holds for the activities upon which they supervene: aversion (the basis of pain) is the privation of desire (the basis of pleasure).

None of these arguments as such are taken from the *Philebus*. Why, then, does Damascius advance them so emphatically? In fact, they serve as the basis for the explicit dissent from Plato at §206. Damascius makes use of the notion of 'true pleasure' as found in the *Philebus* to argue for a fundamental distinction between pleasure and pain, as well

---

[94]   Cf. Arist., *Met.* IV 2, 1004 b 26-27; quoted by Westerink 1959, *ad loc.*
[95]   205.1-13.
[96]   There is a slight discrepancy between lack and repletion in Plato's theory of true pleasure: the lack is too small to be experienced, and so it does not yield distress, whereas the repletion apparently is experienced, since it furnishes pleasure. Nevertheless, the general outline remains valid: true pleasure is never a 'violent' pleasure, precisely because the preceding lack was very small.
[97]   *Phil.* 44 a 12 – d 6.

as between the activities from which each of them stems. This allows him to modify Plato's definition: in its 'highest', paradigmatical form, pleasure is not linked to any previous lack, and its existence is not dependent on a 'movement by which a lack is restored'. Indeed, the natural condition does not have any lack. If, then, Damascius (unlike Plato) claims that we can attain the natural condition, life according to nature must contain some pleasure, if it is to be desirable. This pleasure is *by definition* without any previous lack.

This step is made at §206. Initially, Damascius subscribes to the Platonic explanation: true pleasure is the repletion (πλήρωσις, 1.5-6) of a lack (ἔνδεια, 1.6-7), but a lack that is not great enough to be perceptible, and thus not great enough to cause pain. Then, however, Damascius' commentary takes a peculiar turn:

> It is better to put it like this: when the natural prevails, replenishment is afforded by something that is somehow of a higher order than the natural, and of this we are entitled to say that the organism has need, not because anything has been lost, but because it was not present. (206.9-11)

So, true pleasure does not imply the repletion of a lack; it implies, rather, the gift of something that was not previously present, and that, accordingly, did not cause any lack. Damascius allows that one can call this a 'need', but only in a very specific sense. The break with Plato is obvious[98]: the typical correction of a provisional explanation ('ἤ, τό γε ἀληθέστερον...') is made here against the explanation that *Plato himself* had given. True pleasure is not the repletion of an imperceptible lack, but the gratuitous gift from a higher realm of something that the lower was not previously lacking. The lack is not too small to be perceived; it is simply absent.

Plato's definition is modified here, with the aim of 'saving' it in the new theory of pleasure. The stable pleasure is genuine 'pleasure' because it is the replenishment of something previously absent. This is the remaining 'residue' of the Platonic definition: eventually it is regarded as a 'replenishment'. But it is no longer the replenishment of a lack. This position, which is absolutely fundamental for Plato's theory of pleasure, is *de facto* overruled by means of a very subtle interpretation.

---

[98] Cf. Westerink 1959, *ad loc.*: 'either Dam. overlooked that the rejected explanation is Plato's own (51 b 5-7), or else the redactor must have taken for criticism what was meant as a supplement'.

If one regards this as a 'stable' pleasure — as Damascius would have it — then one has to accept that the gift from the higher realm never comes to an end, for that would give rise to a lack. Thus, the replenishment under discussion cannot be understood in a temporal sense, but rather 'arche-logically'; i.e., the natural condition is always already fulfilled by the higher. The pleasure that by its nature is attendant upon this fulfilment, occurs from the moment man actualises his highest faculty, i.e., intellect.

What, then, is this 'gift'? The terms 'εὐπάθεια', 'εὐφροσύνη', and 'ῥᾳστώνη', which Damascius uses to describe the natural condition[99], help to clarify this. Damascius uses these terms in accordance with Proclus, although he deviates from the latter by considering this state to be a genuine kind of pleasure. As we saw already, these terms are used to indicate the 'absence of burden' and the 'bliss' with which the gods perform their activity — an activity that consists in two elements: providence and transmitting the good to lower realms[100]. Damascius thus implies that the 'gift' from the higher consists in maintaining the lower and transmitting the good to it[101]. The happiness of intellect consists, then, precisely in its transmitting this good to that which is situated below it in reality. This implies that the good is always already 'given' to intellect itself. The stable pleasure of the intellect occurs when it experiences this gift.

This pleasure is not an accidental or accessory characteristic of the intellect. Indeed, if the gift of the higher is essentially and always already present, then the affection that is attendant on it must belong to the very essence of intellect. Damascius clearly states this:

> The mixed life has the characteristics of the preferable, for it is the only life that is perfect, adequate, and desirable; intellect has the characteristics of cognition; while the soul is the first to show those of pleasure. It is true that pleasure also exists in intellect, but as the essence of intellect and a kind of thought; for there is, in intellect, no division that could make thought and pleasure distinct functions. (257.1-5)

Again, Damascius initially follows Plato: the desirable lies in the mixed life, and the specificity of cognition lies in intellect, whereas the proper

---

[99]   *DP* I 58.5-12.
[100] Cf. supra, p.127.
[101] Cf. Proclus, *In Parm.* V 1030.26-28: κάτεισι δὲ ὁμῶς [i.e., Parmenides, despite his hesitation in front of the many] τοῦ ἀγαθοῦ ἕνεκα ἐπ᾽ εὐεργεσίᾳ τῶν δευτέρων· ἡ γὰρ χάρις αὕτη μίμησίς ἐστι τῆς προνοίας τῶν θεῶν.

characteristic of pleasure occurs for the first time in the soul. But then he qualifies this immediately: intellect, too, has its own pleasure, and the internal relation between them is stated as radically as possible. It is, Damascius says, a pleasure that belongs to the essence of the intellect, indeed, a pleasure *that even is this essence*. The cognition of intellect *is* its pleasure. It experiences nothing other than the pleasurable, natural condition, a permanent and invariable pleasure.

Yet, despite this *de facto* identity of cognition and pleasure, Damascius draws a distinction in principle between them, calling pleasure an 'accompanying element' (παρακολούθημα) throughout[102]. Moreover, when one takes these terms very strictly, there is a distinction between stable pleasure and the 'ῥαστώνη'. 'Ῥαστώνη' is understood as the act of transmitting the good to the lower, and thus stresses the relation of intellect with the lower. Stable pleasure, on the contrary, is the experience of the gift that comes from the higher (the Good), and is thus based upon the relation of intellect with the higher.

8. *A Hierarchy of the Kinds of Pleasure*

On the basis of the preceding analyses it has now become possible to demonstrate a hierarchical structure within Damascius' theory of pleasure. At §13 the distinction between process and end is established, and the double definition of pleasure is based upon this distinction. This double definition, however, does not cover the entire scheme implied at §13. Of the four terms mentioned there (rational and irrational, movement and end), only the two extremes are discussed in the preceding text. The distinction between the two kinds of pleasure corresponds to the distinction between the irrational desire and the rational end. The intermediate terms are not discussed explicitly.

At §155 the space between the two extremes (i.e., the two poles of the double definition of pleasure) is filled up. Here, Damascius establishes an entire hierarchy of seven different species of pleasure, each of which corresponds to a specific level of reality:

> There are a great many phases of pleasure: (1) some pleasures are of the body, attending a change towards the natural condition; (2) others, which belong to the soul, have a similar origin, namely, a movement from the preternatural to the natural; (3) or from one natural

---

[102] 35.1; 94.5; 218.7.

condition to another, as in the case of ever-perfect souls, which, as they pass on from one object of cognition to another, delight in each, but above all in that which has last presented itself; (4) some pertain to a changeless condition of the soul, if it exists; (5) then there is the pleasure of intellect that attends its activity; (6) and that which belongs to its essence, as heat belongs to the essence of fire, and this I call the very paradigm of pleasure; (7) and above this the Goddess herself. What transcends these is beyond pleasure. (155.1-9)

These seven forms of pleasure are divided into four large groups: corporeal pleasure, pleasure of the soul, pleasure of intellect, and the goddess 'Pleasure'[103].

Concerning corporeal pleasure, the situation is clear: it occurs in the movement towards the natural condition. We have seen that for this class the Platonic definition remains unchanged.

Pleasure of the soul is divided into three species. The first has the same structure as bodily pleasure: it occurs in the restoration of a condition contrary to nature. The second alludes to the specific natural activity of the rational soul, which consists in a discursive transition from one form to another. Unlike intellect, which contemplates 'everything at once', the soul acquires knowledge by directing itself towards the multitude of different forms[104]. Damascius now states that the performance of this natural activity gives rise to pleasure, a pleasure which, thus, does not consist in the transition from a condition against nature to the natural one. Every single act of contemplation of a form is a performance of the natural condition of the soul; and thus the pleasure that occurs in this case is attendant upon the transition from one natural condition to another. As regards the third species, pleasure in the unchanging condition of the soul, Damascius immediately doubts whether it exists. As we saw already, Damascius cannot accept that the substance of the soul is unchangeable[105].

Pleasure of the intellect is divided into two: pleasure of the activity of the intellect and pleasure of its substance. As Damascius explains at *DP* II 80.5-82.15, 'ἐνέργεια of the intellect' refers to the transitive activity directed towards what is outside the intellect itself. The 'οὐσία', then, indicates that which in *In Phil.* 155 is termed 'internal activity of the intellect': a state of rest in the substance of the intellect.

---

[103]   At §35 this hierarchy is combined with the hierarchy of the different kinds of 'activity', although the classification here is much less nuanced.

[104]   Cf. Procl., *In Parm.* III 808.6-14.

[105]   Cf. supra, p.143-144.

The pleasure attendant upon this state, which was discussed in the previous section, is explicitly characterised here as the 'very paradigm of pleasure' (αὐτο τὸ παράδειγμα τῆς ἡδονῆς). This statement is of essential importance for Damascius' theory of pleasure: he confirms that this kind of pleasure is *genuine* pleasure (and not pleasure in a metaphorical sense), and that the entire range of 'pleasures', from the highest to the lowest, belongs together under one single heading.

This paradigm of pleasure is surpassed only by the goddess 'pleasure'. We have seen that at §19 Damascius calls this the Grace Euphrosune, by which he apparently means that there is a henad 'pleasure' that heads the entire series of pleasures[106]. This implies that pleasure *is* a 'primary good' (προηγούμενον ἀγαθόν). In holding this thesis, Damascius radically (though implicitly) dissents from Proclus[107]. The henad pleasure is good *in se* and transmits its goodness to all lower forms of pleasure, which are set out in one line in a gradual πρόοδος.

The culmination point of Damascius' dissent from tradition is his position that there is genuine pleasure in the natural condition. According to Damascius, in other words, there is pleasure (in the true sense of the word) that does not attend a movement towards the natural condition. In fact, in holding this, Damascius accepts the existence of a katastematic pleasure as defended by Epicurus: the highest pleasure does not consist in remedying pain, but in a condition of rest. This notion is rejected by the entire Platonic tradition, on the basis of Plato's assertion that a condition without any pain or pleasure can itself be no pleasure: misjudging this neutral state, Plato says, by regarding it as a kind of pleasure, is a form of 'false pleasure'[108]. Unlike traditional Platonists, Damascius considers the affection we experience in this state to be the highest kind of pleasure. Consistently, then, he recognises this affection in the natural condition as the Epicurean katastematic pleasure:

> Even supposing that we experience a pleasure of this kind [i.e., pleasure in the unimpeded actualization of the natural condition], it is attended by a perception equally devoid of violence; and so, if you

---

[106] Westerink 1959, *ad loc.*

[107] For the discussion of this issue between Damascius and Proclus in §19: cf. supra, p.123-124. Damascius' statement was announced already in §13, where the προηγουμένη was opposed to the ἑπομένη ἡδονή; cf. supra, p.158.

[108] *Phil.* 42 c 5 – 44 a 11; cf. supra, p.25-27.

> take changes that cause no perception at all, you will have the life that
> is here called 'neutral' in a very appropriate way. Even Epicurus
> speaks of pleasure in accordance with nature, calling it 'katastematic'.
> (190.3-7)

Damascius presents this issue as an *a fortiori* reasoning. Pleasure in the
natural state, he argues earlier on, is always 'quiet': it only leads to
non-violent experiences. However, it is possible that one undergoes
'movements' in the natural condition without having experiences of
them, not even 'non-violent' experiences. This, then, is what Plato
means by the 'neutral life': a pleasure the movement of which is not
experienced. That this *is* pleasure is clear from the reference to
Epicurus: the non-experienced movement is his katastematic pleasure.

How can Damascius maintain that a 'movement that is not
attended by experience' is pleasant after all? Once again, he takes as
his presupposition the distinction he introduced earlier in the Platonic
definition: Plato's assertion that 'pleasure is always attendant on a
movement towards the natural condition' was interpreted so as to
allow pleasure to consist in the movement as well as in the result. The
stable pleasure under discussion now is a pleasure that consists in the
attained result. It is clearly presented as a replenishment of something
that was never lacking. So, in other words, there is no replenishment of
a lack. The only thing experienced here is the *post factum* awareness of
repletion. It is the state of repletion that yields pleasure, whereas the
process of replenishment is not felt.

The position of Epicurus is not defended here (a view that could
hardly be accepted by the Platonic school), but neither is it rejected.
On the contrary, Damascius quotes it to reinforce his own point of
view. Thus, in a subtle move, tradition is pushed aside after all.

CONCLUSION

Although Plato's authority is never questioned in the Neoplatonic tradition, his theory of pleasure undergoes thorough modifications on three major points: the definition of pleasure itself, the 'natural condition', and 'true pleasure'. The main inspiration behind these changes is Aristotle's theory, although the influence of Stoicism and (particularly in the case of Damascius) Epicureanism should not be neglected.

In Plato the definition of pleasure is based on the idea that our life is constantly subject to lack and replenishment. The ultimate aim of every replenishment is a state of perfect harmony. The essential point, however, is that this 'natural condition' can never be fully attained. Of course we can partially fulfil our needs, but these fulfilments will always be thwarted by a new lack. A real attainment of this natural condition would mean an escape from the flux of lack and replenishment, which is impossible for living beings. This negative inference, however, guarantees the occurrence of pleasure: if pleasure coexists (or coincides) with the replenishment of a lack, then the absence of all lack would never be pleasurable.

This natural condition should not be confused with what Plato labels the 'neutral condition'. Whereas the natural condition concerns the (*de facto* unattainable) absence of lack and replenishment, the neutral condition consists in the absence of pleasure and distress. In the *Philebus* Plato bases the difference between them on a theory of perception: in some cases lack and replenishment are too small to be perceived, which means that they do not yield pleasure or distress.

Plato's theory also grounds the notion of 'true', or 'pure', pleasure. That this kind of pleasure is not contaminated by distress is explained by the hypothesis that in this case the lack is too small to be perceived (and thus does not cause distress), whereas the replenishment does reach the senses, and thus yields pleasure. There remains an ambiguity, however, regarding the way in which this 'pure' pleasure (which clearly is the highest pleasure) relates to the intellect in the good life. Pure pleasure is not confined to intellectual pleasure (although some pure pleasures are intellectual in nature, most of the examples given by Plato are physical pleasures); nor are intellectual pleasures always pure pleasures (indeed, most of them pertain to the class of 'mixed pleasures', since they remedy perceived lacks).

The Neoplatonists appropriate this definition, agreeing with Plato that pleasure occurs in the movement towards the natural condition. At the same time, however, they take over the Aristotelian view that the natural condition not only is the most desirable state for a living being but is also a perfectly attainable state, in which all activities are performed as they should be. For human beings, this natural condition is the perfect performance of the highest activity, i.e., intellectual activity.

It becomes very difficult, then, to accept without qualifications one inference of the Platonic definition of pleasure, namely, that the natural condition is devoid of pleasure. Later thinkers, in order to uphold the desirability of this life, maintain that at least a kind of 'pleasure' occurs in the intellectual life. The changed perspective forces them to interpret Plato in such a way as to allow for the existence of a 'pleasure' in the attained natural condition. A certain ambiguity in Plato's writings concerning the nature of 'higher' pleasure allows the Neoplatonists to use their interpretive skills. We have been able to detect two general answers to the problem, in both of which the influence of Aristotle plays a decisive role.

Plotinus and Proclus accept the Aristotelian idea that the natural condition is identical with the neutral condition. The former is a life entirely devoted to intellect, which is detached from the whirl of pleasure and distress. In this scheme, 'pleasure' merely indicates an 'affection' (in the Stoic sense) that is to be eradicated if one wants to attain the good life. Plato was thus right to infer that the natural condition does not yield pleasure at all.

In order to affirm the high value of this life, Plotinus and Proclus allow that a certain kind of 'additional element' (a term taken over from the Aristotelian definition) occurs in the attained natural condition. Since, however, this 'element' is not found in the Platonic definition, it is called 'pleasure' only in a metaphorical sense. The 'pleasure' that, according to Plato, is combined with intellect in the good life is a kind of 'well-being', or 'joy', that we feel when detaching ourselves from lower reality (and thus also from genuine pleasure). In this way, 'pure pleasure' loses its initial meaning. It now becomes — again in accordance with the Aristotelian scheme — the 'pleasure' that is the furthest removed from the afflictions of the body.

Damascius, for his part, elaborates an alternative reading that could be called 'Aristotelian' rather than 'Platonic', although the author does not explicitly reject the Platonic account. He adopts the general lines of his predecessors' interpretation: the natural condition is the neutral condition, which in turn is the unimpeded activity of the intellect. The definition of pleasure, however, is now interpreted in such a way that it actually loses its initial meaning. In contradistinction to his predecessors, who accepted the Platonic definition, and who used Aristotle's account merely to demonstrate the existence of an 'additional element' (but not pleasure) in every activity, Damascius takes over the essentials of Aristotle's definition. Pleasure no longer is the replenishment of a lack; it is rather the supervenient effect of an activity, in movement as well as at rest. The natural condition of intellect, essentially characterised as a state of rest, yields a *genuine* kind of pleasure: pleasure-at-rest, or the katastematic pleasure of Epicurus. This pleasure is true pleasure (or 'the very paradigm of pleasure'), occurring when the intellect experiences the gracious gift of the Good.

Damascius presents his ideas in the following way: he presupposes the traditional viewpoint (i.e., the doctrine of Proclus), which is then subtly replaced by his own views. Despite the subtleties, however, the departure from tradition is significant. Damascius offers a completely different definition of pleasure, even introducing the katastematic pleasure of Epicurus into the Platonic doctrine.

Thus, the last phase of Athenian Neoplatonism contains a substantial innovation in the theory of pleasure, although this innovation is presented in Platonic terminology and is disguised, as it were, as traditional material[1].

To conclude, we would like to address the issue of why Damascius deviates (though never openly) from the Platonic tradition. Why does he feel obliged to correct the earlier views on pleasure?

The main problem of Proclus' (and Plotinus') theory of pleasure resides in the absence of a real link between 'genuine' pleasure (to be situated on the level of the body) and the intellectual 'affection' (if one is entitled to use this term) that occurs in the good life. Along with the

---

[1] Thus, for Damascius' commentary on the *Philebus* we can make the same inference as does Steel 1978, 80, with regard to the commentary on the *Parmenides*: 'And so we find a very original vision of the soul in his interpretation of the *Parmenides* even though he remains, especially terminologically, indebted to the tradition.'

dualism that characterises the system there is a gap between (corporeal) pleasure, which always presupposes distress, and (intellecual) 'pleasure', without any 'προλύπησις. The two 'universes' have their own standards: the lower pleasure, which consists in the movement towards the natural condition, can never belong to the same order as the well-being that is experienced in the attained natural condition.

In fact, the need to recognise a kind of katastematic pleasure made itself felt already in Plotinus' theory. Strictly speaking, the natural condition can only be 'desirable' if it promises to yield pleasure: nobody would prefer a life without pleasure (i.e., one devoted only to the intellect). From the moment the natural condition is seen as an attainable ideal (which it is not in Plato), one should be able to attribute pleasure to this state. For how can one explain that this ultimate aim of human activity could not be desirable? Thus that pleasure which by its definition fits this condition is the katastematic pleasure of Epicurus': a pleasure at rest, transcending the whirl of lack and replenishment. According to Plotinus (and Proclus) this is not pleasure: Plato only uses the term here as a metaphor. But as we saw, it is very difficult to define the nature of this metaphorical 'pleasure': if indeed it is not pleasure, then what is it?

The ambiguity, however, precedes the Plotinian interpretation. Actually it goes back to the *Philebus*, and to the entire Platonic theory of pleasure, as it is very difficult to deduce a positive doctrine of the 'higher' pleasure. After all, Plato's discussions of pleasure are always dominated by his apparent desire to oppose 'lower' pleasures rather than to draw a positive counterbalance.

In essence, Damascius' solution is quite simple: there is no reason to introduce any gap between higher 'pleasure' and genuine pleasure. The natural condition yields genuine pleasure, too; indeed, it constitutes the paradigm of pleasure, from which the characteristics of all other kinds of pleasure can be deduced. This is a clear (though implicit) 'return to Aristotle', for whom intellectual pleasure is genuine pleasure. Even more: intellectual pleasure is a more authentic kind of pleasure than is that yielded by the replenishment of a lack; the latter can only be called pleasurable *per accidens*. This enables Damascius to affirm unambiguously that pleasure is good *per se*. All forms of pleasure are derived from their paradigm that is coexistent with the gift of the Good.

But this result renders untenable Plato's definition of pleasure. For, in order to be adapted to the natural condition itself, the notion of pleasure must be detached from the 'movement towards the natural condition'. As we have seen in discussing *In Phil.* 206, Damascius himself makes this inference. In an original interpretation he first states that Plato's definition actually implies two stages: the movement towards the natural condition and the attained natural condition itself. Next he points out that this definition also holds for 'true' pleasure, i.e., pleasure in the attained natural condition: here, too, we experience a 'replenishment', though not the replenishment of a lack. It involves the gift of something that we did not miss beforehand. Damascius in fact rejects the physiology that lies at the basis of the Platonic definition, without however (and unlike Aristotle) rejecting the definition as such.

Although the implications of this new viewpoint are primarily metaphysical (in the context of the gift of the Good to Intellect), we do find a (partial) solution to a problem that we raised in the discussion of Plato's theory of pleasure. Damascius indicates that true pleasure occurs without any previous lack. So, in his view, it is possible to detach pleasure from any lack that is replenished. For Plato this is impossible. Whereas a lack or a replenishment might occur without yielding distress or pleasure, a pleasure and distress cannot occur without a lack or its replenishment. We criticised this view because it suggests that pleasure arises automatically when certain conditions are fulfilled, as if the replenishment of a lack, when perceived, necessarily yields pleasure. Damascius' interpretation is immune to this criticism, since it implies that pleasure can occur without any previous lack. Thus, the distinction drawn between a physiological scheme and the definition of pleasure (which, although initiated by Plato, remains unfinished in his theory) is further elaborated by Damascius. One can even reconcile his view of true pleasure with that which we advanced when criticizing Plato: true pleasure is a pleasure that occurs without our expecting its arrival, without our being 'fixated' on it. In other words, true pleasure is always a 'gift'. As a matter of fact, we should like to extend this idea to include all kinds of pleasure. For the very nature of pleasure implies its unexpectedness. It cannot be manipulated, neither by consciously aspiring to replenish a lack, nor by seeking the perfection of an activity.

BIBLIOGRAPHY

I. *Ancient Sources*

[Translations and commentaries are listed in the general bibliography.]

Plato
[For the abbreviation of the titles of Plato's works we have followed Brandwood 1976, xvii]
Burnet, J. 1900-1907. *Platonis Opera*, 5 vol. (*Oxford Classical Texts*), Oxford [repr. 1988].

Aristotle (Arist.)
Bekker, I. 1970. *Aristotelis Opera ex recensione Immanuelis Bekkeri*, editio altera quam curavit O. Gigon, 5 vols., vol. 1-2 *(textus graecus)*. Berlin *(Academia Regia Borussica)* [= 1960²; 1ˢᵗ ed. 1831].
De an. = Ross, W.D. 1961. *Aristotle. De Anima.* Edited with Introduction and Commentary. Oxford [repr. 1967].
Phys. = Ross, W.D. 1936. *Aristotle's Physics.* A Revised Text with Introduction and Commentary. Oxford.
Met. = Ross, W.D. 1953. *Aristotle. Metaphysics.* A Revised Text with Introduction and Commentary, 2 vols. Oxford (1ˢᵗ ed. 1924) [repr. 1970].
EN = Bywater, J. 1894. *Aristotelis Ethica Nicomachea.* Oxford (*Oxford Classical Texts*) [repr. 1970].
    Rackham, H. 1926. *Aristotle. The Nicomachean Ethics.* Text and Translation. London and Cambridge/Mass. (*The Loeb Classical Library. Aristotle,* XIX) [repr. 1968].
MM = Susemihl, F. 1883. *Aristotelis Magna Moralia.* Leipzig (*Bibliotheca scriptorum graecorum et romanorum Teubneriana*).
Pol. = Ross, W.D. 1957. *Aristotelis Politica.* Oxford (*Oxford Classical Texts*) [repr. 1973].

Epicureans and Stoics
Cicero (Cic.):
    De fin. = Rackham, H. 1914. *Cicero, De finibus bonorum et malorum.* With an English Translation. Cambridge (*The Loeb Classical Library*) [2ⁿᵈ ed. 1931].
    Tusc. = Pohlenz, M. 1918. *Tusculanae Disputationes.* Leipzig (*Bibliotheca scriptorum graecorum et romanorum Teubneriana*) [repr. Stuttgart 1965].
Diog. Laërt. = Diogenes Laërtius, *Vitae philosophorum*, ed. Hicks, R.D. 1925. *Diogenes Laërtius. Lives of Eminent Philosophers.* With an English Translation. 2 vol. London/Cambridge-Mass. (*The Loeb Classical Library*) [repr. 1972].
Epicurus (Epic.):
    Ep. ad Menoec. = *Epistula ad Menoeceum*
    RS = *Ratae Sententiae*
    SV = *Sententiae Vaticanae* [*Gnomologium Vaticanum*]

Conche, M. 1987. *Épicure. Lettres et Maximes.* Introduction, texte et traduction avec notes. Nouvelle édition augmentée. Paris (1st ed. Villers-sur-Mer, 1977).

Diano, C. 1946. *Epicuri Ethica.* Firenze [repr. 1974. *Epicuri Ethica et Epistulae*].

Usener, H. 1887. *Epicurea.* Leipzig [editio stereotypa editionis primae Stuttgart 1966].

See also Long-Sedley 1987 [in the general bibliography].

Galen, *Plac.* = De Lacy, P. 1978.1980.1984. *Galeni De placitis Hippocratis et Platonis.* 3 vol. Berlin (*Corpus Medicorum Graecorum* V 4, 1, 2).

Posidonius: Edelstein, L., and Kidd, I.G. 1972. *Posidonius, vol. 1: The Fragments.* Cambridge.

Sen., *Ep.* = Reynolds, L.D. 1965. *L. Annaei Senecae ad Lucilium epistulae morales.* 2 vol. Oxford (*Oxford Classical Texts*).

Stobaeus (Stob.), *Ecl.* = Wachsmuth, C. 1884. *Ioannis Stobaei Anthologii libri duo priores qui inscribi solent Eclogae Physicae et Ethicae.* Berlin.

SVF = Arnim, H. von. 1903-1905. *Stoicorum Veterum Fragmenta.* 3 vols. Vol. 4 Indices ed. Adler, M. 1924. Leipzig [repr. Stuttgart 1968].

See also Long-Sedley 1987 [in the general bibliography].

Plotinus (Plot.)

Enn. = *Enneades,* ed. Henry, P., and Schwyzer, H.R. *Plotini Opera,* see H-S[1].

See also Bréhier I-VI[2]; Armstrong I-VII [in the general bibliography].

H-S[1] = Henry, P., and Schwyzer, H.R. 1951.1959.1973. *Porphyrii De vita Plotini. Plotini Opera*: *Editio maior* (*Museum Lessianum,* Series philosophica, XXXIII-XXXV), 3 t., Paris/Bruxelles/Leiden, 1951 (*V. Plot.; Enn.* I-III), 1959 (*Enn.* IV-V), 1973 (*Enn.* VI).

H-S[2] = Henry, P., and Schwyzer, H.R. 1964.1977.1982. *Porphyrii De vita Plotini. Plotini Opera*: *Editio minor.* Oxford (*Oxford Classical Texts*).

See also Schwyzer, H.R. 1987. 'Corrigenda ad Plotini Textum', in *Museum Helveticum,* 44, p.191-210.

Proclus (Procl.)

ET = *Elementatio Theologiae,* see Dodds 1933 [in the general bibliography].

TP I-VI = Saffrey, H.D., and Westerink, L.G. 1968-1998. *Proclus. Théologie Platonicienne.* Texte et traduction, 6 t. Paris (*Collection des Universités de France*).

In Parm. I-VII :

Cousin, V. 1864[2]. *Procli Philosophi Platonici Opera inedita. Pars tertia continens Procli Commentarium in Platonis Parmenidem.* Paris [Hildesheim, 1961].

Steel, C. 1982. *Proclus. Commentaire sur le Parménide de Platon.* Traduction de Guillaume de Moerbeke. Edition critique, 2 vols. Leuven/Leiden (*Ancient and Medieval Philosophy, De Wulf-Mansion Centre,* ser. I, 3-4).

K-L = Klibansky, R., and Labowsky, Carlotta. 1953. *Parmenides usque ad finem primae hypothesis nec non Procli commentarium in Parmenidem, pars ultima adhuc inedita, interprete Guillelmo de Moerbeka,* ediderunt, praefatione et adnotationibus instruxerunt — . London (*Corpus Platonicum Medii Aevi, Plato Latinus,* III).

Steel, C. 1997. 'The Final Section of Proclus' Commentary on the *Parmenides.* A Greek Retroversion of the Latin Translation', in *Documenti e Studi sulla tradizione filosofica medievale,* 8, p. 211-267.

In Tim. = Diehl, E. 1903-1906. *Procli Diadochi Commentarium in Platonis Timaeum,* 3 vol. Leipzig.

In Remp. = Kroll, W. 1899-1901. *Procli Diadochi commentarium in Platonis Rem Publicam*, 2 t. Leipzig.

In Alc. = *Proclus. Sur le Premier Alcibiade de Platon*, see Segonds 1985-86 [in the general bibliography].
> See also Westerink, L.G. 1954. *Proclus, Commentary on the First Alcibiades of Plato*. Critical Text and Indices. Amsterdam.

In Crat. = Pasquali, G. 1908. *Proclus, In Cratylum*. Leipzig [repr. with Ital. trans. and comm. in Romano, F. 1989. *Proclo: Lezioni sul Cratilo di Platone*. Catania/Roma (*Symbolon*, 7)].

Dec. Dub. = *De decem dubitationibus circa providentiam*, in Boese, H. 1960. *Procli tria Opuscula*. Latine Guilemo de Moerbeka vertente et Graece ex Isaacii Sebastocratoris aliorumque scriptis collecta. Berlin. p.3-108.

Prov. = *De providentia et fato et eo quod in nobis, ibid.* p.109-171.

De mal. subsist. = *De malorum subsistentia, ibid.* p.172-265.

In Eucl. = Friedlein, G. 1873. *Procli In Primum Euclidis Elementorum librum commentarii*. Leipzig.

Chald. Philos. = Des Places, E. *Proclus, De Philosophia Chaldaïca*, in Des Places, E. 1971. *Oracles Chaldaïques*. Texte et traduction. Paris (*Collection des Universités de France*). p.202-212.

Damascius (Dam.)

DP = Combès, J., and Westerink, L.G. 1986.1989.1991. *Damascius. Traité des premiers principes*, 3 vol. Paris (*Collection des Universités de France*).

In Parm. = Westerink, L.G., and Segonds, A.P. 1997- . *Damascius. Commentaire du Parménide de Platon, adhuc* 2 vol. Paris (*Collection des Universités de France*).
> Ruelle, C.E. 1889. *Damascius, Dubitationes et Solutiones de Primis Principiis*. Paris. Vol. II, p.5-322.
> See also Chaignet, A.E. 1897. 'Damascius. Fragment de son commentaire sur la 3ᵉ hypothèse du *Parménide*', in *Compte Rendu de l'Académie des Sciences Morales et Politiques*. p.3-42.

In Phil. = Damascius, *In Philebum*, see Westerink 1959 [in the general bibliography].

In Phaed. = Damascius, *In Phaedonem*, see Westerink 1976-77 [in the general bibliography].

Vit. Isid. = Zintzen, C. 1967. *Damascii Vitae Isidori Reliquiae*. Hildesheim.

Other Authors

Alcinous, *Didascalicus* (*Didasc.*) = Whittaker, J., and Louis, P. 1990. *Alcinoos, Enseignement des doctrines de Platon*. Introduction, texte établi et commenté par Whittaker J., et traduit par Louis P. Paris (*Collection des Universités de France*).

Aristippus: Mannebach, E. 1961. *Aristippi et Cyrenaicorum Fragmenta*. Leiden.

Aristoxenus: Macran, H.S. 1902. ΑΡΜΟΝΙΚΩΝ ΣΤΟΙΧΕΙΩΝ. *The Harmonics of Aristoxenus*. Oxford [repr. Hildesheim, 1974].

Eudoxus: Lasserre, F. 1966. *Die Fragmente des Eudoxos von Knidos*. Berlin.

Michael: Heylbut, G. 1892. *Eustratii et Michaelis et anonyma In Ethica Nicomachea Commentaria*. Berlin (*Commentaria in Aristotelem Graeca*, XX).

Or. Chald. = Des Places, E. 1971. *Oracles Chaldaïques, avec un choix de commentaires anciens*. Texte et traduction. Paris (*Collection des Universités de France*).
> See also Lewy 1956 [in the general bibliography].

Proleg. = *Prolégomènes à la philosophie de Platon*, see Westerink-Trouillard 1990 [in the general bibliography].

Simplicius (Simplic.):
  In Cat. = Kalbfleisch, K. 1907. *Simplicii in Aristotelis Categorias Commentarium.* Berlin (*Commentaria in Aristotelem Graeca*, VIII).
  In Phys. = Diels, H. 1882.1895. *Simplicii in Aristotelis Physicorum Commentaria*, 2 vol. Berlin (*Commentaria in Aristotelem Graeca*, IX-X).
Speusippus: see Tarán 1981 [in the general bibliography].
Syrianus, *In Metaph.* = Kroll, G. 1902. *Syriani in Aristotelis Metaphysica commentaria.* Berlin (*Commentaria in Aristotelem Graeca*, VI/1).

II. *General Bibliography*

Ackrill, J.L. 1965[a]. 'Aristotle's Distinction between *Energeia* and *Kinesis*', in Bambrough (ed.), *New Essays on Plato and Aristotle.* London. p.121-141.
Ackrill, J.L. 1965[b]. *Aristotle's Ethics.* London.
Ackrill, J.L. 1981. *Aristotle the Philosopher.* Oxford.
Ackrill, J.L. 1997. *Essays on Plato and Aristotle.* Oxford.
Algra, K., Barnes, J., Mansfeld, J., and Schofield, M. 1999. *The Cambridge History of Hellenistic Philosophy.* Cambridge.
Annas, Julia. 1980. 'Aristotle on Pleasure and Goodness', in Rorty 1980[b], p.285-299.
Annas, Julia. 1981. *An Introduction to Plato's Republic.* Oxford.
Armstrong I-VII = Armstrong, A.H. 1966-1988. *Plotinus. The Enneads.* With an English Translation, 7 vol. Cambridge-Mass./London (*The Loeb Classical Library*).
Armstrong, A.H. 1940. *Plotinus. The Architecture of the Intelligible Universe in the Philosophy of Plotinus.* Amsterdam [repr. 1970].
Armstrong, A.H. 1979. *Plotinian and Christian Studies.* London.
Armstrong, A.H. 1984. 'Dualism, Platonic, Gnostic, and Christian', in Runia, D.T. (ed.). 1984. *Plotinus amid Gnostics and Christians.* Amsterdam. p.37-41. [Repr. in Armstrong 1990, ch. XII].
Armstrong, A.H. 1990. *Hellenic and Christian Studies.* London.
Aubenque, P. 1962. *Le problème de l'être chez Aristote.* Essai sur la problématique Aristotélicienne. Paris.
Aubenque, P. 1971. 'Plotin et le dépassement de l'ontologie grecque classique', in *Le Néoplatonisme.* Actes du colloque international du Centre National de la Recherche Scientifique, Royaumont, 9-13 juin 1969. Paris. p.101-109.
Aubenque, P. 1986. *La Prudence chez Aristote.* 3ème édition revue et augmentée d'un appendice sur la prudence chez Kant. Paris [1st ed. 1963].
Barnes, J. 1982. *Aristotle.* Oxford.
Beierwaltes, W. 1971. 'Andersheit. Zur neuplatonischen Struktur einer Problemgeschichte', in Schuhl-Hadot 1971, p.365-372.
Beierwaltes, W. 1972. 'Andersheit: Grundriss einer neuplatonischen Begriffsgeschichte', in *Archiv für Begriffsgeschichte*, 16, p.166-197.
Beierwaltes, W. 1975. 'Das Problem der Erkenntnis bei Proklos', in *De Jamblique à Proclus.* Vandœuvres/Genève (*Entretiens de la Fondation Hardt sur l'antiquité classique*, 21). p.153-183.
Beierwaltes, W. 1979. *Proklos. Grundzüge seiner Metaphysik.* Frankfurt (*Philosophische Abhandlungen*, 24) [2. durchgesehene und erweiterte Auflage, 1st ed. 1965].

Beierwaltes, W. 1985. *Denken des Einen*. Studien zur Neuplatonischen Philosophie und ihrer Wirkungsgeschichte. Frankfurt.

Beierwaltes, W. 1990. 'Einheit und Identität als Weg des Denkens', in Melchiorre, V. (ed.). *L'uno e i Molti*. Milano. p.3-47.

Benitez, E.E. 1989. *Forms in Plato's Philebus*. Assen.

Bentham, J. 1948. Lafleur, Laurence J. (ed.). *An Introduction to the Principles of Morals and Legislation*. New York/London.

Beutler, R. 1939. art. 'Olympiodoros, 13', in *Paulys Realencyclopädie der classischen Altertumswissenschaft*, XVIII, 1. Stuttgart. col. 207-227.

Beutler, R. 1957. art. 'Proklos', in *Paulys Realencyclopädie der classischen Altertumswissenschaft*, XXIII, 1. Stuttgart. col. 186-247.

Bidgood, R.A. 1982. *Hedonism in Plato's Protagoras and Gorgias*. Ph.D. diss. Univ. Massachusetts.

Blumenthal, H.J. 1971. *Plotinus' Psychology*. His Doctrine of the Embodied Soul. The Hague.

Blumenthal, H.J. 1972. 'Aristotle in the Service of Platonism', in *International Philosophical Quarterly*, 12, p.340-364.

Blumenthal, H.J., and Lloyd, A.C. (eds.). 1982. *Soul and the Structure of Being in Late Neoplatonism*. Liverpool.

Blumenthal, H.J. 1987. 'Plotinus in the Light of Twenty Years' Scholarship, 1951-1971', in *Aufstieg und Niedergang der Römischen Welt*, II, 36.1. Berlin/New York. p.528-570.

Bodéus, R. 1983. 'L'autre homme de Plotin', in *Phronesis*, 28, p.256-264.

Bolotin, D. 1985. 'Socrates' Critique of Hedonism: A Reading of the *Philebus*', in *Interpretation*, 13, p.1-13.

Bos, E.P., and Meijer, P.A. (eds.). 1992. *On Proclus and his Influence in Medieval Philosophy* Leiden (*Philosophia antiqua*, 53).

Boss, G., and Seel, G. (eds.). 1987. *Proclus et son Influence*. Actes du Colloque de Neuchâtel, juin 1985, éd. par -, avec une introduction de Brunner, F. Zürich.

Bostock, D. 1986. *Plato's Phaedo*. Oxford.

Bostock, D. 1988. 'Pleasure and Activity in Aristotle's Ethics', in *Phronesis*, 33, p.251-272.

Brandwood, L. 1976. *A Word Index to Plato*. Leeds (*Compendia*, 8).

Bréhier I-VI^2 = Bréhier, É. 1924-1938. *Plotin, Ennéades*. Texte et traduction, 7 t. Paris (*Collection des Universités de France*).

Bréhier, É. 1928. *La philosophie de Plotin*. Paris [repr. 1961].

Breton, S. 1985. 'L'Un et l'être', in *Revue philosophique de Louvain*, 83, p.5-13.

Broadie, Sarah. 1991. *Ethics with Aristotle*. New York/Oxford.

Burnet, J. 1900. *The Ethics of Aristotle*. London [repr. 1973].

Bury, R.G. 1926. *Plato. Laws*, 2 vols. Cambridge-Mass./London (*The Loeb Classical Library*).

Bussanich, J.R. 1988. *The One and Its Relation to Intellect in Plotinus*. A Commentary on Selected Texts. Leiden (*Philosophia Antiqua*, 49).

Bussanich, J.R. 1990. 'The Invulnerability of Goodness: the Ethical and Psychological Theory of Plotinus', in Cleary, J. (ed.). 1990. *Proceedings of the Boston Area Colloquium in Ancient Philosophy*, 6, p.151-184.

Charrue, J.-M. 1978. *Plotin, lecteur de Platon*. Paris.

Chrétien, J.-L. 1980. 'Le Bien donne ce qu'il n'a pas', in *Archives de Philosophie*, 43, p.263-277.

Chrétien, J.-L. 1989. 'L'analogie selon Plotin', in *Les Etudes Philosophiques*, 3/4, p.305-318.

Combès, J. 1987[a]. 'Les trois monades du *Philèbe* selon Proclus', in Pépin-Saffrey 1987, p.177-190 [repr. in Combès 1989, p.223-243].

Combès, J. 1987[b]. 'Proclus et Damascius', in Boss-Seel 1987, p.221-246 [repr. in Combès 1989, p.245-271].

Combès, J. 1989. *Études Néoplatoniciennes*. Grenoble.

Cooper, J. 1977. 'Plato's Theory of the Human Good in the *Philebus*', in *Journal of the History of Philosophy*, 74, p.714-730.

Cooper, N. 1968. 'Pleasure and Goodness in Plato's *Philebus*', in *Philosophical Quarterly*, 18, p.12-15.

Cornford, F.M. 1937. *Plato's Cosmology*. The *Timaeus* of Plato Translated with a Running Commentary, London [repr. 1966].

Corrigan, K., and O'Cleirigh, P. 1987. 'The Course of Plotinian Scholarship from 1971 to 1986', in *Aufstieg und Niedergang der Römischen Welt*, II, 36.1. Berlin/New York. p.571-623.

Cosenza, P. (ed.). 1996. *Il Filebo di Platone e la sua fortuna*. Atti del Convegno di Napoli, 4-6 novembre 1993. Napoli.

Cropsey, J. 1988-89. 'On Pleasure and the Human Good: Plato's *Philebus*', in *Interpretation*, 16, p.167-192.

Davidson, D. 1949. *Plato's Philebus*. Ph.D. diss. Harvard University (repr. with new Preface, New York 1990).

de Gandillac, M. 1952. *La sagesse de Plotin*. Paris [repr. 1966].

Des Places, E. 1971. *Oracles Chaldaïques. Avec un choix de commentaires anciens*. Paris (*Collection des Universités de France*).

Diès, A. 1927. *Autour de Platon*, 2 vols. Paris. II. 385-399.

Diès, A. 1941. *Platon. Philèbe*. Paris (*Collection des Universités de France*) [repr. 1993].

Dillon, J. 1996. 'Speusippus on Pleasure', in Algra, K.A., van der Horst, P.W., and Runia, D.T., *Polyhistor*. Studies in the History and Historiography of Ancient Philosophy Presented to Jaap Mansfeld on his Sixtieth Birthday. Leiden (*Philosophia Antiqua*, 72). p.99-114.

Dixsaut, Monique (ed.). 1999. *La fêlure du plaisir*. Etudes sur le *Philèbe* de Platon. Vol. 1: *Commentaires*. Vol. 2: *Contexte*. Paris.

Dodds, E.R. 1933. *Proclus, The Elements of Theology*. A Revised Text with Translation, Introduction and Commentary. Oxford [1963[2], repr. 1992].

Dodds, E.R. 1959. *Plato: Gorgias*. A Revised Text with Introduction and Commentary. Oxford.

Dörrie-Baltes I-IV = Dörrie, H. 1987-1993. *Der Platonismus in der Antike*. Grundlagen, System, Entwicklung. Begründet von H. Dörrie, fortgeführt von M. Baltes unter Mitarbeit von F. Mann. 4 Bde. Stuttgart/Bad Canstatt.

Edwards, R.B. 1979. *Pleasures and Pains*. A Theory of Qualitative Hedonism. Ithaca/London.

Elster, J. 1983. *Sour Grapes*. Studies in the Subversion of Rationality. Cambridge/Paris.

Emilsson, E.K. 1988. *Plotinus on Sense-Perception: A Philosophical Study*. Cambridge.

Erler, M. 1994. 'Epikur. Die Schule Epikurs. Lukrez', in Flashar H. (ed.). 1994. *Grundriss der Geschichte der Philosophie*. Begründet von Friedrich Ueberweg. Völlig neubearbeite Ausgabe. *Die Philosophie der Antike*. Band 4: *Die hellenistische Philosophie*, 2 Halbbände. Basel. p.29-490.

Festugière, A.-J. 1936ᵃ. 'La doctrine du plaisir des premiers sages à Epicure', in *Revue des sciences philosophiques et théologiques*, 25, p.233-268.

Festugière, A.-J. 1936ᵇ. *Le Plaisir (Eth. Nic. VII, 11-14; X, 1-5)*. Introduction, traduction et notes. Paris [1960³].

Festugière, A.-J. 1950. *Contemplation et vie contemplative selon Platon*. Paris.

Festugière, A.-J. 1966-1968. *Proclus, Commentaire sur le Timée*. 5 vol. Paris.

Festugière, A.-J. 1970. *Proclus, Traité sur la République*. 3 vol. Paris.

Festugière, A.-J. 1971. 'L'ordre de lecture des dialogues de Platon aux Vᵉ/VIᵉ siècles', in Festugière, A.-J. 1971. *Etudes de Philosophie grecque*. Paris. p.535-550.

Foucault, M. 1984. *L'usage des plaisirs (Histoire de la sexualité, 2)*. Paris.

Fowler, H.N. 1925. *Philebus*. London (*The Loeb Classical Library*).

Frede, Dorothea. 1985. 'Rumpelstiltskin's Pleasures: True and False Pleasures in Plato's *Philebus*', in *Phronesis*, 30, p.151-180.

Frede, Dorothea. 1992. 'Disintegration and Restoration: Pleasure and Pain in Plato's *Philebus*', in Kraut, R. (ed.). 1992. *The Cambridge Companion to Plato*. Cambridge. p.425-463.

Frede, Dorothea. 1993. *Plato, Philebus*. Translated, with Introduction and Notes. Indianapolis/Cambridge.

Fuhrer, Therese, and Erler, M. (eds.). 1999. *Zur Rezeption der hellenistischen Philosophie in der Spätantike*. Akten der 1. Tagung der Karl-und-Gertrud-Abel-Stiftung vom 22.-25. September 1997 in Trier. Stuttgart (*Philosophie der Antike. Veröffentlichungen der Karl-und-Gertrud-Abel-Stiftung*, 9).

Gadamer, H.-G. 1931. *Platos Dialektische Ethik*. Phänomenologische Interpretation zum *Philebus*. Leipzig [repr. 1968 in *Platos Dialektische Ethik und andere Studien zur platonischen Philosophie*. Hamburg. 103-115].

Gallop, D. 1975. *Plato: Phaedo*. Translation and Notes. Oxford.

Galpérine, Marie-Cl. 1990. 'Damascius entre Porphyre et Jamblique', in *Philosophie (Paris)*, 26, p.41-58.

Gardeya, P. 1993. *Platons Philebos*. Interpretation und Bibliographie. Würzburg.

Gauthier, R.-A., and Jolif, J.Y. 1958.1959. *Aristote, l'Éthique à Nicomaque*. Introduction, traduction et commentaire. 2 vol. Louvain/Paris.

Gersh, S.E. 1973. Κίνησις ἀκίνητος. A Study of Spiritual Motion in the Philosophy of Proclus. Leiden.

Gersh, S.E. 1978. *From Iamblichus to Eriugena*. An Investigation of the Prehistory and Evolution of the Pseudo-Dionysian Tradition. Leiden (*Studien zur Problemgeschichte der antiken und mittelalterlichen Philosophie*, 8).

Gerson, L.P. 1994. *Plotinus*. London/New York (*The Arguments of the Philosophers Series*).

Gigon, O. 1988. 'Die Gestalt des Philebos in Platons gleichnamigen Dialog', in *Mélanges M. Plezia*, p.79-84.

Goldschmidt, V. 1951. 'Remarques sur le *Philèbe*', in *L'Information Philosophique*. p.45ss. [repr. in Goldschmidt, V. 1970. *Questions Platoniciennes*. Paris. p.35-47].

Gonzalez, F.J. 1991. 'Aristotle on Pleasure and Perfection', in *Phronesis*, 36, p.141-160.

Gosling, J.C.B. 1969. *Pleasure and Desire*. The Case for Hedonism Reviewed. Oxford.

Gosling, J.C.B. 1973-74. 'More Aristotelian Pleasures', in *Proceedings of the Aristotelian Society*, 74, p.15-34.

Gosling, J.C.B. 1975. *Plato: Philebus*. Translation and Notes. Oxford.

Gosling, J.C.B., and Taylor, C.C.W. 1982. *The Greeks on Pleasure*. Oxford.

Gosling, J.C.B. 1996. 'Metaphysik oder Methodologie? : *Philebos*', in Kobusch, T., and Mojsisch, B. (ed.). 1996. *Platon*. Seine Dialogen in der Sicht neuer Forschungen. Darmstadt. p.213-228.

Grant, A. 1885. *The Ethics of Aristotle*. Illustrated with Essays and Notes. London [repr. 1973].

Guthrie, W.K.C. 1978. *A History of Greek Philosophy*. vol. V: *The Later Plato and the Academy*. Cambridge.

Hackforth, R. 1945. *Plato's Examination of Pleasure*. Cambridge [repr. 1972. *Plato's Philebus*. Cambridge].

Hadot, P. 1963. *Plotin ou la simplicité du regard*. Paris [repr. 1973].

Hadot, P. 1987. 'Structure et thèmes du *Traité 38* (VI, 7) de Plotin', in *Aufstieg un Niedergang der Römischen Welt*, II, 36.1. Berlin/New York. p.624-676.

Hadot, P. 1988. *Plotin. Traité 38*. Introduction, traduction, commentaire et notes. Paris.

Halfwassen, J. 1993. *Der Aufstieg zum Einen*. Untersuchungen zu Platon und Plotin. Stuttgart.

Hampton, Cynthia. 1987. 'Pleasure, Truth, and Being in Plato's *Philebus*: A Reply to Professor Frede', in *Phronesis*, 32, p.253-262.

Hampton, Cynthia. 1989. 'Plato's Later Analysis of Pleasure', in *Essays in Ancient Greek Philosophy*. III, p.41-49.

Hampton, Cynthia. 1990. *Pleasure, Knowledge, and Being*. An Analysis of Plato's *Philebus*. Albany.

Hardie, W.F.R. 1968. *Aristotle's Ethical Theory*. Oxford [2nd ed. 1980].

Harris, R.B. (ed.). 1976. *The Significance of Neoplatonism*. Albany.

Harris, R.B. (ed.). 1982. *The Structure of Being, A Neoplatonic Approach*. Albany (*Studies in Neoplatonism: Ancient and Modern*, vol. IV).

Haynes, R.P. 1962. 'The Theory of Pleasure of the Old Stoa', in *American Journal of Philology*, 83, p.412-419.

Heath, R.G. (ed.). 1964. *The Role of Pleasure in Behavior*. New York.

Inge, W.R. 1929. *The Philosophy of Plotinus*. 2 vols. London [repr. 1968].

Inwood, B. 1985. *Ethics and Human Action in Early Stoicism*. Oxford.

Irwin, T. 1979. *Plato: Gorgias. Translation and Notes*. Oxford.

Irwin, T. 1985. *Aristotle. Nicomachean Ethics*. Indianapolis.

Isenberg, M.W. 1940. 'The Unity of Plato's *Philebus*', in *Classical Philology*, 35, p.154-179.

Joachim, H.H. 1951. *Aristotle, the Nicomachean Ethics*. ed. by Rees, D.A. Oxford.

Kenny, A. 1978. *The Aristotelian Ethics*. Oxford.

Klein, J. 1971-72. 'About Plato's *Philebus*', in *Interpretation*, 2, p.157-182.

Krämer, H.J. 1964. *Der Ursprung der Geistmetaphysik*. Untersuchungen zur Geschichte des Platonismus zwischen Platon und Plotin. Amsterdam (1974²).

Kristeller, P.O. 1987. 'Proclus as a Reader of Plato and Plotinus, and his Influence in the Middle Ages and in the Renaissance', in Pépin-Saffrey 1987, p.191-211.

Letwin, O. 1981. 'Interpreting the *Philebus*', in *Phronesis*, 26, p.187-206.

Lewy, H. 1956. *Chaldaean Oracles and Theurgy:* Mysticism, Magic and Platonism in the Later Roman Empire. Cairo [Paris, 1978²].

LSJ = Liddell, H.G., Scott, R., and Jones, H.S. 1985. *A Greek — English Lexicon*. Oxford.

Lieberg, G. 1958. *Die Lehre von der Lust in dem Ethiken des Aristoteles*. München (*Zetemata*, 19).

Liske, M.-Th. 1991. 'Kinesis und Energeia bei Aristoteles', in *Phronesis*, 36, p.161-178.

Long, A.A., and Sedley, D.N. 1987. *The Hellenistic Philosophers*. 2 vols. Vol. 1: *Translations of the Principal Sources with Philosophical Commentary*; vol. 2: *Greek and Latin Texts with Notes and Bibliography*. Cambridge/London/New York.

MacClintock, S. 1961. 'More on the Structure of the *Philebus*', in *Phronesis*, 6, p.46-52.

Mackinnon, F.J. 1925. 'The Doctrine of Measure in the *Philebus*', in *Philosophical Review*, 33, p.114-153.

McGinley, J. 1977. 'The Doctrine of the Good in the *Philebus*', in *Apeiron*, 11, p.25-57.

Merlan, P. 1960. *Studies in Epicurus and Aristotle*. Wiesbaden.

Merlan, P. 1963. *Monopsychism, Mysticism, Metaconsciousness*. Problems of the Soul in the Neoaristotelian and Neoplatonic Tradition. The Hague (*Archives internationales d'histoire des idées — International Archives of the History of Ideas*, 2).

Merlan, P. 1975. *From Platonism to Neoplatonism*. The Hague. [3rd, rev. ed.; 1960^{2}].

Mill, J.S. 1998. *Utilitarianism*. Oxford.

Mitsis, P. 1988. *Epicurus' Ethical Theory*. The Pleasures of Invulnerability. Ithaca/London.

Monan, J.D. 1968. *Moral Knowledge and its Methodology in Aristotle*. Oxford.

Mooradian, N. 1996. 'Converting Protarchus: Relativism and False Pleasures of Anticipation in Plato's *Philebus*', in *Ancient Philosophy*, 16, p.93-112.

Moravcsik, J.M. 1979. 'Forms, Nature and the Good in the *Philebus*', in *Phronesis*, 24, p.81-104.

Moravcsik, J.M. 1992. *Plato and Platonism*. Plato's Conception of Appearance and Reality in Ontology, Epistemology, and Ethics, and its Modern Echoes. Oxford/Cambridge-Mass.

Moreau, J. 1970. *Plotin ou la gloire de la philosophie antique*. Paris (*Bibliothèque d'histoire de la philosophie*).

Moreschini, C. 1996. 'Temi delle *Lezioni sul Filebo* di Damascio', in Cosenza 1996, p.73-92.

Morrow, G.R., and Dillon, J. 1987. *Proclus' Commentary on Plato's Parmenides. Translated with Introduction and Notes*. Princeton.

Mueller, G.E. 1954-55. 'The Unity of Plato's *Philebus*', in *Classical Journal*, 50, p.21-27.

Murphy, N.R. 1938. 'The 'Comparison of Lives' in Plato's *Philebus*', in *The Classical Quarterly*, 32, p.116-124.

Narbonne, J.-M. 1994. *La métaphysique de Plotin*. Paris.

O'Daly, G.J.P. 1973. *Plotinus' Philosophy of the Self*. Shannon.

O'Meara, D.J. 1975. *Structures hiérarchiques dans la pensée de Plotin*. Etude historique et interprétative. Leiden (*Philosophia Antiqua*, 27).

O'Meara, D.J. 1999a. 'Epicurus neoplatonicus', in Fuhrer-Erler 1999, p.83-91.

O'Meara, D.J. 1999b. 'Lectures néoplatoniciennes du Philèbe', in Dixsaut 1999, vol. 2, p. 191-204.

O'Neill, W. 1965. *Proclus, In Alcibiadem*. English Translation. The Hague.

Owen, G.E.L. 1971-72. 'Aristotelian Pleasures', in *Proceedings of the Aristotelian Society*, 72, p.135-152 [repr. in Barnes, J., Schofield, M., and Sorabji, R. (eds.). 1977. *Articles on Aristotle*. vol. II. London. 92-103].

Pépin, J. 1962. *Les Stoïciens*. Paris (*Bibliothèque de la Pléiade*).

Pépin, J., and Saffrey, H.D. (eds.). 1987. *Proclus lecteur et interprète des anciens*. Actes du Colloque International du CNRS, Paris, 2-4 oct. Paris.

Pétrement, Simone. 1947. *Le dualisme chez Platon, les gnostiques et les manichéens.* Brionne.

Philippson, R. 1925. 'Akademische Verhandlungen über die Lustlehre', in *Hermes*, 60, p.444-481.

Polansky, R. 1983. '*Energeia* in Aristotle's *Metaphysics* ix', in *Ancient Philosophy*, 3, p.160-170.

Price, A.W. 1995. *Mental Conflict*. London/New York.

Ricken, F. 1976. *Der Lustbegriff in der Nikomachischen Ethik des Aristoteles*. Göttingen (*Hypomnemata*, 46).

Ricken, F. 1995. 'Wert und Wesen der Lust', in Höffe, O. (ed.). 1995. *Aristoteles: Die Nikomachische Ethik*. Berlin (*Klassiker Auslegen*, 2). p.207-228.

Rist, J.M. 1964. 'Mysticism and Transcendence in Later Neoplatonism', in *Hermes*, 102, p.213-225.

Rist, J.M. 1967[a]. *Plotinus. The Road to Reality*. Cambridge.

Rist, J.M. 1967[b]. 'Integration and the Undescended Soul in Plotinus', in *American Journal of Philology*, 88, p.410-422.

Rist, J.M. 1969. *Stoic Philosophy*. Cambridge.

Rist, J.M. 1972. *Epicurus : An Introduction*. Cambridge.

Rist, J.M. 1974. 'Pleasure: 360-300 B.C.', in *Phoenix*, 28, p.167-179.

Rist, J.M. 1989. *The Mind of Aristotle*. A Study in Philosophical Growth. Toronto/Buffalo/London (*Phoenix*, Supplementary Volume, 25).

Rorty, Amélie O. 1974. 'The Place of Pleasure in Aristotle's Ethics', in *Mind*, 83, p.481-493.

Rorty, Amélie O. (ed.). 1980[a]. *Essays on Eudaemonia*. Berkeley.

Rorty, Amélie O. (ed.). 1980[b]. *Essays on Aristotle's Ethics*. Berkeley.

Ross, W.D. 1951. *Plato's Theory of Ideas*. Oxford.

Ross, W.D. 1953. *Aristotle. Metaphysics*. A Revised Text with Introduction and Commentary. 2 vols. Oxford [1st ed. 1924, repr. 1970].

Rudebusch, G. 1999. *Socrates, Pleasure, and Value*. New York.

Ryle, G. 1954. 'Pleasure', in *Dilemmas*, Ch. 4. Cambridge-Mass.

Saffrey, H.-D. 1984. 'Quelques aspects de la spiritualité des philosophes néoplatoniciens, de Jamblique à Proclus et Damascius', in *Revue des Sciences Philosophiques et Théologiques*, 68, p.169-182.

Saffrey, H.-D. 1987. 'La Théologie Platonicienne de Proclus et l'histoire du néoplatonisme', in Boss-Seel 1987, p.29-44.

Saffrey, H.-D. 1990. *Recherches sur le néoplatonisme après Plotin*. Paris.

Salem, J. 1989. *Tel un dieu parmi les hommes*. L'éthique d'Epicure. Paris.

Schofield, M. 1971. 'Who Were οἱ δυσχερεῖς in Plato, *Philebus* 44 a ff.?', in *Museum Helveticum*, 28, p.2-20; 181.

Schubert, V. 1973. *Plotin. Einführung in sein Philosophieren*. Freiburg/München.

Schuhl, P.M., and Hadot, P. (eds.). 1971. *Le Néoplatonisme*. Actes du Colloque International organisé dans le cadre des colloques Internationaux du CNRS à Royaumont du 9 au 13 juin 1969. Paris.

Schwyzer, H.R. 1951. art. 'Plotinos', in *Paulys Realencyclopädie der classischen Altertumswissenschaft*, XXI, 1. Stuttgart. col. 471-592.

Schwyzer, H.R. 1970. 'Plotin und Platons *Philebos*', in *Revue internationale de philosophie*, 91, p.181-193.

Scoti Muth, Nicoletta. 1993. *Proclo negli ultimi quarant'anni*. Bibliografia ragionata della letteratura primaria e secondaria riguardante il pensiero procliano e i suoi influssi storici (anni 1949-1992). Milano.

Sedley, D. 1976. 'Epicurus and his Professional Rivals', in Bollack, J., and Laks, A., *Etudes sur l'Epicurisme antique*. Lille (*Cahiers de Philologie*, 1). p.119-159.

Segonds, A.Ph. 1985.1986. *Proclus. Sur le Premier Alcibiade de Platon*. Texte et traduction. 2 vols. Paris (*Collection des Universités de France*).

Siegmann, G. 1990. *Plotins Philosophie des Guten*. Eine Interpretation von *Enneade* VI 7. Würzburg (*Epistemata*, Reihe Philosophie, 82).

Sleeman, J.H., and Pollet, G. 1980. *Lexicon Plotinianum*. Leiden (*Ancient and medieval Philosophy*, De Wulf-Mansion Centre Ser. 1, II).

Sparshott, F. 1994. *Taking Life Seriously*. A Study of the Argument of the *Nicomachean Ethics*. Toronto.

Stallbaum, G. 1820. *Platonis Philebus*. Recensuit prolegomenis et commentariis illustravit — . Lipsiae (*Bibliotheca scriptorum graecorum et romanorum Teubneriana*).

Steel, C.G. 1978. *The Changing Self*. A Study on the Soul in Later Neoplatonism: Iamblichus, Damascius and Priscianus. Brussel (*Verhandelingen van de Koninklijke Academie voor Wetenschappen, Letteren en Schone Kunsten van België, Klasse der Letteren*, 40, 1978, nr.85).

Steinmetz, P. 1994. 'Die Stoa', in Flashar, H. (ed.). 1994. *Grundriss der Geschichte der Philosophie*. Begründet von Friedrich Ueberweg. Völlig neubearbeite Ausgabe. *Die Philosophie der Antike*. Band 4: *Die hellenistische Philosophie*. 2 Halbbände. Basel. p.495-716.

Strömberg, R. 1946. 'Damascius. His Personality and Significance', in *Eranos*, 44, p.175-192.

Sullivan, R.J. 1977. *Morality and the Good Life*. A Commentary on Aristotle's *Nicomachean Ethics*. Memphis.

Sweeney, L. 1961. 'Another Interpretation of *Enneads* VI, 7, 32', in *Modern Schoolman*, 38, p.289-303.

Szasz, T.S. 1957. *Pain and Pleasure: a Study of Bodily Feelings*. New York (1975[2]).

Tallon, A. 1972. 'The Criterion of Purity in Plato's *Philebus*', in *New Scholasticism*, 46, p.439-445.

Tarán, L. 1981. *Speusippus of Athens*. A Critical Study with a Collection of the Related Texts and Commentary. Leiden (*Philosophia Antiqua*, 39).

Taylor, A.E. 1926. *Plato. The Man and His Work*. London [1960[7]].

Taylor, A.E. 1956. *Plato: Philebus and Epinomis*. Translation and Introduction by –, edited by Klibansky, R. London [1972[2]].

Taylor, C.C.W. 1963. 'Pleasure', in *Analysis*, 23, p.2-19.

Taylor, C.C.W. 1976. *Plato: Protagoras*. Translation and Notes. Oxford.

Taylor, C.C.W. 1988. 'Urmson on Aristotle on Pleasure', in Dancy, J., and Moravcsik, J. (eds.). 1988. *Human Agency*. Language, Duty, and Value. Philosophical Essays in Honor of J.O. Urmson. Stanford. p.120-132.

Tenkku, J. 1956. *The Evaluation of Pleasure in Plato's Ethics*. Helsinki (*Acta Philosophica Fennica*, 11).

Todd, R.B. 1972. 'Epitedeiotes in Philosophical Literature: Towards an Analysis', in *Acta Classica*, 15, p.25-35.

Trevaskis, J.R. 1960. 'Classification in the *Philebus*', in *Phronesis*, 5, p.39-44.

Tricot, J. 1959. *Aristote, Éthique à Nicomaque*. Paris.

Trouillard, J. 1955[a]. *La purification plotinienne*. Paris.

Trouillard, J. 1955[b]. *La procession plotinienne*. Paris.

Trouillard, J. 1965. *Proclus, Eléments de Théologie*. Traduction française. Paris.

Trouillard, J. 1972. *L'Un et l'âme selon Proclos*. Paris.

Urmson, J.O. 1967. 'Aristotle on Pleasure', in Moravcsik, J.M.E. (ed.). 1967. *Aristotle. A Collection of Critical Essays*. New York. p.323-333.

Urmson, J.O. 1984. 'Pleasure and Distress: A Discussion of J.C.B. Gosling and C.C.W. Taylor, *The Greeks on Pleasure*', in Annas, Julia (ed.). 1984. *Oxford Studies in Ancient Philosophy*, 2, p.215-216.

Urmson, J.O. 1988. *Aristotle's Ethics*. Oxford/New York. [97-108: Pleasure].

Van Riel, G. 1993. 'Plato's *Philebus*. De rol van het genot binnen het geluk in de Platoonse traditie', in *Gehelen en Fragmenten*. Acta van de veertiende Vlaams-Nederlandse Filosofiedag te Leuven. Leuven. p.130-134.

Van Riel, G. 1995. 'Hoe zuiver is onbegrensd genot? Plato's *Philebus* of de bekering van een hedonist', in *Tijdschrift voor Filosofie*, 57, p.433-460.

Van Riel, G. 1997a. *Het genot en het goede. Plato's Philebus en zijn invloed in de antieke filosofie*. 2 vol. Diss. doc. Leuven.

Van Riel, G. 1997b. 'The Transcendent Cause. Iamblichus and the *Philebus* of Plato', in *Syllecta Classica*, 8, p.31-46.

Van Riel, G. 1999a. 'Le plaisir est-il la réplétion d'un manque ? La définition du plaisir (*Philèbe* 32 a – 36 c) et la physiologie des plaisirs faux (42 c 44 a)', in Dixsaut 1999, vol. 1, p.299-314.

Van Riel, G. 1999b. 'Platon, *Philèbe*: Bibliographie Compréhensive', in Dixsaut 1999, vol. 1, p.422-436.

Van Riel, G. 1999c. 'Does a Perfect Activity Necessarily Yield Pleasure? An Evaluation of the Relation between Pleasure and Activity in Aristotle, *Nicomachean Ethics* VII and X', in *International Journal of Philosophical Studies*, 7, p.211-224.

Van Riel, G. [forthcoming]. 'Aristotle's Definition of Pleasure : a Refutation of the Platonic Account', in *Ancient Philosophy*.

Verhaeghe, J. 1980. *Het mensbeeld in de Aristotelische ethiek*. Brussel (*Verhandelingen van de Koninklijke Academie voor Wetenschappen, Letteren en Schone Kunsten van België, Klasse der Letteren*).

Vlastos, G. 1991. *Socrates*. Ironist and Moral Philosopher. Cambridge.

Voigtlaender, H.-D. 1960. *Die Lust und das Gute bei Platon*. Würzburg.

Waterfield, R.A.H. 1993. *Plato, Republic* (translation). Oxford.

Webb, P. 1977. 'The Relative Dating of the Accounts of Pleasure in Aristotle's Ethics', in *Phronesis*, 22, p.235-262.

Westerink, L.G. 1959. *Damascius. Lectures on the Philebus, Wrongly Attributed to Olympiodorus*. Text, Translation, Notes and Indices. Amsterdam.

Westerink, L.G. 1971. 'Damascius, Commentateur de Platon', in *Le Néoplatonisme*. Actes du colloque international du Centre National de la Recherche Scientifique, Royaumont, 9-13 juin 1969. p.253-260. [repr. in Westerink 1980, p.271-278].

Westerink, L.G. 1976.1977. *The Greek Commentaries on Plato's Phaedo*. 2 vols. vol. 1: *Olympiodorus*. vol. 2: *Damascius*. Amsterdam.

Westerink, L.G. 1980. *Texts and Studies in Neoplatonism and Byzantine Literature. Collected Papers*. Amsterdam.

Westerink, L.G., and Trouillard, J., avec la collaboration de Segonds, A.Ph. 1990. *Prolégomènes à la philosophie de Platon*. Paris (*Collection des Universités de France*).

Williams, B. 1972. *Morality. An Introduction to Ethics*. Cambridge.

INDICES

1. *Index rerum*

Greek-English Glossary

αἰσθητικόν	sensitive
ἀνάμνησις	recollection
ἀνδρεία	courage
ἀπάθεια	absence of affections
βούλησις	will
γνῶσις	cognition, or knowledge
διανοητικόν	rational
διάνοια	thought
εἴδησις	knowledge
ἔκτασις	strained attention
ἐνέργεια	activity
ἕξις	disposition
ἐπιθυμία	appetite, or desire
ἐπιθυμητικόν	appetitive
ἐπιστήμη	knowledge, or science
ἐπιτηδειότης	receptivity
ἔρως	love
εὐδαιμονία	happiness
εὐλάβεια	carefulness
εὐπάθεια	good affection, or well-being
εὐφροσύνη	well-being
ζήτησις	inquiry
θεωρία	contemplation
θυμός	passion
θυμοειδές	passionate spirit
κάλλος	beauty
κρίσις	judgment
λεκτά	sayables
λογιστικόν	rational, reasoning
νοῦς	intellect
ὀργή	anger
ὁρμή	impulse
ὄρεξις	desire
πάθος	affection
πεπόνθησις	receptivity
πληγή	shock (Lat. *ictus*)
πληκτικός	violent
πλήρωσις	replenishment
προπάθεια	preliminary affection
ῥαστώνη	easy life
σοφία	wisdom
σπουδαῖος	righteous
συμμετρία	assent
συμμετρία	proportion
τεῦξις	hit, or attainment
φαντασία	mental impression, imagination, or presentation
φρόνησις	(in Plato) understanding, (from Aristotle onwards) prudence, or practical wisdom
φυτικόν	vegetative
χαρά	joy
ὠδίς	travail

2. *Index locorum* *

---

*   References to translated passages are *italicised*.

3. *Index nominum*

PHILOSOPHIA ANTIQUA

A SERIES OF STUDIES ON ANCIENT PHILOSOPHY

EDITED BY

J. MANSFELD, D.T. RUNIA
AND J.C.M. VAN WINDEN

34. Epiktet. *Vom Kynismus.* Herausgegeben und übersetzt mit einem Kommentar von M. Billerbeck. 1978. ISBN 90 04 05770 6

35. Baltes, M. *Die Weltentstehung des platonischen Timaios nach den antiken Interpreten.* Teil 2. Proklos. 1979. ISBN 90 04 05799 4

37. O'Brien, D. *Theories of Weight in the Ancient World.* Four Essays on Democritus, Plato and Aristotle. A Study in the Development of Ideas 1. Democritus: Weight and Size. An Exercise in the Reconstruction of Early Greek Philosophy. 1981. ISBN 90 04 06134 7

39. Tarán, L. *Speusippus of Athens.* A Critical Study with a Collection of the Related Texts and Commentary. 1982. ISBN 90 04 06505 9

40. Rist, J.M. *Human Value.* A Study in Ancient Philosophical Ethics. 1982. ISBN 90 04 06757 4

41. O'Brien, D. *Theories of Weight in the Ancient World.* Four Essays on Democritus, Plato and Aristotle. A Study in the Development of Ideas 2. Plato: Weight and Sensation. The Two Theories of the 'Timaeus'. 1984. ISBN 90 04 06934 8

44. Runia, D.T. *Philo of Alexandria and the Timaeus of Plato.* 1986. ISBN 90 04 07477 5

45. Aujoulat, N. *Le Néo-Platonisme Alexandrin: Hiéroclès d'Alexandrie.* Filiations intellectuelles et spirituelles d'un néo-platonicien du Ve siècle. 1986. ISBN 90 04 07510 0

46. Kal, V. *On Intuition and Discursive Reason in Aristotle.* 1988. ISBN 90 04 08308 1

48. Evangeliou, Ch. *Aristotle's Categories and Porphyry.* 1988. ISBN 90 04 08538 6

49. Bussanich, J. *The One and Its Relation to Intellect in Plotinus.* A Commentary on Selected Texts. 1988. ISBN 90 04 08996 9

50. Simplicius. *Commentaire sur les Catégories.* Traduction commentée sous la direction de I. Hadot. I: Introduction, première partie (p. 1-9, 3 Kalbfleisch). Traduction de Ph. Hoffmann (avec la collaboration d'I. et P. Hadot). Commentaire et notes à la traduction par I. Hadot avec des appendices de P. Hadot et J.-P. Mahé. 1990. ISBN 90 04 09015 0

51. Simplicius. *Commentaire sur les Catégories.* Traduction commentée sous la direction de I. Hadot. III: Préambule aux Catégories. Commentaire au premier chapitre des Catégories (p. 21-40, 13 Kalbfleisch). Traduction de Ph. Hoffmann (avec la collaboration d'I. Hadot, P. Hadot et C. Luna). Commentaire et notes à la traduction par C. Luna. 1990. ISBN 90 04 09016 9

52. Magee, J. *Boethius on Signification and Mind.* 1989. ISBN 90 04 09096 7

53. Bos, E.P. and Meijer, P.A. (eds.) *On Proclus and His Influence in Medieval Philosophy.* 1992. ISBN 90 04 09429 6

54. Fortenbaugh, W.W., et al. (eds.) *Theophrastes of Eresos.* Sources for His Life, Writings, Thought and Influence. 1992. ISBN 90 04 09440 7 *set*

55. Shankman, A. *Aristotle's* De insomniis. A Commentary. ISBN 90 04 09476 8

56. Mansfeld, J. *Heresiography in Context.* Hippolytos' *Elenchos* as a Source for Greek Philosophy. 1992. ISBN 90 04 09616 7

57. O'Brien, D. *Théodicée plotinienne, théodicée gnostique.* 1993. ISBN 90 04 09618 3

58. Baxter, T.M.S. *The Cratylus.* Plato's Critique of Naming. 1992. ISBN 90 04 09597 7

59. Dorandi, T. (Hrsg.) *Theodor Gomperz. Eine Auswahl herkulanischer kleiner Schriften (1864-1909).* 1993. ISBN 90 04 09819 4

60. Filodemo. *Storia dei filosofi. La stoà da Zenone a Panezio* (PHerc. 1018). Edizione, traduzione e commento a cura di T. Dorandi. 1994. ISBN 90 04 09963 8

61. Mansfeld, J. *Prolegomena.* Questions to be Settled Before the Study of an Author, or a Text. 1994. ISBN 90 04 10084 9

62. Flannery, s.J., K.L. *Ways into the Logic of Alexander of Aphrodisias.* 1995. ISBN 90 04 09998 0

63. Lakmann, M.-L. *Der Platoniker Tauros in der Darstellung des Aulus Gellius.* 1995. ISBN 90 04 10096 2

64. Sharples, R.W. *Theophrastus of Eresus.* Sources for his Life, Writings, Thought and Influence. Commentary Volume 5. Sources on Biology (Human Physiology, Living Creatures, Botany: Texts 328-435). 1995. ISBN 90 04 10174 8

65. Algra, K. *Concepts of Space in Greek Thought.* 1995. ISBN 90 04 10172 1   66. Simplicius. *Commentaire sur le manuel d'Épictète.* Introduction et édition critique de texte grec par Ilsetraut Hadot. 1995. ISBN 90 04 09772 4

67. Cleary, J.J. *Aristotle and Mathematics.* Aporetic Method in Cosmology and Metaphysics. 1995. ISBN 90 04 10159 4

68. Tieleman, T. *Galen and Chrysippus on the Soul.* Argument and Refutation in the *De Placitis* Books II-III. 1996. ISBN 90 04 10520 4

69. Haas, F.A.J. de. *John Philoponus' New Definition of Prime Matter.* Aspects of its Background in Neoplatonism and the Ancient Commentary Tradition. 1997. ISBN 90 04 10446 1

71. Andia, Y. de. *Henosis.* L'Union à Dieu chez Denys l'Aréopagite. 1996. ISBN 90 04 10656 1

72. Algra, K.A., Horst, P.W. van der, and Runia, D.T. (eds.) *Polyhistor.* Studies in the History and Historiography of Ancient Philosophy. Presented to Jaap Mansfeld on his Sixtieth Birthday. 1996. ISBN 90 04 10417 8

73. Mansfeld, J. and Runia, D.T. *Aëtiana.* The Method and Intellectual Context of a Doxographer. Volume 1: The Sources. 1997. ISBN 90 04 10580 8

74. Slomkowski, P. *Aristotle's* Topics. 1997. ISBN 90 04 10757 6

75. Barnes, J. *Logic and the Imperial Stoa.* 1997. ISBN 90 04 10828 9

76. Inwood, B. and Mansfeld, J. (eds.) *Assent and Argument.* Studies in Cicero's *Academic Books.* Proceedings of the 7th Symposium Hellenisticum (Utrecht, August 21-25, 1995). 1997. ISBN 90 04 10914 5

77. Magee, J. (ed., tr. & comm.) *Anicii Manlii Severini Boethii* De divisione liber. Critical Edition, Translation, Prolegomena, and Commentary. 1998. ISBN 90 04 10873 4

78. Olympiodorus. *Commentary on Plato's* Gorgias. Translated with Full Notes by R. Jackson, K. Lycos & H. Tarrant. Introduction by H. Tarrant. 1998. ISBN 90 04 10972 2

79. Sharples, R.W. *Theophrastus of Eresus.* Sources for his Life, Writings, Thought and Influence. Commentary Volume 3.1. Sources on Physics (Texts 137-223). With Contributions on the Arabic Material by Dimitri Gutas. 1998. ISBN 90 04 11130 1

80. Mansfeld, J. *Prolegomena Mathematica.* From Apollonius of Perga to Late Neoplatonism. With an Appendix on Pappus and the History of Platonism. 1998. ISBN 90 04 11267 7

81. Huby, P. *Theophrastus of Eresus.* Sources for His Life, Writings, Thought and Influence. Commentary Volume 4. Psychology (Texts 254-327). With Contributions on the Arabic Material by D. Gutas. 1999. ISBN 90 04 11317 7

82. Boter, G. *The* Encheiridion *of Epictetus and Its Three Christian Adaptations.* Transmission and Critical Editions. 1999. ISBN 90 04 11358 4

83. Stone, M.E. and Shirinian, M.E. *Pseudo-Zeno. Anonymous Philosophical Treatise.* Translated with the Collaboration of J. Mansfeld and D.T. Runia. 2000. ISBN 90 04 11524 2

84. Bäck, A.T. *Aristotle's Theory of Predication.* 2000. ISBN 90 04 11719 9

85. Riel, G. Van. *Pleasure and the Good Life.* Plato, Aristotle, and the Neoplatonists. 2000. ISBN 90 04 11797 0